SUFFERINGS
OF EARLY QUAKERS

Westmorland 1651 to 1690
Cumberland 1653 to 1690
Durham & Northumberland
1658 to 1690
Isle of Man 1656 to 1685
Lancashire 1652 to 1690

Facsimile of part of the 1753 edition
by JOSEPH BESSE

with new Introduction and
newly compiled Index of People and Places
by Michael Gandy BA FSG

SESSIONS BOOK TRUST
York, England

Facsimiles of Volume II (Chapter I) and of Volume I (Chapters IX,
XIII, XX and XXII) have been reprinted in reduced size with
new introduction and indexes

© 2000
by William Sessions Limited
The Ebor Press, York, England

ISBN 1 85072 242 0

06262344

*The 'Swarthmoor Hall' panel on the back cover is the copyright of The Quaker
Tapestry Scheme©. Seventy seven original embroideries of their internationally
famous Quaker Tapestry are on view at the Exhibition Centre of the Friends
Meeting House, Kendal, Cumbria, England (Tel. 01539 722975) between
spring and late autumn annually.*

FOREWORD

IN 1753, JOSEPH BESSE published his detailed account of the sufferings of Quakers throughout England, Ireland, Scotland, Wales and New England from 1650, when Quakers were 'first distinguished by that name', to approximately 1689, when the Act of Toleration at last gave some protection to Dissenters. The work has now become a standard source for Quaker genealogy and social history.

The two volumes of this substantial work, long out-of-print, comprise 824 and 648 pages, subdivided into regions and English counties. So for cost and other reasons our small family Book Trust (a registered charity) decided to publish a series of regional volumes beginning with Yorkshire in 1998 and continuing in 1999 with this present second regional volume.

Skilled indexing services have again been provided by Michael Gandy BA, Fellow of the Society of Genealogists and founding chairman of the Quaker Family History Society, who has many Quaker branches in his ancestry. Trustees wish to express their appreciation to him for these specifically compiled Indexes of People and of Places.

Given further ordering support for copies of these first two regional volumes, Trustees intend to continue in subsequent years with more newly indexed volumes embracing other areas.

William K Sessions
Chairman Sessions Book Trust

INTRODUCTION

Michael Gandy

EVER SINCE IT APPEARED IN 1753, Joseph Besse's *Collection of the Sufferings of the People called Quakers* has been the first port of call for anyone interested in 17th century Quakerism at local level. Arranged county by county, and then extending to New England and Maryland, the Caribbean (especially Barbados), Ireland, Scotland and continental Europe, Joseph Besse drew together the most interesting or indicative examples of what individual Quakers had suffered for the Truth between approximately 1650 and 1689. The work is densely packed with names, dates and places; snapshots from the lives of ordinary people, our ancestors, the atmosphere built up by an unrelenting chronological catalogue of persecutions, sometimes thwarted but usually bravely borne, 'for the testimony of a good conscience'.

The work is particularly valuable because it pre-dates the establishment of the Quakers in Pennsylvania. A great many of the families of the early settlers appear in the *Sufferings* and so their home area can be identified.

The background to publication was described by Norman Penney in 'The Story of a Great Literary Venture' (1). In 1727 London Yearly Meeting had passed the following minute:

> On a proposition made to this Meeting by James Dickinson, seconded by divers countyes, this Meeting desires Friends of ye meeting for sufferings to take upon them ye care of collecting and digesting by proper persons ye sufferings and imprisonments of Friends for Tythes and on all other accounts, into proper heads from ye beginning of our being a People to this time.

Under the supervision of a committee, Joseph Besse (the final 'e' is pronounced) began the work of sorting the material already held at Gracechurch Street Meeting House in London and of bringing up to date the records of sufferings in the provinces. The work took twenty six years to complete, though there were a number of very valuable interim volumes. In 1753 1000 copies of the final work were printed of which 719 were sent straight to subscribers. The remainder were advertised at 22 shillings (£1.10p) and in 1755 100 were distributed to 43 Quarterly Meetings

> expressly intended for the use of such Friends as are not of ability to purchase the Work, or to be lent occasionally to People of other Persuasions, where there is Prospect of Service.

Fifty copies were sent to Philadelphia and it was also proposed to present copies to 'some great Personages...as proper and seasonable Occasion may offer'.

As the above implies Besse's *Sufferings* commanded immediate respect and was used as both an authority and a source of inspiration. It was by its nature an abstract and there is plenty more material in the sources from which it was drawn. W.C.Braithwaite says of it, 'The work is conscientiously done, and may be generally relied on' (2). Its great value is its accessibility. Once Quakers have been identified and localised in Besse, researchers know that a much longer search in the Quarter Sessions, the Books of Sufferings, the Digests of Births, Marriages and Deaths and elsewhere, is likely to be worthwhile.

In a more recent article (3) David M.Butler uses the *Sufferings* to plot the peaks and troughs of Quaker persecution in each county and attempts some analysis. He demonstrates not only that persecution came in waves according to the national political climate but that there were local variations depending on the attitude of the local magistrates and, above all, of the local vicar or the lay impropriator who was the immediate financial loser when Quakers refused to pay tithes. After the Restoration in 1660 Quakers were never seen as politically dangerous and in many cases they were respected for their moral stand even while the Letter of the Law was invoked against them. On the other hand many of those in authority were outraged by their refusal to conform and persecuted them with enthusiasm.

In a short introduction Besse himself described 'the principal Points wherein their conscientious Nonconformity rendered them obnoxious to the Penalties of the Law'. These were:

- **Their refusal to pay Tithes** which they esteemed a Jewish Ceremony abrogated by the Coming of Christ. They also considered that the Levitical Priesthood, which took Tithes, being changed, a change also of the Law which enjoined the Payment of them did necessarily follow: And that there being no Precept either of Christ or his Apostles, enjoining them to be paid under the Gospel, his Disciples are totally freed from all Obligation thereunto.

- **Their refusal to pay Rates or Assessments** for building and repairing Houses or Places appropriated to the Exercise of such a Worship as they did not approve of; the pretended Consecration of which Places they looked upon as an unwarrantable Superstition

- **Their constant Obedience to the Precept of Christ** *Swear not at all* which they would not in any case transgress. For they did not believe that any human Law or Power upon Earth could justify them in the known Breach of a positive Command such as they esteemed that of our Saviour to be in respect of Swearing. In this point they were acted by an invincible Constancy, and supported steadfast in the Faith, through Bonds, Imprisonments, Banishments, and even Death itself.

- **Their Disuse of the Custom of uncovering their Heads,** or pulling off their hats, by way of Homage to Men, which they accounted an undue and unscriptural Respect of Persons and a Misapplication of that outward Signification of Honour and Address which they appropriated to God only. This Custom had not the sanction of any written Law yet the omission of it was deemed a Contempt, and frequently punished by Fines and Imprisonment.

- **Their Christian Resolution of assembling publickly for the Worship of God** in such manner as was most agreeable to their Consciences, from which nothing could deter them; and in which they stood much exposed to the malice of their Adversaries, who always knew where to find them. In this they manifested an intrepidity, sometimes astonishing, even to those who came to their Meetings on purpose to molest them.

- **The Necessity many of them found themselves under of publishing the Doctrine of Truth** which they were persuaded of, and of reproving Vice and Immorality openly in the Streets and Markets, and sometimes even in the Places appointed for the publick national Worship. From the worst of those whom they so reproved they met with ungrateful Returns of manifold and barbarous Abuses, which were too often encouraged by Authority of the Magistrates, who ought to have restrained them.

- **Their refusing to make Use of the established Priests or Ministers,** either in Marrying, Burying, or any other Case, and conscientiously withholding the fees customarily paid on those Occasions. Hence proceeded many Prosecutions against them, especially in the Ecclesiastical Courts, where they generally issued in Excommunications, the Consequences of which often were Imprisonments on Writs *de Excommunicato capiendo*, during the pleasure of holy Church. By this means many of this People were buried alive, and became sacrifices to the Interest of domineering Ecclesiasticks, in causes of which the secular Power never had any Cognizance, but through their Misrepresentations.

- **Their Testimony against Wars and Fighting;** the Practice whereof they judged inconsistent with those Precepts of Christ, *Love your*

Enemies. Do Good to them that hate you. Wherefore they refused either to bear Arms themselves, or to hire others in their Stead. This exposed them to Fines, and Seizures of their Goods, and sometimes even to corporal Punishments at the arbitrary Will of Military Officers.

These Points of their religious Dissent were to them of very great Weight and Consequence; in the Observance of which they experienced an inward Peace and Tranquillity of Mind, strengthening and enabling them to persevere in the Way of their Duty; and indeed their Patience and Constancy in enduring so great a Fight of Afflictions, for the sake of their religious Testimony, was as cogent and convincing a Demonstration of the Sincerity therein, as can reasonably be expected.'

About this edition

This facsimile of part of Besse's *Sufferings* is taken from the 1753 edition in *two volumes, independently numbered*. All the counties published here appear in Volume One with the exception of Westmorland which has been placed first to produce standard numerical order. The text is straight-forward and no alterations have been made. Modern indexes of surnames and places have been compiled but original spellings and pagination have been retained and no distinction has been made between towns, villages or farms, in the case of places, or between variant spellings of what looks like the same surname. References such as 'at the same meeting' have been indexed under the appropriate name so that the number of refer-ences stated may be more than the number of appearances of the actual word.

Researchers in local history will find it worthwhile to look up the names of all people identified as attending a particular meeting and family historians should look up all the references to the places where their ances-tors lived. Breaking up a meeting, imprisonments or a campaign of distraint of goods affected everyone connected with a meeting, not just those who were directly involved. In the same way readers are reminded how well-informed Quakers were of what was happening elsewhere in the Quaker world and are strongly advised to read the general histories listed overleaf. All except Lloyd are in print, (the first two with Sessions of York).

The text contains the names of various ministers, magistrates and informers. All of these have been included.

December 1999

Recommended reading:

Braithwaite, Wm.C. *The beginnings of Quakerism to 1660.* (1912. 2nd ed 1981)

Braithwaite, Wm.C. *The second period of Quakerism.* (1919. 2nd ed 1979)

Lloyd, A. *Quaker social history 1669-1738.* (1950)

Milligan, E.H. and Thomas, M.J. *My ancestors were Quakers: How can I find out more about them?* (1983. 2nd ed 1999). SoG

Nickalls, J.L. (ed.) *The Journal of George Fox.* (1975)

Penney, N. *The First Publishers of Truth.* (1907)

Punshon, J. *Portrait in Grey: a short history of the Quakers.* (1984)

Notes:

1. Penney, N. Journal of the Friends Historical Society Vol 23 Nos 1-2 (1926)

2. Braithwaite, Wm.C. *The Second Period of Quakerism* (1919; reprint 1979) p285n

3. Butler, D.M. 'Friends' Sufferings 1650 to 1688: a comparative summary'. Journal of Friends Historical Society Vol 55 No 6 (1988)

Contents

Illustrations

A
COLLECTION
OF THE
SUFFERINGS
Of the PEOPLE called
QUAKERS.

VOL. II.

CHAP. I.

WESTMORLAND.

ANNO 1651.

I N this Year *Chriſtopher Biſbrown*, of *Arnſide*, was convinced of the Truth, as profeſſed by the *Quakers*, and being at that Time Churchwarden of the Pariſh, had a conſcientious Scruple of acting in that Office, and forbore to collect the Moneys called *Church-Dues*, for which Neglect he had Goods taken from him worth 5 s.

A conſcientious Scruple to act in the Office of Church-warden.

ANNO 1652. In this Year, *James Naylor* having been at a Meeting in the Houſe of *Edward Briggs* on the Firſt-day of the Week, where many came to hear him, was deſired by ſome of his Friends to meet next Day again at the Widow *Cock*'s about a Mile from *Kendal*; whereof the Prieſt having Notice, raiſed the Town of *Kendal* againſt him, but being long in getting their Company together, the Time of their Meeting was over; however, they had placed Spies on the Steeple and other high Places, to obſerve *James*, which Way he paſſed, and as he was coming toward *Kendal*, two Prieſts with a Juſtice of the Peace and ſome other Magiſtrates, with a great Multitude following them, met him, and one of the Prieſts ſaid to him, Naylor, *I have a Meſſage from the Lord Jeſus Chriſt to thee, but this is not a convenient Place.* To which *James* anſwered, *The Lord Jeſus Chriſt is no Reſpecter of Places.* The Prieſt then delivered what he called his Meſſage thus, *I conjure thee to tell me,*

Conferences between ſome Prieſts and J. Naylor.

by what Power thou * *inflictest such Punishment upon the Bodies of Creatures?* James answered, *Dost thou remember who it was that did adjure Christ to tell him if he were the Son of God*, and asked *by what Authority he did those Things?* But the Priest still conjured him to tell, *By what Power he did it?* James said, *Dost thou acknowledge it to be done by a Power? Yea*, said the Priest, *I have the Spirit of God, and thereby I know it is done by a Power.* James said, *If thou hast the Spirit of God, as thou sayst thou hast, then thou canst tell by what Power it is done.* The Priest said, *When God cometh, he comes to torment the Souls, and not the Bodies.* James replied, *He comes to redeem the Souls.* After which Discourse the Priest began to accuse him of many Things before the Justice and Magistrates, as *that he taught People to burn their Bibles, Children to disobey their Parents, Wives their Husbands, People to disobey their Magistrates*, and such like Accusations. To which James answered, *Thou art a false Accuser, prove one of these Things here if thou canst before the Magistrates.* But not being able to prove any Thing, he went on accusing James for *holding a Light that doth convince of Sin, which*, said the Priest, *all have not.* James replied, *Put out one of this great Multitude that dare say he hath it not.* He answered, *These are all* Christians, *but if a* Turk *or* Indian *were here, he would deny it.* James said, *Thou goest far for a Proof, but if a* Turk *were here, he would witness against thee.*

The People growing disorderly, the Priest turned away, saying, *There will be a Disturbance.* James said, *These are thy* Christians, *and this is the Fruit of thy Ministry.* The Justices endeavoured to keep the People from abusing him, yet many ran before to a Bridge, which he was to pass over, swearing *they would throw him off the Bridge into the Water*, but he undismayed passed through the Midst of them, testifying against their Fury, and received no Harm ; thus he passed through the Town and Market-place, declaring boldly the Word of the Lord, who restrained the rude People from hurting him, though they continued shouting, crying out, and throwing Stones at him for above a quarter of a Mile out of the Town.

At another Time James being at a Meeting at *Orton*, five Priests came thither, and many People from all Parts. The Priests asked him many Questions, to which he gave such Answers as prevented their Purpose of ensnaring him in his Words ; however the next First-day they had prepared their Sermons against him, representing him to the People as a *Blasphemer*, and as denying *the Resurrection and Humanity of Christ, and contemning all Authority.* And some of them, as their Hearers reported, said, *It would be doing God good Service to knock him down.* Having thus prepared the ruder Sort of People, one of the Priests Sons got a great Company of them together next Morning, who beset the House where *Naylor* was, threatning to *knock out his Brains against the Wall, and to pull the House down if he would not come out.* But he answered them thus, *You did not use me so civilly the last Time I was among you, but if any have a Mind they may come in, the Doors are*

open : Which Answer being told to the Priests, the Rabble rushed violently into the House, took him by the Throat, and dragged him into a Field, where a Justice, sent for by the Priests, was present. Then they struck off *James's* Hat with a Pitch-fork, and the Justice commanded him to answer such Questions as the Priests should ask him : Whereupon one of the Priests asked him many Questions, as concerning the *Resurrection*, the *Humanity of Christ*, the *Scriptures*, and other Things, to which he answered scripturally : At length, being asked, *If Christ was in him?* he answered, *I witness him in me in Measure.* The Priest asked him, *If Christ was in him as Man?* he answered, *Christ is*
not

---

* The divine Power which attended the Ministry of *Naylor*, and others of those early Witnesses to the Truth, wrought so effectually on the Spirits of some of their Hearers, that their Bodies were affected therewith to the Surprize of the Priests, and such as were not acquainted with the Nature of those Operations ; and which therefore this Priest ignorantly called *inflicting Punishment.*

not divided, for if he be, he is no more Chrift ; but I witnefs that Chrift is in me, in Meafure, who is God and Man. The Prieft faid, *Chrift is in Heaven with a carnal Body.* To which *James* anfwered, *Chrift filleth Heaven and Earth, and is not carnal, but Spiritual: For if Chrift be in Heaven with a carnal Body, and the Saints with a fpiritual Body, that is not proportionable, neither was that a carnal Body which came among the Difciples, the Doors being fhut : For Chrift is a Myftery, and thou knoweft him not.*

When after much Conference, the Prieft got little Advantage, he became angry, and warned the People not to receive him into their Houfes, and fo turned from him. Then the People began to abufe fome of the Friends prefent, but *James Naylor* faid to the Juftice, *Surely you will fet us peaceably into the Houfe again,* but he alfo turning away, as if he meant to leave them to the Mercy of the Rabble, *James* faid, *The Will of the Lord be done.* At which the Juftice being mov'd, returned, faying, *We will fet them in the Houfe again ;* and did fo : This difpleafed the Priefts, who were heard to fay, *If we let him go thus, all People will run after him.* Whereupon they agreed that he fhould be brought before the Juftice again : Then the Priefts and Juftice mounted their Horfes, and went to an Alehoufe at fome Diftance, and the Rabble having feized *James* again, hurried him after them. When they came, the Juftice told him, *If he would not put off his Hat, he would fend him to Prifon ;* and alfo becaufe he faid *Thou* to him, *for,* faid the Juftice, *my Commiffion runs Ye.* To which *James* anfwered, *I do it not in Contempt, for I own Authority, and honour it according to the Scriptures, but I find no fuch Honour commanded in Scripture, but forbidden.* Then they concluded to commit him to Prifon for that pretended Contempt, and alfo as being a Vagabond, faying, *None there knew whence he came :* Which was but a Quibble, for they had fhut his Acquaintance out of Doors. Then faid he to the Juftice, whofe Name was *Arthur Scarfe, Thou knoweft me, I was in the Army with thee eight or nine Years. It's no Matter,* faid the Juftice, *thou art no Soldier now.* So they made his *Mittimus,* and carried him that Night to *Kirkby-Steven,* and placed a Guard over him in a Chamber. Several of his Friends followed him, and among them, *Francis Howgill,* who took an Opportunity to preach to the People, who were got together in the Street to a great Number. Complaint of his Preaching being made, he was fent for before a Juftice, who commanded him *to put off his Hat :* He anfwered, *I know no fuch Law.* One of the Priefts, five of whom were prefent, faid, *He will tread both Miniftry and Magiftracy under Foot.* *Francis* replied, *Thou art a falfe Accufer ; prove wherein.* Then one of the Standers-by took off his Hat, and threw it into the Fire : Then faid the Juftice, *What is this thou fpeakeft againft the Minifters ?* He anfwered, *What haft thou to accufe me of ?* Whereupon one affirmed that he faid, *All Minifters that taught for Hire, and in the Steeple-houfes, were Enemies and Liars againft* Jefus Chrift, *and no Minifters of* Jefus Chrift. Upon that the Juftice faid, *Thou fpeakeft againft the Law, for the Law gives them their Maintenance.* He faid, *I meddle not with the Law, but with their Practice.* Then faid *Francis* to the Prieft, *Didft thou ever know a Minifter of Chrift that was a Perfecutor, or did labour to imprifon any ?* And after fome more Difcourfe, he faid to the Prieft, *I have feen a great deal of Tyranny and Perfecution in this Day's Actions.* Then faid the Juftice to the People, *Take Notice, he faith the Law I act by is Tyranny and Perfecution :* To which the People affented. Then faid *Francis, Thou mayft give out to the People what thou wilt, but I fpeak not of the Law, but of your Actions.* Upon that they made a *Mittimus* to fend him to Prifon, placing over him a Guard of eight Men, who fpent that Night in Drinking, Swearing, and filthy Talking, and the more they were reproved, the oftner they repeated their Wickednefs : On the Morrow he was, together with *Naylor,* fent to *Appleby* Goal.

At the Seffions, held at *Appleby* in the Month called *January* 1652, *James Naylor* was tried on an *Indictment for Blafphemy :* His Trial being as follows, *viz.*

Imprifonment of J. Naylor.

F. Howgill *alfo convened before the Juftice.*

Examined,

and fent to Prifon.

Juftice

W E S T-
M O R-
L A N D.
1652.

Trial of James
Naylor *at*
Appleby
Seffions for
Blafphemy.

Juftice *Pearfon.* P *U T* *off your Hat.*

Naylor. I do it not in Contempt of Authority ; for I honour the Power as it is of God, without Refpect of Perfons, it being forbidden by Scripture. He that refpects Men's Perfons commits Sin, and is convinced of the Law as a Tranfgreffor.

Juftice *Pearfon.* *That is meant of refpecting Perfons in Judgment.*

Naylor. If I fee one in goodly Apparel and a Gold Ring, and fee one in poor and vile Raiment, and fay to him in fine Apparel, *Sit thou in an higher Place than the Poor,* I am partial, and judged of evil Thoughts.

Colonel *Briggs. If thou waft in the Parliament-Houfe, wouldft thou keep it on?*

Naylor. If God fhould keep me in the fame Mind I am in now, I fhould.

Colonel *Briggs. I knew thou wouldft contemn Authority.*

Naylor. I fpeak in the Prefence of God : I do not contemn Authority, but I am fubject to the Power, as it is of God, for Confcience-fake.

Juftice *Pearfon. Now Authority commands thee to put off thy Hat : What fayft thou to it ?*

Naylor. Where God commands one Thing, and Man another, I am to obey God rather than Man.

Colonel *Briggs. See whether the Law commands it, or your own Wills.*

The Indictment was read, wherein he was charged with faying, that *Chrift was in him* ; and that *there was but one Word of God.*

Colonel *Briggs. Where waft thou born ?*

Naylor. At *Ardiflaw,* two Miles from *Wakefield.*

Colonel *Briggs. How long livedft thou there ?*

Naylor. Until I was married : Then I went into *Wakefield* Parifh.

Colonel *Briggs. What Profeffion waft thou of ?*

Naylor. An Hufbandman.

Colonel *Briggs. Waft thou a Soldier ?*

Naylor. Yea : I was a Soldier betwixt eight and nine Years.

Colonel *Briggs. Waft thou at* Burford *among the Levellers ?*

Naylor. I was never there.

Colonel *Briggs. I charge thee by the Lord, that thou tell me whether thou waft or no.*

Naylor. I was then in the *North,* and was never taxed for any Mutiny, or any other Thing, while I ferved the Parliament.

Colonel *Briggs. What was the Caufe of thy Coming into thefe Parts ?*

Naylor. If I may have my Liberty I fhall declare it : I was at the Plough, meditating on the Things of God, and fuddenly I heard a Voice, faying unto me, *Get thee out from thy Kindred, and from thy Father's Houfe :* And I had a Promife given in with it. Whereupon I did exceedingly rejoice, that I had heard the Voice of that God which I had profeffed from a Child, but had never known him.

Colonel *Briggs. Didft thou hear that Voice ?*

Naylor. Yea, I did hear it ; and when I came Home, I gave up my Eftate, and caft out my Money ; but not being obedient in going forth, the Wrath of God was on me, fo that I was made a Wonder to all, and none thought I would have lived. But (after I was made willing) I began to make fome Preparation, as Apparel and other Neceffaries, not knowing whither I fhould go : But fhortly after going a Gateward with a Friend from my own Houfe, having on an old Sute, without any Money, having neither taken Leave of Wife or Children, nor thinking then of any Journey, I was commanded to go into the *Weft,* not knowing whither I fhould go, nor what I had to do there, but when I had been there a little while, I had given me what I was to declare ; and everfince I have remained, not knowing To-day what I was to do To-morrow.

Colonel *Briggs. What was the Promife thou hadft given ?*

Naylor. That *God would be with me :* Which Promife I find made good every Day.

Colonel *Briggs. I never heard fuch a Call as this in our Time.*

Naylor. I believe thee.

Juftice

Juſtice *Pearſon.   Is Chriſt in thee ?*

Naylor. I witneſs him in me, and if I ſhould deny him before Men, he would deny me before his Father which is in Heaven.

Juſtice *Pearſon.   Spiritual, you mean.*

Naylor.   Yea, Spiritual.

Juſtice *Pearſon.   By Faith, or how ?*

Naylor.   By Faith.

Juſtice *Pearſon.   What Difference then between the Miniſters and you ?*

Naylor. The Miniſters affirm Chriſt to be in Heaven with a carnal Body, but I with a ſpiritual Body.

Juſtice *Pearſon.   Which of the Miniſters ſay, Chriſt is in Heaven with a carnal Body.*

Naylor.   The Miniſter, ſo called, of *Kirkby-Steven.*

Prieſt *Higginſon* ſtood up, and affirmed it again openly before all the Court.

Naylor. If Chriſt be in Heaven with a carnal Body, and the Saints with a ſpiritual Body, it is not proportionable ; neither was that a carnal Body which appeared among the Diſciples, the Doors being ſhut, and appeared in diverſe Shapes.

Queſt.   *Was Chriſt Man, or no ?*

Naylor. Yea, he was, and took upon him the Seed of *Abraham,* and was real Fleſh and Bones ; but this is a Myſtery not known to the carnal Man, for he is begotten of the *immortal Seed,* and thoſe that know him, know him to be Spiritual, for it was the Word that became Fleſh, and dwelt among us ; and if he had not been ſpiritual, he had not wrought by Redemption.

Juſtice *Pearſon.   Is Chriſt in thee as Man ?*

Naylor. Chriſt filleth all Places, and is not divided : Separate God and Man, and he is no more Chriſt.

Juſtice *Pearſon.   If we ſtand to diſpute theſe Things, we ſhould have the Miniſters.*

Naylor perceiving Prieſt *Higginſon* offended, becauſe he had told of his ſaying Chriſt was in Heaven with a carnal Body, ſaid, *Friend, I had not accuſed thee, had I not been aſked,* What was the Difference between the Miniſters and me ? *for I am not come to accuſe any, for I am againſt Accuſations.*

Colonel *Briggs.   Waſt thou not of a Kirk about* Sawrby ?

Naylor.   I was Member of an *Independent* Church at *Weed-church.*

Colonel *Briggs.   Waſt thou not excommunicated for thy blaſphemous Opinions ?*

Naylor. I know not what they have done ſince I came forth ; but before, I was not to my Knowledge.

Colonel *Briggs.   Mr.* Coale, *Did you e'er hear ſuch a Call as this ? Did you hear it ?*

Coale.   Yea, I heard Part of it.

Colonel *Briggs.   Didſt thou not write a Paper, wherein was mentioned, that if thou thinkeſt to be ſaved by that Chriſt which died at* Jeruſalem, *thou art deceived ?*

Naylor. If I cannot witneſs Chriſt nearer than *Jeruſalem,* I ſhall have no Benefit of him ; but I know no other Chriſt but that who witneſſed a good Confeſſion before *Pontius Pilate,* which I witneſs in me now.

Colonel *Briggs.   Wilt thou deny thine Hand ?*

Naylor. I will not deny my Hand if I may ſee it, and I deſire that I may have ſo much Favour, that that Paper may be kept as an Evidence either with or againſt me.

A large *Petition* was read, in which was ſomething againſt *Quaking* and *Trembling.*

Juſtice *Pearſon.   How comes it to paſs, that People* quake *and* tremble ?

Naylor. The Scriptures witneſs the ſame Condition in the Saints formerly, as *David, Daniel, Habakkuk,* and diverſe others.

WEST-
MOR-
LAND.
1652.

Juſtice *Pearſon.*   *Did they fall down ?*

Naylor.   Yea, ſome of them did ſo.

Coale.   David *ſaid,* All his Bones were broken, *but they were whole.*

Naylor.   So are theſe now.

Coale.   Moſes *trembled, for he ſaw the Face of God, and all* Iſrael.

Naylor.   Did all *Iſrael* ſee the Face of God ? that croſſeth the Scriptures.

Coale.   *They ſaw his Glory. I ſhall ſee the Lord with theſe Eyes ;* putting his Finger to his Eyes.

Naylor.   They muſt firſt be made ſpiritual : He cannot be ſeen with carnal Eyes, for he is a Spirit, and no Fleſh can ſee God and live.

Coale.   *That Light by which I am juſtified, is a created Light.*

Naylor.   That Light by which I am juſtified, is *not* a created Light.

Coale.   *That is true.*

Juſtice *Pearſon.*   *To the Word. What ſayſt thou to the Scriptures ? Are they the Word of God ?*

Naylor.   They are a true Declaration of the *Word* that was in them who ſpake them forth.

Higginſon.   *Is there not a written Word ?*

Naylor.   Where readeſt thou in the Scriptures of a written Word ? The Word is Spiritual, not ſeen with carnal Eyes ; but as for the Scriptures, they are true, and I witneſs them true, in Meaſure fulfilled in me, as far as I am grown up.

Juſtice *Pearſon.*   *Why doſt thou diſturb the Miniſters in their publick Worſhip ?*

Naylor.   I have not diſturbed them in their publick Worſhip.

Juſtice *Pearſon.*   *Why doſt thou ſpeak againſt* Tithes, *which are allowed by the States ?*

Naylor.   I meddle not with the States : I ſpeak againſt them that are Hirelings, as they are Hirelings. Thoſe that are ſent of Chriſt, never took *Tithes,* nor never ſued any for Wages.

Juſtice *Pearſon.*   *Doſt thou think we are ſo beggarly as the* Heathen, *that we cannot afford our Miniſters Maintenance ? We give it them freely.*

Naylor.   They are the Miniſters of Chriſt, who abide in the Doctrine of Chriſt.

Juſtice *Pearſon.*   *But who ſhall judge ? How ſhall we know them ?*

Naylor.   By their Fruits you ſhall know them : They that abide not in the Doctrine of Chriſt, make it appear they are not the Miniſters of Chriſt.

Juſtice *Pearſon.*   *That is true.*

J. Naylor
diſcharged.

Thus it appearing, after a long Examination, that the Prieſts could not make out the Charge of Blaſphemy exhibited againſt *Naylor,* he was diſcharged by the Juſtices from his Impriſonment, which had continued about twenty Weeks. Whether *Francis Howgill's* Confinement was at this Time of longer or ſhorter Continuance than his, our Accounts do not mention.

Death of
R. Hebſon.

ANNO 1656. *Thomas Alexander* and *Richard Hebſon,* for ſome Oppoſition to one of the Prieſts, were impriſoned at *Appleby,* where they were cruelly beaten and abuſed by the unmerciful Goaler, inſomuch that the ſaid *Richard Hebſon,* being put out of Priſon, in a few Days after died of the Hardſhips there received.

Thomas Taylor, Chriſtopher Taylor, and *Anne Airey,* were impriſoned in the ſame Goal for ſpeaking to one of the Prieſts. The ſaid *Chriſtopher Taylor* gave forth in Writing a *Repreſentation* of the Uſage they met with there, which he directed to the Officers and Magiſtrates, being as follows, viz.

C. Taylor's
*Repreſentation
of the Pri-
ſoners Uſage.*

" IF we were Thieves and Murderers, by your Law we ſhould not be thus " uſed as we are, and have been by this Goaler. Some of our Friends, " who have come to ſee us, coming no farther than the common Liberty " which ſhould be granted to any whatſoever, to bring us a little Water, " have been by him pulled down by the Legs, and others beaten, and others, " five or ſix, impriſoned by him many Hours, who ſome of them at that

" Time

" Time came to bring us our natural Food : Some of us beaten till he hath
" shed our Blood, with several other Cruelties and Abuses, as the imprisoning
" others at other Times, and cruel Threatnings : Our Meat and Water hath
" been hindred by him from coming to us, the rude People being suffered to
" abuse us, throwing Stones at us in the Goal. Some have drawn their Swords,
" thrusting them into the Goal to us full of Rage, gnashing with their Teeth
" because they could not get in to us to execute their bloody Intents. 'Tis well
" known to you how long the most of us have been here imprisoned, well
" near a whole Year, in a cold raw Place, in the Winter Season : Some, for
" want of Fire, for any Pity there is in you, may perish ; and in the hot
" Summer our Bodies may faint through smothering Heats, and ill Savours,
" which do arise up out of the lower Goal from among the Felons, and the
" Smells which cannot be avoided from being among our selves. Some of us
" in the hot Weather, being faint and weak through these Things, have been
" glad of a little Air through the Grate, as we have been of our natural Food,
" being both equally useful for the preserving of our natural Lives, and yet
" there is nothing in you that can pity us : Also he has often kept the Out-
" door lockt through Envy, left our Friends should come near us to the Bars,
" and yet we could not any Way get a little Water to relieve our Thirst. His
" Rage and Cruelty hath formerly been laid before you, beating of us bloodily
" and desperately, searching our Pockets several Times, breaking nine of our
" Knives, holding two of them against our Breasts with the Points in a des-
" perate Manner, breaking them, tearing and throwing under Foot our Pen,
" Ink, and Paper, Candle and Candlestick down the Stairs, threatning with
" manacling us, and binding us in Chains by the Neck, charging us for light-
" ing a Candle in the Winter Season, we having no Fire ; taking away our
" Steel, and throwing away our Flint ; causing our Meat to be carried back,
" and us to fast or starve ; holding a blazing Candle under one Friend's Chin,
" and afterward, like a cruel Tyrant, to his Nose, till the Breath of his Nostrils
" blew it out.
    " The most of these Things have been formerly laid before you, and you
" have been *prone* to it, and there was no Redress, but he was afterward, it
" seems, more encouraged from you, which hath made him since persecute
" so bloodily without Fear or Care, having since, as it seems, Murder both
" in his Heart and Hands, as by his Words and Works to his Power did ap-
" pear against *John Spooner*, but that his own Wife understanding it, did at
" that Time restrain him, for which he beat her, and imprisoned her above
" fixteen Hours, with two of the Town that came to deliver her from his
" Cruelty at that Time. Was there ever the like Cruelty acted upon any who
" were Prisoners ? Though we are imprisoned by you only for the satisfying
" your Wills, and crying against your Sins, and the Sinners of these Times,
" which cry unto God for Vengeance, which will be freely poured upon you,
" if you speedily repent not. And these Things, with many more of your
" Cruelties against the Servants of the Lord, shall stand as a Record against
" you to after Ages, that they may see your bloody Minds, and all may see
" that God is clear when he judgeth, and justified in his Judgments, and the
" Hand of the Lord will lie heavy upon you, who scoff and laugh at these
" Things when they are laid before you, and thereby you strengthen the Hands
" of the evil Doers, and bear the Sword in vain, which should be turned
" against your selves, Drunkards, Swearers, Adulterers, bloody Persecutors,
" and such like, who are encouraged through you. *Woe*, *Woe*, unto you, often
" have you been warned of the Judgments of God which are to come upon
" you, and you have not believed nor repented, but harden your Hearts like
" cruel Oppressors, and make Authority your Cloak for persecuting the
" Innocent, and say you do it in the Name of his Highness the *Lord-Protector*
" of *England*, but the Lord God of Heaven and Earth, who is our *Protector*
" and Keeper, will plead our Cause, and it is and will be a Day of Joy to us,
" when to you it will be a Day of bitter Weeping and Lamentation, and to
                                                      " all

WEST-
MOR-
LAND.
1656.

" all bloody Perfecutors whatfoever, who are hardened againſt the Fear of the
" Lord, and in giving you Warning, we are clear of your Blood if you
" periſh.

" CHRISTOPHER TAYLOR,

" *Priſoner in the Goal at* Appleby *for the Truth's Sake.*"

To this we ſhall annex the Cafe of *John Spooner,* one of thoſe who viſited the
Priſoners there, as penned by himſelf, *viz.*

Cafe of John
Spooner.

" UPON the 16th Day of this Month, the Goaler, *George Beck,* who
" is alfo in the Conſtable's Place, came down to the Goal about two of
" the Clock in the Afternoon, to let out a Priſoner, one of the Felons, to beg
" in the Town, who, it feems, knowing me, or ſome of us, to be upon the
" Stairs, did haſtily pull to him the outer Door, and locked it : About two
" Hours after, he came to let the Priſoner into the Goal again, and when the
" outer Door was open, I came down, thinking to go peaceably away :
" and then he aſked me, *What I had to do there ?* I ſaid, *I came to ſee my*
" *Friends.* Then he lockt me in, and fell in a Rage, and beat me bloodily
" with the Keys about my Head and Face, and bruiſed me till Blood came
" forth at my Mouth, until the Strings broke ; he broke my Head, and jolled
" me ſeveral Times againſt the Wall, and when he had done fo, I bid him
" *See how he had bloodied me :* He anſwered, *Rogue, I ſhall blood thee :* And
" then he gathered up the Keys again, and ſtruck me again with the Keys,
" and jolled me to and fro : Then I would have gone my Way, and he thruſt
" me violently back, and lockt the Door, and kept me there till after nine
" of the Clock at Night. Then he afterward, in his Houſe, boaſted to *Georgе*
" *Teeber,* of *Orton,* how *He did beat me till the Keys flew about my Ears, and*
" *he intended to go down again,* and ſaid, *What he had done, was but Earneſt, or*
" in that Manner, and ſaid, *He would give me more.* His Wife privately
" hearing him ſay fo, and the Intent of his farther Cruelty, followed after him,
" and when he had opened the Door, he called on me, and I came down, and
" he took me by the Throat, and bringing a Cudgel with him, fell deſpe-
" rately a beating me with it, and then his Wife ſtepped in, and got faſt hold
" on him, and fo I went forth, and then he fell a beating his Wife in much
" Cruelty and Rage, and two Men of the Town feeing him, they came to
" help her, and intreat him, or hold him, and he locked them all within the
" Goal-door, and kept them there till almoſt four of the Clock in the Morning.

" JOHN SPOONER."

Diſtreſſes

ANNO 1660. In this and ſome preceding Years were taken for Tithes
demanded from divers Perfons in this County, amounting to 36 *l.* 8 *s.* 5 *d.*
Cattle, Corn, and other Goods, worth 140 *l.* 12 *s.* 4 *d.* Alfo for Claims of
Church-Rates and *Eaſter-Offerings,* amounting to no more than 9 *s.* Goods to
the Value of 1 *l.* 6 *s.* 4 *d.*

*and Impriſon-
ments for
Tithes,*

William Hebſon, for his conſcientious Refuſal to pay Tithes, fuffered forty
Weeks Impriſonment : And *John Fothergill,* for the fame Caufe, was impriſoned fourteen Months : *William Cartmell* and *Mabell Camm,* were alfo impriſoned for the fame Caufe.

*Richard Sill, Edward Robinſon, Thomas Robertſon, Thomas Atkinſon, Henry
Ward, Thomas Wright,* and *Iſabel Garnet,* were profecuted in the *Exchequer* for
refuſing to pay Tithes. Alfo *Robert Story,* of *Birkrigg-Park,* was fued at
Common Law by *Edward Wilſon,* of *Dallan-Tower,* Efq; for feven Years
Tithe, and fuffered the Lofs of more than 50 *l.*

*and for
for refuſing
to Swear.*

Arthur Burrow, Thomas Sill, Richard Sill, and *Daniel Tompſon,* all of *Preſton-
Patrick, Robert Atkinſon* of *Birkrigg-Park, Edward Burrow* of *Lapton, Richard
Parke* of *Wood-houſe,* and *William Cartmell* of *Warth-Sadden,* were all taken

from

from their own Houfes by Order from Captain *John Lowther*, and upon their
Refufal to take the Oath of Allegiance were committed to Prifon, fome at
Kendal, and others at *Appleby*, where they continued feveral Weeks.

On the coming forth of the King's Proclamation in the Month called
January this Year, the Deputy-Lieutenants of the County iffued forth Warrants
to the High-Conftable, who in Purfuance of their Inftructions, fent the following
Orders, *viz.*

" *To the Conftables of the Parifh of* ————

" Weftmorland *fs.*

" W HEREAS I have received a Warrant from his Majefty's Deputy-
" Lieutenants of this County, for the fuppreffing of all numerous and
" unlawful Meetings, by Virtue of a certain fpecial Order from his Majefty :
" Thefe are to require you to give publick Notice within your Conftable-
" wick, that from the 11th of this Inftant *January*, there be no numerous
" Meetings of *Quakers*, *Sectaries*, or other difaffected Perfons, in any fecret or
" unufual Places, upon any Pretence whatfoever, as they will avoid the
" Penalties and Forfeitures which by the Laws of this Nation are to be im-
" pofed upon fuch Offences. Dated the 5th Day of *January* 1660.

" THO. RIGG, *High-Conftable.*"

In Confequence of thefe Orders many of the People called *Quakers* were
foon apprehended at their feveral Meetings in this County, of whom fifty two
were imprifoned at *Appleby*, and fixty four at *Kendal*, in all one Hundred and
fixteen. Of thofe at *Appleby*, *Thomas Holme*, *Edmund Arlington*, and four
others, were kept clofer than the reft, being denied the common Privileges
granted to Felons, the only Reafon of which, fo far as they could learn, was,
that the Oath had been tendred to them, and refufed before their Commitment.
Among thofe at *Kendal* were *John Audland*, *Miles Halhead*, *Miles Huberfty*,
and *Stephen Huberfty*, who in the following Letter, pathetically expreffes the
Innocence and Conftancy of himfelf, and his Fellow-fufferers, *viz.*

STEPHEN HUBERSTY's L E T T E R *to* FRANCIS HOWGILL,

" Kendal, *the 9th of the Twelfth Month* 1660.

" *My Dear and Well beloved Friend and Brother in the Lord !*

" M Y dear and everlafting Love in the Lord Jefus Chrift is unto thee,
" and to our Brethren, and knowing affuredly, that thou art a Pillar
" in the Church of our God, whereof Chrift Jefus is the Head, who is the
" Head of Principalities and Powers, and who is our Head, *God bleffed for*
" *ever and ever*, Amen, to whom we and the Saints owe Subjection in all
" Things, who is become our exceeding great Reward, and eternal Portion
" for ever. Dearly doth my Soul falute thee, and embrace thee in the Spirit
" of Life, and in God's holy Covenant, in which the Faithful are united and
" joined firmly together, in this Day of Trial and Sufferings, which is come
" upon many to try their Faith and Patience, and who will ftand by the
" Lord in the Day of Trial and Sufferings, and who will not. And this we
" are affured, and that from the Lord, that we are innocent and harmlefs
" as Lambs, and had no fuch Thing in our Heart, for which they feem to
" accufe us, and for which we thus fuffer, and are haled to Prifon, and per-
" fecuted. O Lord, lay not this Sin to their Charge. And we are clear,
" God knows, and redeemed out of Wars, and that for which they pretend
" to lay this heavy Yoke and Bondage upon us, though we are free in the
" Lord, and we know that we are delivered from the Evil to come, though
" we fuffer. Friends here-aways are pretty well generally, as far as I know,

WEST-
MOR-
LAND.
1660.

" through great Sufferings and Spoilings, and twining up and down the
" innocent Lambs of Chrift. The Lord give all Patience to perfevere unto
" the End, that we may inherit Eternal Life, and that Crown of Glory
" which is in the Lord's Hand for the Faithful, and God give us Patience,
" we knowing that in Heaven there is laid up a better and more enduring Sub-
" ftance. Friends of *Kendal* have been tolfed up and down, of which it is
" likely thou haft heard, and divers taken out of *Prefton* Meeting, and with
" fome of *Kendal* carried to *Appleby*. *Underborough* Meeting has efcaped yet
" pretty well, only *Miles B—* was taken at *Kendal*. God's Love is large to
" us, and, I believe, we fhall not ftart afide like a broken Bow, but God give
" us Courage to go through that Suffering which he permits to come upon us,
" which I hope in Time may tend to fome of our Good. So God Almighty
" be with us, and keep us for ever, *Amen*. And let thy Prayers be to God for
" us, that we may be preferved if harder Trials come. So, Dear *Francis*,
" farewel, whom I much honour in the Lord. I am

" *Thy Loving and Dear Friend, whom thou knoweft,*

" Stephen Hubersty."

More Prifoners at Kendal,

The Number of Prifoners at *Kendal* was fhortly after enlarged by the Commitment of *Robert Story, John Audland, James Sill, Henry Horfeman, John
Middleton, William Story, Charles Story,* and fome others, who being taken
at a Meeting at *Birkrigg-Park,* and carried before *Allen Bellingham* Juftice, he
tendred them the Oath, and upon their Refufal to take it committed them to
Prifon.

and at Apple-by.

About the fame Time *Henry Ward, Thomas Robertfon, Peter Mofer, Edward
Fawcet, James Beck, Allen Wilfon, James Rowlandfon, William Farrer,* and
Thomas Ayrey, of *Blakethwaite,* having been at a Meeting at the faid *Henry
Ward's* Houfe, were taken before *James Ducket,* of *Grayrigg,* a Juftice of the
Peace, who tendred them the Oath of Allegiance, and upon their refufing to
take it committed them to *Appleby* Goal, where they were detained till the
next Quarter Seffions.

Diftreffes for Tithes.

ANNO 1661. *Jane Johnfon,* of *Stubbe,* Widow, after a Profecution in the
Exchequer for Tithes, had her Goods taken away to the Value of 40*l*. *Ifabel
Garnet,* for Tithe of four Acres, had Goods taken from her to the Value
of 40*s.* *John Dickinfon,* of *Grayrigg,* was feveral Times imprifoned, and put
to more than 10*l.* Charge, for not paying Tithes.

Imprifonment.

Peter Mofer, of *Grayrigg,* was imprifoned for a trivial Sum demanded for an
Eafter-Offering, at the Suit of *William Brownfwood,* Prieft of *Kendal :* He remained in Prifon till the Parfon had prevailed on the Affection of his Mother
to pay 40*s.* for his Difcharge.

ANNO 1662. The three Perfons next under-named, were taken at a religious Meeting on the 14th of the Month called *July,* and conftrained to
appear at the Quarter Seffions at *Appleby* the next Day, where they were fined,
and by Order of Court fhortly after had Goods taken as follows, *viz.*

	l.	*s.*	*d.*
Diftreffes for Meeting. William Hobfon, for a Fine of 5*l.* two Cows worth	7	0	0
John Boulton, for a Fine of 5*l.* Leather worth	6	0	0
Michael Langhorne, for a Fine of 4*l.* 10*s.* two Cows worth	5	0	0
For Fines of 14*l.* 10*s.* 0*d.* Taken	17	0	0

Imprifon-ments.

At the fame Seffions *Thomas Langhorne* was fined 5*l.* and *Robert Hutchinfon* 4*l.*
and both of them were committed to Prifon for Non-payment.

Chriftopher Bifbrown, for 6*d.* claimed for a Church-Rate, had Goods taken
from him to five Times that Value.

ANNO

ANNO 1663. *William Cartmell*, for a Demand of 7 *s. Richard Thompson*, for 2 *s.* and *Arthur Burrow*, for 5 *d.* ¼ *d.* demanded for Tithes, were caſt into Priſon, at the Suit of *Richard Brown*, Prieſt of *Barton*, and were continued Priſoners thirty three Weeks.

Taken this Year from *Chriſtopher Biſbrown*, for 4 *s.* 4 *d.* claimed for Church-dues, Goods worth 12 *s.* 6 *d.*

Imprisonments and Distresses.

About the ſame Time *Elizabeth Story*, a Widow of *Preſton-Patrick*, was proſecuted for 1 *d.* ¼ *d.* demanded for Communicant-Money by *Richard Brown*, Prieſt of *Barton*, for which trifling Claim ſhe was put to an Expence of 4 *l.*

About the End of the Month called *July* this Year, *Francis Howgill* being in the Market-place at *Kendal* about his ordinary Buſineſs, was ſummoned by the High-Conſtable to appear before the Juſtices, then ſitting at a Tavern, who tendred him the Oath of Allegiance, and committed him to Priſon till the Aſſizes to be held in the next Month at *Appleby* : Being brought thither, the Oath was again tendred him, and upon Refuſal to take it, an Indictment was drawn up againſt him, which he traverſing, had Liberty till the next Aſſizes to anſwer thereto. Accordingly at the following *Lent* Aſſizes he appeared, where Sir *Philip Muſgrave*, a violent Man, endeavoured to incenſe the Judges againſt him as *a dangerous Perſon, a Ringleader of the* Quakers, *and a great Upholder of their Meetings.* A Copy of his Examination at that Aſſizes, held before Judge *Twiſden* at *Appleby*, is as follows, *viz.*

Commitment of F. Howgill.

Being brought to the Bar, the Judge proceeded very calmly, and ſpake as follows, *viz.*

His Examination at the Assizes.

Judge. *The Time being dangerous, and Things having now a worſe Appearance than at the laſt Aſſizes, and People, under Pretence of Conſcience, violating the Laws, and hatching Treaſons and Rebellions, although I have nothing of that Kind to charge againſt you, yet ſeeing you did refuſe to take the Oath of Allegiance at the laſt Aſſizes, the Law doth preſume ſuch Perſons to be Enemies to the King and Government, however I ſhall give you Time to prepare for your Trial till the next Aſſizes, only you muſt enter into Recognizance for your Appearance then, and for your good Behaviour in the mean Time.*

F. H. I deſire I may have Liberty of Speech : *Which being granted, he proceeded,*

Thou very well knoweſt, Judge *Twiſden*, upon how ſlender an Account, or none, I was brought before thee the laſt Aſſizes, where thou waſt pleaſed to tender me the Oath of Allegiance, though, I believe, both thou and the reſt of the Court did know that it was a received Principle amongſt us, *Not to Swear at all* : Many Reaſons I then gave to ſhew, that I did not refuſe the Oath out of Obſtinacy, but conſcientiouſly, and that I was none of them that made Religion a Cloak of Maliciouſneſs, nor Conſcience a Cloak to carry on Plots and Conſpiracies : The Lord hath redeemed me and many more out of ſuch Things. I deſire therefore that my verbal Promiſe and Engagement to appear at the next Aſſizes may be accepted.

Judge. *You muſt enter into Bond in this dangerous Time : I would have you conſider of it, and either give me your Anſwer now, or before we go out of Town.*

A Day or two after he was called again, and appeared.

Judge *Twiſden* made a Speech concerning Treaſons and Rebellions, ſaying, *Theſe Things were carried on under Pretence of Conſcience and Religion,* and reflected on the *Quakers.*

F. H. As to thoſe Things, I am clear : I hope neither the Court nor Country have any Thing to lay to my Charge : I bleſs the Lord I have nothing to accuſe my ſelf with, for I have Peace, and ſeek it with all Men ; and ſeeing the Court is pleaſed to give me Time, to anſwer my Indictment, till the next Aſſizes, and ſince it is a Matter of great Conſequence to me, on which my Liberty and Eſtate depends, I hope the Court will not be againſt my having Liberty for theſe five Months to prepare for my Trial.

Judge. *We do not deſire your Impriſonment, if you will be of good Behaviour.*

Juſtice *Flemming. My Lord, he is a great Speaker, it may be the* Quakers *cannot do without him.*

Judge.

Judge. *Let him be what he will, if he will enter into Bond. What do you tell us of Conscience, we meddle not with that, but you contemn the Laws, and keep up great Meetings, and go not to Church.*

F. H. It has been a Doctrine always held by us, and a received Principle as any Thing we believed, that Christ's Kingdom could not be set up with carnal Weapons, nor the Gospel propagated by Force of Arms, nor the Church of God builded with Violence ; but the Prince of Peace is manifest among us, and we cannot learn War any more, but can love our Enemies, and forgive them that do Evil to us : And though this unhappy Contrivance hath fallen among some Men, who have brought Trouble on the Country, and Misery on themselves, we have had no Hand in it : This is the Truth, and if I had twenty Lives, I would engage them all, that the Body of the *Quakers* will never have any Hand in War, or Things of that Nature, that tend to the Hurt of others, and if any such, whom you repute to be *Quakers*, be found in such Things, I do, before the Court here, and before all the Country, deny them : They are not of us.

Justice Musgrave. *My Lord, we have been remiss toward this People, and have striven with them, and put them in Prison again and again, and as soon as they are out they meet again.*

Sir John Lowther. *My Lord, they grow insolent, notwithstanding all Laws, and the Execution of them, yet they grow upon us, and their Meetings are dangerous.*

Justice Musgrave. *My Lord, it happened that some of the* Quakers *being sent to Prison, one of them died there, and they carried his Corps through the Country, and set this Paper on the Coffin,* This is the Body of such an one, who was persecuted by *Daniel Flemming* to Death.

He pulled out the * Paper, and they handed it from one to another, but did not publickly read it.

F. H. Notwithstanding here has been diligent Enquiry made by the Grand Jury concerning this Plot, what have you found against the *Quakers* ?

Justice Musgrave. *There was one* Reginald Fawcett, *a Quaker, that is run away, that was an Intelligencer from the County of* Durham.

F. H. *Fawcett* has been disown'd by us these six Years, nor do I believe he hath pretended to come among us these two Years : And if perhaps any reputed by you *Quakers*, should be found Offenders in this Nature, I believe they would testify for us against themselves, that *the Body of our Friends and Meetings every where did disown them.* It is therefore unkind to represent us so hardly to the Country. God is with us, and hath kept us from Evils and Temptations of this Nature, of plotting and fighting, notwithstanding all the Provocations and Sufferings we have passed through.

Judge. *The Gentlemen and I have spent much Time with you, and I shall not discourse with you any longer.*

F. H. I acknowledge your Moderation towards me, and I shall not trouble you much longer. I shall be willing to appear to answer my Indictment at the Assizes, and shall in the mean while live peaceably and quietly as I have always done.

Judge. *You must enter into Bond, and come at no more Meetings.*

F. H. I cannot do that, if I should, I must be treacherous to God and my own Conscience, and even you your selves, and this People, would think me an Hypocrite.

The

---

* A Copy of the Paper affixed to the Coffin of *Samuel Sandys*, of *Roger-Ground* near *Hawkshead.*

" This was a Prisoner for the Lord Jesus Christ, and for the Testimony of the Truth of
" God as it is in Jesus, hath he offered up his Life for a Witness thereof, and for an Example
" and Encouragement to all that shall be in the Truth, and a Warning to them that perse-
" cute the Truth, that make Widows and fatherless Children, that they may consider the
" dreadful Judgment Day, and Everlasting Sentence from Christ in that Day, which saith,
" *Go into Everlasting Punishment* to them that did not visit Christ in Prison, and what will
" become of them that cast into Prison, where he is manifested in his Members."

The Court ordered him to Prison, and as he was going out he turned to the People, saying, *The Fear of God be amongst you all.*

The People generally appeared very loving and affectionate to him, and much pitied his Case.

On the 19th of *October*, fifteen Friends were taken at a Meeting in the House of the Widow *Cocke* at *Birkhagge*, for which they were afterward indicted at the Sessions, and several of them fined. Three of them, *John Ayrey, Robert Barrow*, and *Brian Lancaster*, were committed to Prison, where they lay above eleven Months.

On the 8th of *November, Anthony Bownas, Nicholas Denkin, Robert Bowman*, and *Thomas Sourby*, were forced from a religious Meeting, and committed to Prison ; as were on the 22d of the same Month, *John Morland, Edward Guy, John Salkeld, John Brown*, and *John Kendal* ; and on the 29th of the same, *John Bolton, William Hebson, Thomas Langhorn, Robert Robinson, Thomas Langhorn* jun. and *George Denison* : On the 6th of *December, Robert Hutchinson, William Berwick, George Berwick, Edward Winter*, and *Thomas Smith* ; and on the 13th of the same, *William Fallowfield, William Bland, Richard Ayrey*, and *Henry Bowman*. At the next Sessions, in the Month called *January*, they were all fined, and generally had their Goods distrained. But the said *William Hebson, John Bolton*, and *Thomas Langhorn*, having been before fined for a first Offence, were now fined for the second Offence, and it was thought the Magistrates had an Intention of proceeding to banish them, if taken the third Time.

On the 28th of *December, Edward Robinson* was taken at a Meeting, and committed to Prison, at the Sessions fined 40 *s.* and for Non-payment committed to the House of Correction three Months.

On the 13th of the Month called *March* 1663-4, *Anthony Bownas, William Fallowfield, Thomas Langhorn, Thomas Langhorn* jun. *Robert Winter, Henry Bowman, George Dennison, John Hobson*, and *Thomas Hobson*, being assembled to worship God, were taken out of their Meeting, and carried before a Justice of the Peace, who made a *Mittimus*, and sent them from Constable to Constable, to the County Goal : Whither also *Lancelot Fallowfield* and *John Ayrey* had been sent on the 10th of the same Month.

ANNO 1664. *Miles Walker*, of *Middleton*, for a Demand of 1 *l.* 13 *s.* for Tithes, had Goods taken from him worth 12 *l.* Also *Robert Atkinson*, of *Middleton*, had taken from him for Tithes, two Mares, two Caldrons, and six Pewter Platters, worth 10 *l.*

In this Year *Christopher Bisbrown* was sued for Tithes to an Outlawry, and taken up on a Commission of Rebellion by *Robert Wilkinson*, a Bayliff of *Kendal*, at the Suit of *James Ducket*, of *Grayrigg* : The Plantiff, instead of having him carried up to *London*, as the Writ required, to appear personally in the Court of *Exchequer*, found Means to keep him close Prisoner in the Bayliff's House above sixteen Months, endeavouring by that Means to force him to a Compliance : But the old Man, who was then seventy seven Years of Age, bore his Confinement with *Christian* Patience, and at length died in the said Bayliff's House, the Place of his long Imprisonment.

Richard Burrough, of *Arnside*, Son-in-Law to the old Man last mentioned, was taken at the same Time with his Father, and detained Prisoner in the said Bayliff's House two Years and nine Months.

Robert Story, of *Birkrigg-Park*, and *Thomas Pearson* and *John Pearson*, both of *Powbank*, were sued in the *Exchequer* for Tithes, at the Suit of *Thomas Briggs*, Priest of *Haversham*, and upon a Commission of Rebellion, were attached by *Robert Wilkinson*, who was both Bayliff and one of the Commissioners. But after their Apprehension, it was discovered that the Priest had proceeded illegally against them, and that they had a manifest Advantage both against him and the Commissioners for their false Imprisonment : Nevertheless, they rendred not Evil for Evil, but freely forgave them, having learned the

Margin notes:

WESTMORLAND. 1663.

His Recommitment to Prison.

Imprisonments for Meeting.

Distresses for Tithes.

Outlawry.

Patience and Death of an aged Sufferer.

More Imprisonments.

Christian Forgiveness.

W E S T-
M O R-
L A N D.
1664.

*Diſtreſſes for
Steeple-houſe
Rates.*

Chriſtian Doctrine of *loving Enemies,* of *doing Good* to thoſe that *hated* them, and *praying* for thoſe who *deſpitefully uſed* and *perſecuted* them.

In this Year *John Watſon,* of *Thirmby,* had his Goods taken by Diſtreſs for his own and his Wife's not receiving the Sacrament, though his Wife was then dead. But it was not unuſual with Informers to be guilty of ſuch Miſtakes. In this Year alſo, *Miles Walker,* for 1 *s.* 6 *d.* demanded for an *Eaſter-Reckoning,* by *John Smith,* Prieſt of *Kirby-Lonſdale,* had Goods taken from him to the Value of 18 *s.*

In our Relation of the laſt Year, we left *Francis Howgill* returned to Priſon till another Aſſizes, which were in the Month called *Auguſt* this Year. At the Coming of the Judges, he cauſed two Papers to be preſented them ; one of them was a Declaration containing the Subſtance of the Oath, and the other a modeſt Defence of himſelf for refuſing to Swear : Both which he was informed the Judges read. We ſhall in the next Place lay before our Reader,

The P R O C E E D I N G S *againſt the ſaid* FRANCIS HOWGILL, *before Judge* TURNER, *at the Aſſizes at* Appleby, *the* 22*d and* 23*d of the Month called* Auguſt 1664.

Clerk. *B* R I N G Francis Howgill *to the Bar.*

Judge. *Here is an* Indictment *againſt you for refuſing to Swear, you muſt plead* Guilty, *or* Not Guilty.

F. H. May I have Liberty to ſpeak and make my Defence ?

Judge. *Yes, you may.*

F. H. I will lay the true State of the Caſe before thee, ſeeing Judge *Twiſden* is not here, who was privy to all the Proceedings hitherto againſt me. I was born and brought up in this County ; my Carriage and Converſation is known, that I have walked peaceably toward all Men, as I hope, my Country-men can teſtify. About a Year ago, being in a neighbouring Market-Town, about my reaſonable and lawful Occaſions, I was ſent for, by an High-Con-ſtable, out of the Market to the Juſtices of the Peace, before whom I went : They had nothing to lay to my Charge, but fell to aſking Queſtions to enſnare me about our Meetings, and when they could find no Occaſion, they ſeemed to tender me the Oath of Allegiance, though they never read it to me, nor did I poſitively deny it ; yet they committed me to Priſon. At the next Aſſizes Judge *Twiſden* declared that my *Mittimus* was *inſufficient :* Nevertheleſs, he there tendred me the Oath, and engaged me to appear the next Aſſizes after, which I did, and then refuſing to give Bond for the good Behaviour, and not to be preſent at any of our Meetings, I was committed to Priſon, where I have been theſe five Months, ſome of that Time under great Reſtraint, and my Friends not ſuffered to ſpeak to me. Now as to the Oath, the Subſtance thereof, with the Repreſentation of my Caſe, is already preſented to the Court, unto which I have ſet my Hand, and ſhall in thoſe Words teſtify the ſame in open Court, if required ; and ſeeing it is the very Subſtance of what the Law doth require, I deſire it may be accepted, and that I may be cleared from my Impriſonment.

Judge. *I am come to execute the Law ; and the Law requires an Oath, and I cannot alter it : Do you think the Law muſt be changed for you, or only for a few ? If this be ſuffered, the Adminiſtration of Juſtice is hindred ; no Action can be tried, nor Evidence given for the King : Your Principles are altogether incon-ſiſtent with the Law and Government : I pray you ſhew me which Way we ſhall proceed : Shew me ſome Reaſon, and give me ſome Ground.*

F. H. I ſhall : In the Mouth of two or three Witneſſes every Truth is confirmed, and we never denied to give, and ſtill are ready to give Evidence for the King in any Matter for the ending of Strife between Man and Man, in Truth and Righteouſneſs, and this anſwers the Subſtance of the Law.

Judge. *Is this a good Anſwer, think you ? Whether to be given with an Oath or without an Oath ? The Law requires an Oath.*

F. H.

F. H. Still Evidence may be given in Truth, according to the Substance of the Law, so that no Detriment cometh unto any Party, seeing true Testimony may be born without an Oath ; and I did not speak of changing the Law : Yet seeing we never refused to give Testimony, which answereth the End and Substance of the Law, I thought it reasonable to receive our Testimony, and not to expose us to such Sufferings, seeing we scruple an Oath only on a conscientious Account, for fear of breaking the Command of Christ, the Saviour of the World, which if we do, there is none of you able to plead our Cause for us with him.

Judge. *But why do you not go to Church, but meet in Houses and private Conventicles, which the Law forbids ?*

F. H. We meet together only for the Worship of the true God in Spirit and in Truth, having the primitive *Christians* for our Example, and to no other End but that we may be edified, and God glorified, and where two or three are met together in the Name of Christ, and he in the Midst of them, there is a Church.

Judge. *That is true : But how long is it since you have been at Church, or will you go to the Church the Law doth allow of ? Give me some Reasons why you do not go ?*

F. H. I have many to give, if thou hast Patience to hear me. 1*st*, God dwells not in Temples made with Hands. 2*dly*, The Parish-house hath been a Temple for Idols, and I dare not have Fellowship with Idols, nor worship in Idols Temples ; for what have we to do with Idols, their Temple, or Worship ?

Judge. *Were there not Houses called the Houses of God, and Temples ?*

F. H. Yes, under the Law, but the *Christians*, who believed in Christ, separated from these, and the Temple was made, and left desolate ; and from the *Gentiles* Temple too, and met together in Houses, and broke Bread from House to House, and the Church was not confined then to one particular Place, neither is it now.

Judge. *Will you answer to your* Indictment ?

F. H. I know not what it is. I never heard it, though I often desired a Copy.

Judge. *Clerk, read it.*

The *Indictment* was read, importing, that *he had wilfully, obstinately, and contemptuously denied to Swear, when the Oath was tendred.*

F. H. I deny it.

Judge. *What do you deny ?*

F. H. The *Indictment.*

Judge. *Did you deny to Swear ?*

F. H. I gave unto the Court the Substance of the Oath, as you all know : I also told you, that *I did not deny it out of Obstinacy or Wilfulness,* neither in Contempt of the *King's Law and Government,* for I would rather chuse my Liberty than Bonds, and I am sensible it is like to be a great Damage to me : I have a Wife and Children, and some Estate, which we might subsist upon, and do Good to others : And I know all this lies at Stake, but if it were my Life also, I dare not but do as I do, lest I should incur the Displeasure of God ; and do you judge, I would lose my Liberty wilfully, and suffer the Spoiling of my Estate, and the Ruining of my Wife and Children in Obstinacy and Wilfulness, surely not.

Judge. *Jury, you see he denies the Oath, and will not plead to the* Indictment, *only excepts against it because of the Form of Words, but you see he will not Swear, and yet he says he denies the* Indictment, *and you see upon what Ground.*

Then the Goaler was called, and gave Evidence, that *the Oath was tendred to him at a former Assizes, which he did refuse to take.*

So the Jury, without going from the Bar, gave in their Verdict *Guilty,* and the Court broke up for that Night.

The

The next Day, toward Evening, he was again brought to the Bar to hear his Sentence.

Judge. *Come : The* Indictment *is proved againſt you : What have you to ſay, why Sentence ſhould not be given ?*

F. H. I have many Things to ſay, if you will hear them. 1ſt, As I have ſaid, I deny not Swearing out of Obſtinacy or Wilfulneſs, but am willing to teſtify the Truth in this Matter of Obedience, or any other Matter wherein I am concerned. 2dly, Becauſe Swearing is directly againſt the Command of Chriſt. And 3dly, Againſt the Doctrine of the Apoſtles. 4thly, Even of ſome of the principal Members of the Church of *England*, as Biſhop *Uſher*, ſometime Primate of *Ireland*, who ſaid in his Works, that *the* Waldenſes *denied all Swearing in their Age, from that Command of Chriſt, and the Apoſtle* James, *and that it was a ſufficient Ground.* And Dr. *Gauden*, late Biſhop of *Exeter*, in a Book of his I lately read, cites many ancient Fathers, proving, that *the* Chriſtians, *for the firſt three Hundred Years, did not Swear,* ſo that it is now no new Doctrine.

Judge. *Surely you miſtake.*

F. H. I have not their Books here.

Judge. *Will you ſay upon your honeſt Word, they denied all Swearing ?*

F. H. What I have ſaid, is true.

Judge. *Why do you not come to Church, and hear Service, and be ſubject to the Law, and to every Ordinance of Man for the Lord's Sake ?*

F. H. I am ſubject : And for that Cauſe do we pay Taxes, Tribute, and Cuſtom, and give unto *Cæſar* the Things that are his, and unto God the Things that are his, *to wit*, Worſhip, Honour, and Obedience : But if thou meaneſt the Pariſh Aſſemblies, I tell thee faithfully, I am perſuaded, and that upon good Grounds, that their Teachers are not the Miniſters of Chriſt, nor their Worſhip, the Worſhip of God.

Judge. *Why it may be for ſome ſmall Thing in the Service, you reject it all.*

F. H. Firſt of all, it is manifeſt they are *Time-ſervers*, one while preaching up that for *Divine Service* to the People, which another while they are crying down as *Popiſh, Superſtitious*, and *Idolatrous*, and that which they have preached up twenty Years together, they make Shipwreck of all in a Day, and now again call *Divine*, and would have all compelled to that themſelves once made void.

Judge. *Why, never ſince the King came in.*

F. H. Yes, the ſame Men that preached it down once, now cry it up, and are ſo unſtable and wavering, that we cannot believe they are the Miniſters of Chriſt. 2dly, They teach for Hire, and live by forced Maintenance, and would force a Faith upon Men contrary to Chriſt's and the Apoſtle's Rule, who would have *Every one perſuaded in their own Minds*, and ſaid, *Whatſoever is not of Faith, is Sin :* And yet they ſay, *Faith is the Gift of God, and we have no ſuch Faith given*, and yet they will force theirs upon us, and if we cannot receive it, they cry, *You are not ſubject to Authority and the Laws.* And nothing but Confiſcations, Impriſonment, and Baniſhment, is threatned ; and this is their greateſt Plea : I could deſcend to more Particulars.

Judge. *Well, I ſee you will not Swear, nor conform, nor be ſubject, and you think we deal ſeverely with you ; but if you would be ſubject, we ſhould not need.*

F. H. Yes, I do ſo think indeed, that you deal ſeverely with us for Obedience to the Command of Chriſt. I pray thee, *Canſt thou ſhew me that any of thoſe People for whom the Act was made, have been proceeded againſt by this Statute ?* though I envy no Man's Liberty.

Judge. *Oh, yes, I can inſtance you many up and down the Country that are* premunired, *I have pronounced Sentence my ſelf againſt divers.*

F. H. What, againſt the *Papiſts ?*

Judge. *No.*

F. H. What then, againſt the *Quakers ?* ſo I have heard indeed. It ſeems then, that Statute which was made againſt the *Papiſts*, thou letteſt them alone, and executeſt it againſt the *Quakers*.

Judge.

Judge. *Well, you will meet in great Numbers, and do increase, but there is a new Statute, which will make you fewer.*

F. H. Well, if we muft fuffer, it is for Chrift's Sake, and for Well-doing.
Then the Judge pronounced Sentence with a faint and low Voice, thus, *You are put out of the King's Protection, and the Benefit of the Law. Your Lands are confifcate to the King during your Life, and your Goods and Chattels for ever, and you are to be Prifoner during your Life.*

F. H. Hard Sentence for obeying the Command of Chrift ; but I am content, and in perfect Peace with the Lord. And the Lord forgive you all.

Judge. *Well, if you will be yet fubject to the Laws, the King will fhew you Mercy.*

F. H. The Lord has fhewed Mercy to me, and I have done nothing againft the King, nor Government, nor any Man, bleffed be the Lord, and therein ftands my Peace, and it is for Chrift's Sake I fuffer, and not for Evil-doing.
So he returned to Prifon, where he continued to the End of his Days.

In this Year the Mayor of *Kendal* caufed the Goods of many Inhabitants of that Town to be diftrained, for their Abfence from the publick Worfhip, but when their Goods were expofed to Sale, the Neighbours would not buy them, nor could the Juftices get them fold at any Rate, till by bidding for them themfelves, they animated fome mean People to buy them at a very low Price. About the fame Time *William Cartmell* and his Wife, *Edward Burroughs, Robert Atkinfon, Rowland Warrier, William Manfergh,* and *Dorothy Lorimer,* were committed to Prifon. Alfo *Chriftopher Bifbrown,* of *Arnfide ; Miles Walker, John Thurnbeck,* and *Richard Walker,* of *Middleton ; Dorothy Middleton,* and *John Middleton* her Son, had their Goods taken by Diftrefs for Abfence from the National Worfhip. *Difficulty of felling Goods taken by Diftrefs.*

In or about this Year, many were fined for their religious Meetings, and committed either to the Common Goal, or Houfe of Correction, for one, two, or three Months, and fome of them longer, viz. *William Whitehead, Richard Barwick, John Barwick, James Fallowfield, William Bland, Edward Winter, Robert Winter, Eleanor Winter, Thomas Hobfon, Mary Robinfon, John Brown, Mary Ayrey, Thomas Langhorn, Thomas Smith, Jennet Smith, Anne Smith, Frances Lawfon, Elizabeth Wilkinfon, Elizabeth Holme, Ellen Cloudfdale, Jennet Atkinfon, Agnes Whinfall, Margaret Fallowfield, Sarah Whitehead, Dorothy Ayrey, Margaret Bownas, John Boulton, Grace Whitehead, Ifabel Whitehead, John Thompfon, Michael Scaife, William Scaife, Henry Fifher, Richard Holme,* and *Anne Laycock.* Alfo *Elizabeth Moreland,* Wife of *John Moreland,* who, while in the Houfe of Correction, had a young Child fucking at her Breaft. *Hugh Gibfon,* a poor Man, who had been blind from his Birth. *Elizabeth Gibfon,* the faid blind Man's Sifter, a very poor and weak Woman. *Katharine Clark,* a married Woman with a fucking Child. *Jane Winter,* a Servant, the only Perfon left of a Family who were before in Prifon. *Robert Hutchinfon,* who alfo had his Clothes taken out of his Mother's Houfe by one *Jackfon,* an old Informer, without any Warrant appearing for fo doing : When the Sufferer complained of that Injury to the Juftices, he obtained no Redrefs. *Mary Holme,* a Woman then great with Child. And *John Robinfon,* who was committed on a falfe Information, not having been at the Meeting he was accufed of. *Many Sufferings for religious Meetings.*

ANNO 1665. Several of the Perfons laft before-named, were again this Year committed to Prifon for a fecond Offence in meeting together. *Imprifonments for a fecond Offence.*

In this Year alfo, *John Beck,* then Mayor of *Kendal,* fent his Officers to fummon all the *Quakers,* and other *Non-conformifts* in the Town, before him, but none appeared, except twenty *Quakers,* feventeen of whom he fined 3 s. each, and ordered the other three, viz. *Thomas Holmes, Robert Barrow,* and *Brian Lancafter,* to be profecuted on an old Indictment, and committed them to Prifon, but after eight Days Confinement, again difcharged them, fining them 13 s. 4 d. each, for which their Goods were afterwards diftrained. *All Non-conformifts being fummoned, Quakers only appear.*

WEST-MORLAND. 1665.

Commitments on the Act for Banishment.

In the same Year *Thomas Burden*, of *Burden*, in the County of *Durham*, *William Parke*, *Thomas Sill*, *William Chambers*, *Daniel Thompson*, and *Charles Story*, all belonging to *Preston* Meeting, were brought before *Allen Bellingham*, a Justice of the Peace, for being at a Meeting, and he committed the first four of them to the Common Goal, and the two last to the House of Correction at *Kendal*, on the Act of Banishment, for the first Offence.

Josiah Coale, of *Winterbourn* in the County of *Glocester*, was taken out of a Meeting at the House of the Widow *Johnson*, in *Preston-Richard*, by Order of the said Justice *Bellingham*, who committed him to Prison for three Months, on the Act for Banishment.

Morgan Watkins, of *Herefordshire*, was taken from the House of *Elizabeth Story* Widow, and carried before *Daniel Flemming* Justice, who committed him to Prison.

Imprisonment on Writs de Excom. Cap.

ANNO 1666. *William Hebson*, for refusing to pay small Tithes, was imprisoned on a Writ *de Excommunicato capiendo*, above fifteen Months, and had also his Cattle taken away to the Value of 40 *l*.

Fines and Distress for refusing to Swear.

In this Year several Persons were fined by *James Ducket*, Lord of the Manour of *Grayrigg*, because they refused to Swear, and *Thomas Robertson*, for such Fine, had a Cow taken from him worth 3 *l*. 6 *s*. 8 *d*.

Peter Moser, of *Grayrigg*, had also a Cow taken from him for a Fine, which Cow the said *James Ducket* killed, and salted in his own House for the Use of his Family.

Prosecution

ANNO 1667. *Richard Burrough*, of *Arnside*, was prosecuted in the County Court for Tithes, at the Suit of *Elizabeth Ducket*, Widow and Executrix of *James Ducket* deceased. She procured against him eight County-Warrants, the removing of which by *Certiorari* cost him 10 *l*. 3 *s*. 4 *d*.

and Distress for Tithes.

ANNO 1668. The said *Edward Burrough* was prosecuted in *Beethom* Court, at the Suit of the said *Elizabeth Ducket* ; and though that Court had no proper Jurisdiction in the Case of Tithes, yet they fined him 4 *l*. 10 *s*. for which the Bayliff next Day took a Cow and an Horse worth 7 *l*.

Severe Prosecutions for Tithes.

The two Daughters and Executrixes of *Christopher Bishrown* deceased, were also prosecuted by the said *Elizabeth Ducket* in the Manour Court of *Beethom*, for the same Tithe for which their Father had before suffered Imprisonment till Death. *Mary Bishrown*, one of the Executrixes, was summoned to appear, and upon her Non-appearance, a Verdict of 6 *l*. 10 *s*. was obtained against her for thirteen Years Tithes, and a Warrant granted for Distress on her Goods, but she being only a Servant, and having no Effects, the Prosecutrix was disappointed, and the other Executrix was out of their Manour or Jurisdiction. Soon after this *Robert Barrow*, of *Kendal*, who had married *Margaret Bishrown*, the other Executrix, was summoned into the Court at *Kendal*, by the said *Elizabeth Ducket*, upon the aforesaid Verdict obtained at *Beethom* Court, where he demurred to the *Jurisdiction* of the Court. Some Time after, he was again summoned to the said Court, and four Actions were brought against him, at the Suit of the said *Elizabeth Ducket*, and on the 2d Day of the Month called *March* 1668, those Actions were tried, and a Verdict obtained against him for 4 *l*. for eight Years, for which the Bayliffs took one Cow which cost him 4 *l*. 5 *s*. and Hay valued at 15 *s*. also four Pewter Plates, five Brass Pans, and one great Kettle or Caldron. It was observed, that the said *Elizabeth Ducket*, and her Servant *Michael Langcake*, were very warm in this Prosecution, she declaring, that *She would spend* 100 *l*. *upon the Executors of* Christopher Bishrown ; and he affirming, that *He would spend* 40 *l*. *out of his own Purse*, *rather than that they should not be subjected to their Wills.*

John Bishrown, for a Demand of 1 *l*. 4 *s*. for Tithes, had taken from him, at the Suit of the said *Elizabeth Ducket*, a Cow worth 3 *l*.

Prosecution in the Ecclesiastical Court for Tithes.

Miles Bateman the Elder, *Robert Barrow*, and *John Fell*, all of *Kendal*, were prosecuted in the Ecclesiastical Court at *Richmond*, for small Tithes and *Easter-Offerings*, at the Suit of *William Brownswood*, Priest of *Kendal*, and were committed to Prison, where the former remained five Weeks, and the other two

nine

nine Weeks: After which, they being informed of some Illegality in the Proceeding againſt them, appealed to the Eccleſiaſtical Court at *York*, upon which they were ſet at Liberty during the Appeal, and were likely to recover Charges of the Prieſt: But by the Advice of one Dr. *Burwell*, the Prieſt took an Oath of the Legality of his Proſecution, and thereupon they alſo were cited to take an Oath in the Cauſe, otherwiſe they would again incur a Contempt. But while theſe Matters were depending, both the Prieſt and Dr. *Burwell* died, having firſt put the ſaid *Robert Barrow* and *John Fell* to about 7 *l.* Charge, beſide their falſe Impriſonment. The Apprehending of *Robert Barrow* in this Caſe, was attended with an ill-natur'd Circumſtance: When the Bayliffs came to his Houſe he was ſick, and had taken Phyſick, wherefore he deſired them to forbear taking him from Home till the next Day. The Bayliff accordingly applied to the Prieſt, telling him, that *It might endanger the Man's Health to take him away at that Time:* But the Prieſt churliſhly anſwered, that *Unleſs he would pay, he ſhould go immediately to Goal.* So they hurried him away to the apparent Danger of his Health.

In the ſame Year *John Biſbrown*, for a Claim of *Church-Dues*, amounting to 1 *s.* 3 *d.* had Goods taken away worth 4 *s.* 8 *d.* And *Thomas Camm*, of *Cammſgill*, for a Demand of 1 *s.* had Goods taken by Diſtreſs worth 2 *s.* 6 *d.*

ANNIS 1670 and 1671. After the coming forth of the ſecond Act againſt Conventicles, the following Perſons had their Goods taken by Diſtreſs, in Conſequence of Warrants granted by the Juſtices, upon Informations of their being at religious Meetings, *viz.* *Chriſtopher Birket*, for permitting a Meeting at his Houſe near *Kendal*, was fined 20 *l.* for which the Conſtable took Beaſts, Sheep, Horſes, and Houſhold Goods, and lockt up the Barn-doors, taking the Keys with him. The Woman of the Houſe being ſick, he took the Kettle off the Fire, and threw the Victuals out of Doors. From *Miles Bateman*, for preaching at that Meeting, for a Fine of 20 *l.* they made a Seizure of two Kine, one Heifer, and eight or nine Acres of Corn: At another Time he was fined 20 *l.* for permitting a Meeting at his Houſe, and 10 *l.* for his own being there, for which Fines they took nine Beaſts, above fifty Sheep, and a Mare. A Juſtice of the Peace directed the Officers to ſell the Goods for whatſoever was offered them, though never ſo little, and then to go again and take more, and lock up the Barn-doors. *Miles Huberſty*, for preaching at that Meeting, had above ſixty Sheep, his Corn, Hay, and Houſhold Goods taken away, the Value of which much exceeded the Sum demanded, yet did the rapacious Spoilers threaten his Tenant for preventing them from taking more. *Dorothy Bateman* and *John Holme*, being fined 10 *s.* each, they took from her Corn on the Mow, and from him his Bedding. From *Thomas Holme*, for a Fine of 5 *s.* they took the Coat from his Back. From *Thomas Cooper*, for a Fine of 5 *s.* they took Pewter, Braſs, and other Goods worth 7 or 8 *s.* and alſo an Heifer. From *Miles Halhead*, *Miles Huberſty*, and *Mary Pepper*, for Fines of 5 *s.* each, they took from the *firſt* a Braſs Pot, the *ſecond* a Pair of Racks, and the *third* a Chair. For the like Fines they took from *Peter Bateman* a Rugg, *Dorothy Bateman*, Pewter worth 7 *s.* *John Tompſon*, a Pot worth 10 *s.* *Richard Crewdſon*, a Pair of Shoes, a Shirt, and other Things. And from *Roger Backhouſe* a Parcel of Yarn. *Richard Holme* was not at the Meeting, yet was he fined on a falſe Information, as were ſeveral others, whom the Informers at random ſwore to be there. From *Thomas Graham*, for 10 *s.* Fine for himſelf and Wife, they took Braſs, Pewter, and other Things. And from the Widow *Graham*, fined 10 *s.* for her ſelf and her Daughter, they took about thirty Yards of Cotton. For Fines of 5 *s.* each, they took from *John Holme* three Kettles. *James Nuby* a Pair of Sheerman's Sheers. And from *Elizabeth Kitchen* a Braſs Pot: At another Time they took from the ſaid *Elizabeth Kitchen*, for a Fine of 10 *s.* Braſs and Pewter worth 13 *s.* From *Anthony Bownas*, of *Shapp*, for Fines of 2 *l.* 15 *s.* for himſelf and others, they took two Kine, one Steer, and a little Heifer, worth about 7 *l.* And at ſeveral other Times, for Fines amounting to 2 *l.* 15 *s.* they took Goods worth 3 *l.* 6 *s.* 4 *d.* From *John Sutton*, of *Cliſton*,
they

WEST-
MOR-
LAND.
1670 *and*
1671.

they took a Caldron and a Brafs Pot worth 14 *s.* From *Thomas Savage*, of *Clifton*, for 1 *l.* 5 *s.* they took Goods of twice that Value. From *William Whitehead*, of *Waters*, for 20 *s.* for himfelf and *Thomas Langhorn*, they took four Stone of Wool worth 24 *s.*

John Bolton, of *Bongate*, was at feveral Times fined 45 *s.* for himfelf and others, which his Son, not of his Perfuafion, being Conftable, paid, rather than diftrain his Father's Goods ; though without his Father's Confent.

James Fallowfield, of *Great-Strickland*, for 18 *s.* 4 *d.* for himfelf and *Elizabeth Smith*, had his Houfhold Goods taken away to the Value of 4 *l.* From *Edward Winter*, of *Moreland*, for 5 *s.* Fine, they took a Rugg worth 10 *s.* They alfo made Diftrefs on *Lancelot Fallowfield*, of *Great-Strickland*, for 15 *s.* Fine, but a young Man, who boarded with him, redeemed the Goods by paying the Fine. *Thomas Langhorn*, of *Hilton*, being fined 30 *s.* for himfelf and others, they took from him a Cow worth 40 *s.* From *Richard Simpfon*, of *Bampton-Scarr*, for 10 *s.* Fine, they took his working Tools, he being a Plaifterer. From *Thomas Langhorn* jun. they took three Stone of Wool, and two Brafs Pots, worth 1 *l.* 6 *s.* 8 *d.* From *Chriftopher Wilkinfon*, of *Tirrell*, and *Elizabeth* his Sifter, for Fines of 10 *s.* they took wearing Apparel worth 40 *s.* From *John Brown*, a Carpenter of *Afkham*, they feveral Times took away his working Tools. From *Robert Winter*, of *Moreland*, for 10 *s.* Fine, they took a Mare worth 2 *l.* 13 *s* 4 *d.* From *William Muckeld*, of *Over-Stavely*, who was fined 20 *l.* for a Meeting at his Houfe, they took feven Beafts, two Horfes, fome Sheep, and fourteen Acres of Hay and Corn, wherein he was Partner with another Perfon, and fold his Part of them. From *Thomas Smith*, of *Sleagill*, for 40 *s.* Fine, they took two young Beafts worth 2 *l.* 10 *s.* From *Mary Holme*, of *Sleagill*, for 10 *s.* Fine, Goods worth 16 *s.* From *William Savage*, of *Clifton*, for 25 *s.* impofed on him and *Chriftopher Wilkinfon*, they took a Mare worth 2 *l.* 7 *s.* From *Lancelot Fallowfield*, for 40 *s.* laid on himfelf and others, they took Goods worth 4 *l.*

Chriftopher Wilkinfon had Goods taken from him worth 2 *l.* 15 *s.* for 40 *s.* Fine impofed for himfelf and *Thomas Langhorn* jun.

Edward Guy, of *Appleby*, was fined at feveral Times, for being at feveral Meetings, 5 *l.* 5 *s.* and for Part of a Fine of the Houfe where they met, was laid on him 6 *l.* 10 *s.* For the former of which Fines, they took Houfhold Goods worth 9 *l.* 15 *s.* and for the latter, they feized his Shop Goods, but did not carry them away.

William Whitehead, of *Waters*, was fined 3 *l.* for being at feveral Meetings, for which they took from him at one Time, three Kine worth 9 *l.* and at another Time, a Cow worth 2 *l.*

John Dickinfon, *Anne Ayrey*, and others, were alfo fined for being at Meetings in this County.

J. Jackfon *Informer.*

There was at this Time one *John Jackfon* who acted the Part of an Informer on every Act againft the *Quakers*, it was obferved, that notwithftanding his ill-gotten Gain that Way, he was reduced to fuch extream Poverty as to beg his Bread.

More Dif-trefles for Meetings.

Taken by Warrants granted by *Allen Bellingham* Juftice, from *Thomas Pearfon* the Elder, of *Wetherflack*, for a Fine of 20 *l.* for a Meeting at his Houfe, twenty three Hides of tanned Leather ; and from *John Pearfon*, of the *Pow-bank*, for 10 *s.* for himfelf and Wife, Goods of about that Value.

There were alfo fined, for being at the faid Meeting in *Thomas Pearfon*'s Houfe, feveral Perfons who dwelt in *Lancafhire*, viz. *Richard Simpfon*, of *Cart-mell*, for praying there, 20 *l.* and *James Taylor*, *Richard Brittain*, *Laurence Newton*, *Chriftopher Fell*, and *John Barrow*, for being prefent, 5 *s.* a piece, all which Fines were levied by Diftrefs, and great Spoil and Havock was made of their Goods.

Several others who dwelt in this County, for being at the Meetings at *Sedbergh* in *Torkfhire*, which they at Times frequented, were fined upon

Convictions

Convictions fent to *Henry Wilfon*, a Juftice near *Kirby-Lonfdale* in this WEST-
County, *viz.* MOR-
LAND.
1670 *and*
1671.

	l.	*s.*	*d.*
Richard Walker, of *Middleton*, for himfelf, and *Margaret* his Sifter	1	0	0
James Corney, of *Killington*	0	15	0
Richard Parrott, of the fame	0	15	0
Jofeph Baines, of the fame, for himfelf and for *Margaret Walker*	1	15	0
Robert Atkinfon, of *Middleton*, for himfelf and *John Thirnbeck*	1	5	0
James Corney aforefaid, for himfelf and the faid *John Thirnbeck*	2	15	0
Miles Walker, of *Middleton*	0	5	0
	8	10	0

All which Fines were levied by Diftrefs on their feveral Goods and Chattels,
except that on *Miles Walker*, which was paid by fome of his Relations.

We fhall next infert an Account of the laft dying Words and happy Departure
of *Francis Howgill*, taken from a Relation prefixed to his Works, publifhed in
Folio, *Anno* 1670.

"   A S for the Time of *F. Howgill's* Sicknefs, which he endured with much *An Account of*
"   Patience and Cheerfulnefs, it began the 11th of the Eleventh Month *F. Howgill's*
"   1668, and continued till the 20th of the fame Month, and then he departed *Death.*
"   this Life, having then, for the Teftimony of Jefus, been Prifoner four
"   Years and Eleven Months. He was not infenfible of the Decay of his out-
"   ward Man fome Time before, which moved him to a Difpofal of his
"   outward Eftate, and the fetting of his Houfe in order. His Love was very
"   dear to his Brethren and Fellow-Labourers, with whom he had laboured and
"   travelled in the Work of the Miniftry, in Teftimony whereof he left to each
"   of them fomething as a Remembrance of his Love, and alfo was mindful of
"   the Church, and left a Legacy to be diftributed amongft the Poor of the
"   Houfhold of Faith in the Parts where he lived.
"   And though the Time of his Departure did draw nigh, and his Sicknefs
"   increafed, yet in all that Time he was in perfect and good Remembrance, and
"   oftentimes very fervent in Prayer, and uttered many comfortable Expref-
"   fions to the great Refrefhment of thofe who were with him : And about ten
"   Days before his Departure, being attended by his dear Wife, and feveral
"   Friends, he began to fay unto them, *Friends, as to Matter of Words you*
"   *muft not expect much more from me, neither is there any great Need of it, as*
"   *to fpeak of Matters of Faith to you, who are fatisfied ; only that you remember*
"   *my dear Love to all Friends that enquire of me, for I ever loved Friends well,*
"   *or any in whom Truth appeared, and truly God will own his People, as he has*
"   *ever hitherto done, and as we have daily witneffed, for no fooner had they made*
"   *that Act againft us for Banifhment, to the great Suffering of many good Friends,*
"   *but the Lord ftirred up Enemies againft them, even three great Nations, whereby*
"   *the Violence of their Hands was taken off. I fay again, God will own his*
"   *People, even all thofe that are faithful ; and as for me, I am well, and am*
"   *content to die ; I am not at all afraid of Death, and truly one Thing was of*
"   *late in my Heart, and that I intended to have writ to* G. F. *and others, even*
"   *that which I have obferved ; which Thing is,* That this Generation paffeth faft
"   away. *We fee many good and precious Friends within thefe few Years have*
"   *been taken from us, and therefore Friends had need to watch, and be very*
"   *faithful, fo that we may leave a good, and not a bad Savour to the next fuc-*
"   *ceeding Generation ; for you fee that it is but a little Time that any of us*
"   *have to ftay here.*

" And often in the Time of his Sickness, he said, *He was content to die,*
" *and that he was ready, and praised God for those many sweet Enjoyments and*
" *Refreshments he had received on that his Prison-house Bed, whereon he lay,*
" *freely forgiving all who had an hand in his Restraint.*

" And he said, *This was the Place of my first Imprisonment for the Truth here*
" *at this Town, and if it be the Place of my laying down the Body, I am content.*

" Several Persons of Note, Inhabitants in *Appleby,* as the Mayor and others,
" went to visit him, some of which praying, that *God might speak Peace to*
" *his Soul,* he sweetly replied, *He hath done it.* And they all spake well
" of him.

" And a few Hours before his Departure, some Friends (who lived several
" Miles from that Place) came to visit him, he enquired of all their Welfare,
" and prayed fervently (with many heavenly Expressions) *that the Lord by his*
" *mighty Power might preserve them out of all such Things ·as would spot and*
" *defile.*

" And a little after, he was saying something concerning *Weeks,* or *a Time,*
" after which Persecution should be ended ; but his Weakness was so great,
" and his Voice so low, that it was not fully heard.

" A little Season after, he recovering a little Strength, farther said, *I have*
" *sought the Way of the Lord from a Child, and lived innocently as among Men,*
" *and if any enquire concerning my Latter-end, let them know that I die in the*
" *Faith in which I lived and suffered for.*

" And after these Words, he spake some other in Prayer to God, and
" sweetly finished his Course in much Peace with the Lord."

Thus died *Francis Howgill,* a *faithful Martyr,* who laid down his Life in
Testimony of his Obedience to the Precept of Christ, *Swear not at all.* He
was a Man of *exemplary Patience* and *Meekness,* well beloved, and died much
lamented, in the Fiftieth Year of his Age.

ANNO 1672. *Thomas Robertson,* of *Grayrigg* was prosecuted for seven
Years Tithe of Wool and Lambs, at the Suit of ȷmes, *Archer,* and cast into
Prison at *Kendal,* where he was kept fourteen Days. 'e 'hen some of his Relations, without his Knowledge, paid the Prosecutor 5 *l.* and discharged him. He
afterward expressed such Dislike of this seeming Kindness of his Friends, that
his Persuasions induced them to promise not to offend him in that kind any
more.

ANNO 1673. *Thomas Langhorn,* of *Hiltondale,* was prosecuted in the
Ecclesiastical Court for Tithes by *Lancelot Hutchinson,* Priest of *Askham* ; the
Process went on unknown to him, who had never been summoned to appear,
till a Certificate of Contumacy was issued : Upon this he appealed to the
Bishop's Court at *York,* and was put to 10 *l.* Expence to prevent his being sent
to Prison.

Charles Story, of *Preston-Patrick,* was prosecuted for Tithe-Corn, at the
Suit of *Thomas Wilson,* Tithe-farmer.

William Baines, of *Killington,* for a Demand of 5 *s.* for Priest's Wages, had
Goods taken from him worth 14 *s.* and *Joseph Baines,* for a Demand of 4 *s.*
Goods worth 20 *s.*

ANNO 1674. *Thomas Camm,* of *Cammsgill,* was sued by *John Ormrod,* Priest
of *Burton,* for small Tithes and Oblations, and by a Writ *de Excommunicato
capiendo,* was cast into Prison, where he remained between two and three Years.

William Baines, of *Killington,* was cited into the Court at *Richmond* for a
Claim of *Easter-Offerings,* and put to an Expence of 20 *s.*

ANNIS 1675 and 1676. In the Year 1675, *Joseph Baines, John Hodgson,*
and *John Yeates,* all of *Killington,* were prosecuted for *Easter-Offerings,* and the
said *John Hodgson* also suffered Imprisonment for Tithes, at *Kendal,* thirteen
Weeks, for a trivial Claim of two Lambs, and about six Fleeces of Wool.

In the same Year, *William Baines* and *Joseph Baines* were cited into *Richmond*
Court, at the Suit of *John Wood,* Priest of *Killington,* for Wages by him
demanded.

demanded. Their Appearance there occasioned 10 s. Charge to each of them, but before the Court-day came, in which their Answers were to have been given in, the Priest was taken sick, and died under much Trouble of Mind.

John Thirnbeck, of *Middleton,* for a small Demand of Tithes, was prosecuted by *Thomas Green,* an Attorney, at the Suit of Sir *Thomas Strickland,* and was apprehended by a Writ of Rebellion after the Time of the Return of the Writ was expired. He was kept Prisoner by *John Holme,* a Bailiff, at his House in *Kendal* several Weeks, when getting a Sight of the Writ, he found that the Date of its Return had been scraped out, and another Date of the next Term put in, and sending to search the Record at *London,* found that there was no Writ returnable against him. The Attorney, detected of this treacherous Dealing, was enraged, and procured a fresh Writ against the said *Thirnbeck,* returnable on the 10th of the Month called *April* 1676, and a few Days after that Time sent him up to *London,* about two Hundred Miles, with a Person of ill Morals to attend him, to which Person he gave Directions *to beat the Prisoner if he refused to go:* But by that Time they came to *Nottingham,* the Return of that Writ was also expired, and the Prisoner refusing to go any farther, his Guide, after some Abuses, left him.

Thomas Moor, of *Hutton-Roofe,* and *Dorothy Middleton,* of *Lupton,* were prosecuted in the Bishop's Court at *Richmond,* by *Henry Hogle,* Priest of *Kirby-Lonsdale,* for small Tithes, and in the latter End of the Year 1675, were cast into Prison by a Writ *de Excommunicato capiendo,* where they remained till the Priest died: After whose Death they were kept in Prison by *John Newton,* of *Kirby-Lonsdale,* the Priest's Proctor, till he also died, and then they were set at Liberty, after four Years and about seven Months Imprisonment.

Thomas Camm, of *Cammsgill,* was sued in the Year 1675, in a Court-Baron held at *Preston-hall,* for 3 s. for his Salary, and (the said *Thomas Camm* being then a Prisoner) a Verdict was obtained against him, by Virtue whereof *Richard Lucas,* a Bailiff, took from his House Goods worth 5 s. 6 d.

In these Years were taken by Justices Warrants, for Absence from the National Worship,

	l.	s.	d.
From *Edward Winter,* of *Moreland,* Goods worth	0	9	0
John Shearman, of *Sleasgill,* Goods worth	0	4	0
Mary Holme, of the same, Goods worth	0	6	0
Thomas and *Anne Robinson,* of *Cliburne*	1	4	0
William Barwick and *John Barwick,* of *Shapp*	0	6	0
Matthew Dawson, of *Hilton,* Goods worth	0	5	6
Thomas Kendal the Younger, of *Askham*	0	7	6
John Sutton, Thomas Savage, and *William Savage,* all of *Clifton,* Goods to the Value of	1	2	0
Thomas Cleasby and *William Moorthwaite*	0	18	0
James Scaife, of *Nateby*	0	9	0
	5	11	0

ANNO 1677. About this Time *Richard Thompson, Anne Thompson,* and *Arthur Burrow,* for 8 s. demanded for his Salary by *Richard Robinson,* Reader at *Preston* Chapel, had Goods taken from them by Distress, to the Amount of 1 l. 7 s. 6 d.

In this Year *Thomas Williamson,* of *Bannerigg,* in the Parish of *Windermer,* having a Concern and Pressure upon his Mind to declare the Truth to the People assembled at the Steeple-house there, went thither, and tarried in Silence till *William Wilson,* the Priest, had ended his Sermon, after which he took an Opportunity to speak to the People what he had upon his Mind to declare. For this the Churchwardens, so called, at the Instigation of the Priest, complained against him to Justice *Flemming,* who, upon his refusing to give Sureties, committed

WEST-
MOR-
LAND.
1678.

An Account of Exchequer *Procefs, prefented to the Parliament.*

committed him to Prifon, where he lay till the next Seffions, and then was fet at Liberty.

ANNO 1678. In the Month called *April* this Year, was drawn up, attefted by Witneffes, and prefented to the Parliament,

" An ACCOUNT of the Names of fuch Perfons who are no *Papifts*,
" but *Proteftant* Diffenters, and diftinguifhed by the Name of QUAKERS,
" and have been profecuted upon the Statutes of 23 and 28 of ELIZABETH,
" made againft *Popifh* Recufants, and Levies for the Yearly Profits of their
" Lands thereupon made by the Sheriff's Bayliffs of the faid County, by
" Procefs out of the *Exchequer* for the Year 1677, as followeth, *viz.*

The Perfons Names, and Places of Abode.	Yearly Value of Lands feized			Value of Goods levied		
	l.	*s.*	*d.*	*l.*	*s.*	*d.*
James Clarkfon, John Pindur, and *Anthony Robinfon,* all of *Ravenftondale*	1	19	4	4	12	0
Thomas Atkinfon, of *Orton* Parifh	1	0	0	2	0	0
Thomas Atkinfon, William Whitehead, Richard Ayrey, John Clark, and *Richard Barwick,* all of *Shapp* Parifh	6	4	8	10	13	4
John Sutton, of *Clifton*	0	10	0	0	14	0
Edward Sutton, of *Browham* Parifh	0	5	0	0	9	0
Thomas Langhorn, of *Hiltondale*	0	18	0	2	10	0
Richard Burrough, Jennett Bifhrown, and *John Hudfon,* all of *Beethom* Parifh	0	15	0	1	15	0
Bridget Gregg, of *Milthorp*	0	2	0	0	5	0
Edward Cragg, of *Ackonthwaite*	0	0	8	0	6	0
John Pearfon and *Thomas Pearfon,* of *Heverfham* Parifh	2	0	0	3	10	0
Stephen Crofsfield, of *Heverfham*	1	6	0	2	0	0
Thomas Ayrey, Robert Simpfon, and *William Farrer,* all of *Kendal* Parifh	3	6	0	5	2	0
Peter Mofer, Robert Wilfon, John Dickinfon, Martin Simpfon, and *Elizabeth Holme,* all of *Kendal* Parifh	1	15	$2\frac{1}{2}$	3	18	0
Nicholas Suart and *William Elcray,* of *Toutran*	0	11	8	1	3	6
Richard Birket and *John Thompfon,* of *Crook*	0	14	8	1	11	0
Miles Bateman, of *Underbarrow*	0	7	4	0	0	0
Richard Atkinfon and *John Prefton,* of *Farleton*	0	12	0	2	6	7
George Denifon, of *Manfergh*	0	4	8	0	10	0
	22	12	$2\frac{1}{2}$	43	5	5

Many others alfo had their Goods feized by *Exchequer* Procefs in the Years 1677 and 1678, the Value of whofe Lands are not mentioned, *viz.*

	l.	*s.*	*d.*
Henry Laycock, Thomas Lawfon, Lancelot Fallowfield, James Fallowfield, Rowland Wilfon, Nicholas Denkin, John Hobfon, and *Thomas Fallowfield,* all of *Morland* Parifh	6	14	8
Mary Robinfon, of *Cliburne*	0	6	8
Chriftopher Wilkinfon, of *Barton* Parifh	0	5	0
John Tinker and *Robert Hutchinfon,* of *Afkham*	1	8	0
Carried over	8	14	4

		l.	s.	d.
Brought over		8	14	4
Thomas Langhorn, of Hilton		0	16	0
George Crossfield, of Stainton		0	4	0
Elizabeth Simpson, Isabel Fell, and William Parke, all of Docker	}	0	19	2½
Thomas Hudson, of the same		0	4	0
William Chambers, of Sedgewick		2	0	0
William Bisbrown, of Beethom Parish		0	3	0
Dorothy Middleton, John Middleton, John Sutton, Edward Burrough, and Henry Skyring, all of Lupton	}	1	9	0
Robert Atkinson, John Scaife, William Cartmell, and Roger Wakefield, all of Preston	}	1	1	8
Richard Stevenson, of Over-Stavely		0	6	8
Richard Clarkson, Anthony Pinder, and Thomas Fawcett, all of Ravenstondale	}	1	1	4
John Holme and John Fawcett, of Orton Parish		0	16	8
Michael Aiskell, of Brough		1	0	0
John Thompson and William Skaife, of Warcopp Parish		1	0	0
Robert Teasdale		2	0	0
Edward Gray, of Appleby		5	6	8
John Bolton, of Bongate		0	10	0
		27	12	6½

WEST-
MOR-
LAND.
1678.

Distresses.

In *November* 1678, the following Distresses were made by the Sheriff's Bayliffs upon Process out of the *Exchequer*, viz.

		l.	s.	d.
From	Robert Simpson, of Docker, a Cow worth	3	6	8
	Peter Moser, of Grayrigg, Pewter and Brass worth	0	10	0
	John Dickinson, of the same, Bed-clothes worth	1	4	0
	Martin Simpson, of the same, Goods worth	0	10	0
	Thomas Ayrey, of Sellside, Pewter worth	0	10	0
	William Farrer, of Grayrigg, Goods worth	0	6	8
	Elizabeth Holme Widow, Goods worth	0	8	0
	John Thompson, of Crook, Goods worth	0	10	0
	Miles Bateman, of the same, an Horse worth	4	0	0
	Thomas Pearson, of Powbank, an Heifer worth	1	13	4
	Nicholas Suart, of Toutran, an Horse worth	4	13	4
	William Elcray, of the same, Goods worth	0	8	6
And in *September* the same Year, had been taken				
From	Edward Cragg, of Ackonthwaite, an * Horse worth	3	10	0
	Bridgett Gregg, of Milthorp, a Caldron worth	1	0	0
	Richard Atkinson, of Farleton, a Mare worth	5	0	0
	Richard Burrough, of Arnside, a Cart and Mare worth	2	10	0
	John Hudson, of Hale, a Cow worth	3	5	0
	Jennet Bisbrown, of Arnside, Widow, Pewter worth	0	11	0
In *November* the same Year, more				
From	John Pearson, of Powbank, two Heifers worth	2	6	8
	Stephen Crossfield, of the same, a Cow worth	2	10	0
		38	13	2

More Distresses.

* *Note.* This Horse was seized for a Demand of 8 *d.* in the *Exchequer* Roll. A Neighbour, *Robert Gibson*, observing the Unreasonableness of the Distress, redeemed the Horse by depositing the Money.

W E S T-
M O R-
L A N D.
1678.

Distresses for
Meeting.

On rhe 5th of the Month called *June* 1677, the Mayor of *Kendal* sent three Constables to the Meeting there, who found *Robert Barrow* preaching: At the next Sessions the said *Robert Barrow*, with *John Fell*, and *Peter Jackson*, who were at the same Meeting, were indicted for a *Riot*, fined by the Court, and imprisoned a few Days: After which they had their Goods taken by Distress, *viz.* from *Robert Barrow*, to the Value of 16 s. and from *John Fell*, to the Value of 18 s.

For a Meeting at *Bownass* in the Parish of *Windermere*, on the 15th of *September* 1678, several Persons were fined by *Daniel Flemming* and *Christopher Philipson*, Justices, and some Time after, by their Warrant, had Distresses made on them as follows, *viz.*

	l.	s.	d.
Taken from *Thomas Williamson*, for preaching, Cattle and Sheep worth	28	0	0
William Rawes, for preaching, Cattle and other Goods worth	23	0	0
Isaac Dixon and *George Dixon*, Goods worth	0	18	0
George Dixon, twelve fat Sheep worth	4	10	0
Christopher Dixon and *George Williamson*, Goods worth	1	2	0
Richard Braithwaite, Goods worth	6	19	0
William Wilkinson, Goods worth	4	15	0
Martin Suart, Goods to the Value of	0	6	8
Miles Sawrey, Goods worth	0	7	0
Thomas Grave, of *Hugill*, Goods worth	0	12	0
John Thompson, of *Crook*, Cattle worth	22	0	0
Peter Bateman and *Miles Bateman*, Goods worth	0	10	0
Richard Crewdson, Goods worth	0	7	0
George Thompson and *Richard Burkett*	0	17	0
Robert Thompson and *Thomas Braithwaite*	1	11	0
John Pearson, Goods to the Value of	0	7	0
	96	1	8

William Garnett, fined 5 s. for being at the same Meeting, had his wearing Apparel taken away to the Value of 13 s.

The Sum of the Distresses, for that one Meeting, amounted to about 180 l. many others being included in the same Warrant, some of whose Names were, *Agnes Wilson*, *William Garnett*, and *Agnes Garnett*, of *Under-Milbeck*; *Nicholas Bateman* and *Mary Harrison*, of *Crook*; *James Grave*, *Rowland Suart*, *Nicholas Suart*, and *William Elleray*, of *Hugill*; *Bryan Braithwaite*, of *Kentmire*; *Robert Barrow* and *William Hawden*, of *Kirby-Kendal*; *Thomas Ellwood* and *Thomas Copeland*, of the same; *William Wilson*, of *Langdale*; *John Garnett*, of *Spooner-Close* in *Cartmell* in *Lancashire*; *Thomas Pennington*, *John Bownas*, *Edward Satterthwaite*, *George Holme*, *George Braithwaite*, *William Rigg*, and *William Sands*, of *Hawkshead* in the County of *Lancaster*; *Leonard Fell*, of *Addingham* in the County of *Lancaster*, fined 20 l. for preaching. *John Garnett* and *Jane Garnett*, of *Cartmell* aforesaid; and *William Grave*, of *Hawkside* aforesaid.

Conclusion of
the Warrant.

The Conclusion of the Warrant, after the Persons Names, was in this Form, *viz.* " And two Strangers, whose Names and Habitations are not known, " for taking upon them to preach in the Conventicle aforesaid, are severally " fined 20 l. a-piece, which you are to levy upon the Goods and Chattels of " any

---

* It happened at this Meeting, that certain rude Boys and others were very abusive, threw in a dead Dog, and behaved very insolently; which *John Thompson* observing, advised them to Sobriety and better Manners. This was sworn to be Preaching, and the Justices proceeded accordingly.

" any other of the Offender or Offenders above-mentioned, fo as you lay not
" above ten Pounds upon any Perfon for another's Offence.   All which Fines
" and Sums of Money aforefaid, as you fhall levy the fame, you are hereby
" required forthwith to deliver unto us, that we may diftribute the fame accord-
" ing to the Act of Parliament aforefaid.   And in cafe you cannot, by reafon
" of Poverty, levy all the faid Fines as above directed, you are hereby required
" and authorized to levy fuch in Arrear, by Diftrefs and Sale of Goods and
" Chattels of any other Offender or Offenders above-mentioned, provided you
" levy not above ten Pounds of any Perfon aforefaid for another's Offence :
" And hereof fail not at your Peril.   Given under our Hand and Seal at *Rydall*
" in the faid County of *Weftmorland.*

The 16*th of* September,
   Anno Dom. 1678.   " DANIEL FLEMMING,
                       " CHRISTOPHER PHILIPSON."

On the 13th of *October* 1678, *Edward Wilfon*, a Juftice of the Peace, fent
feveral Informers to a Meeting held in the Houfe of *Edward Cragg* of
Ackonthwaite in the Parifh of *Haverfham*, and upon their Evidence convicted
divers Perfons without being brought before him, and iffued Warrants for Diftrefs, by which was taken

		l.	s.	d.	
From	*Jofeph Gregg*, a young Cow worth	3	10	0	*More Dif-*
	William Walker, a Mare worth	4	5	0	*treffes for*
	Edward Cragg, Goods worth	2	16	0	*Meeting,*
	Simon Thompfon and *George Wharton*, Goods worth	1	10	0	
	Dorothy Lorimer and *Thomas Huggonfon*	0	14	10	
	Richard Thompfon, of *Prefton*, a young Heifer worth	1	5	0	
	Thomas Camm, of *Cammfgill*, for preaching at the faid Meeting, nine Head of * Cattle, and fifty five Sheep, worth	31	10	0	
	Arthur Burrough, an Horfe worth	3	6	8	
	Hugh Cornthwaite, an Heifer worth	2	16	0	
	John Hudfon, a Cow worth	3	5	0	
	Robert Waller, a Cow worth	3	12	0	
	Richard Atkinfon, two Cows worth	7	5	0	
	John Prefton, a young Steer worth	2	10	0	
		68	5	6	

		l.	s.	d.	
ANNO 1679.	Taken for Tithes in Corn,				*and for Tithes.*
From	*Thomas Camm*, to the Value of	4	5	4	
	Edward Cragg, of *Actonthwaite*	2	9	0	
	Bridget Gregg, of *Milthorp*, Widow	0	5	0	
	Jofeph Gregg, of the fame, to the Value of	1	6	0	
		8	5	4	

ANNO 1680.   Taken for Tithe of Hay, from *Richard Atkinfon*, of *Farleton*,
for 4 s. 2 d. demanded, a Pair of Cart-wheels worth 16 s.   And from *Thomas
Prefton*, for a Claim of 12 s. Turf worth 18 s.

Nicholas

---

* When the Officers complained to Juftice *Wilfon*, that they could not fell fome of the
Cattle, he charged them to fell at any Price, and to fetch more till they had enough, and
ordered them to go from one Market to another, and fell cheap, fo as to encourage
Buyers, and threatned them, that if they did not raife all the Fines, they fhould pay the
reft out of their own Pockets.

Nicholas Thompson was prosecuted for Tithes at the Suit of Sir *Thomas Strickland*, and cast into Prison, where he lay five Months, and during his Imprisonment, the Prosecutor's Servants took from his Lands three Acres and an Half of Barley, worth 24 *l*. *John Thirnbeck*, of *Middleton*, also suffered five Months Imprisonment, at the Suit of Sir *Thomas Strickland*.

ANNO 1681. *Joseph Baines*, of *Killington*, and *John Thirnbeck*, of *Middleton*, being summoned to serve on a Jury at the Quarter Sessions, appeared, but refusing to Swear, were fined 20 *s*. each, and had their Goods taken away, the former, to the Value of 40 *s*. and the latter of 2 *l*. 10 *s*.

Richard Atkinson, of *Farleton*, for 1 *l*. 6 *s*. 8 *d*. demanded, being Two-thirds of his Yearly Estate, had taken from him, by the Statute made against *Popish* Recusants, two Kine worth 7 *l*. 10 *s*.

In this Year *Richard Thompson*, of *Milnhouses*, *George Thompson*, *John Thompson*, *Robert Thompson*, *Richard Burkitt*, *John Dickinson*, *John Beck*, *William Elleray*, and *Nicholas Suart*, all of the Parish of *Kirby-Kendal*, were committed to Prison by Warrants granted by *Edward Wilson* and *John Fisher*, Justices, grounded on Certificates of Contumacy out of the Ecclesiastical Court, on Prosecution there for Tithes, where some of them remained Prisoners a long Time, and one of them, viz. *William Elleray*, died a Prisoner there on the 28th of the Month called *August* 1682.

ANNO 1682. *Reginald Holme*, *John Dixon*, *William Rawes*, *William Harrison*, *Thomas Harrison*, and other Inhabitants of the Parish of *Grasmire* in *Westmorland*, were prosecuted in the *Exchequer* for Tithes, at the Suit of *John Ambrose*, Vicar or Curate of that Parish. It was the Usage of that Court, not to receive any Answer to Bills exhibited there, but upon Oath, wherefore these Defendants, being principled against all Swearing, were soon brought into Contempt, and Attachments were issued for apprehending them. Such Attachments are directed to the Sheriff for him to apprehend the Party, but in case the Party absconds or conceals himself, the Sheriff is to make a Return of *Non est inventus* (i. e. *he is not to be found*) and then a Sequestration is issued to seize his Effects. But through a Corruption in the Practice of the Law, the Sheriff frequently, and on purpose, omits to take the Person, and makes a false Return of *Non est inventus*, and so a Sequestration is obtained, as if he had fled. These Defendants did all they could to prevent the Sheriff's making such a Return, for they not only frequented the usual Places of Traffick, but also sent Notice to the Plantiff and his Attorney, where they were, and at what Times and Places they might be met with, and offered to come to them when they pleased : And when, notwithstanding all this Precaution, the Return had been made, and a Writ of Rebellion issued, they offered themselves to the Commissioners, who nevertheless proceeded to make Return of the Writ, as if they were not to be found. Sequestration was thereupon obtained, and by Virtue thereof, the Sequestrators, *George Garnet*, *William Fell*, and *George Mackreth*, entred the House of *William Rawes*, and took thence Brass, Pewter, Bedding, and his own, and his Wife's Apparel, to the Value of 6 *l*. leaving the poor Woman, then lying in Childbed, without Clothes necessary to keep her from the Cold, so that she was obliged to borrow of her Neighbours : One of the Sequestrators observing amongst the Spoil, which they carried away to an Alehouse about four Miles off, a Pair of new Shoes and Stockings, put them on, and left his old torn ones in their Place. On the next Day they came again, and broke open several Doors, and took what else they could find, to the Value of 4 *l*. more. They also took away a Cow worth 3 *l*. So that they took in all to the Value of 13 *l*. though the Tithe, demanded by the Priest, amounted at the most but to 2 *s*. 6 *d*. A grievous Oppression for a trivial Demand : But the Sufferers of such Spoil endured the same with the utmost Patience, esteeming the Peace of their Consciences above all outward Substance.

On the 6th of the Month called *August* this Year, a religious Meeting was held in the Barn of *Richard Atkinson*, of *Farleton*, of which Information being given to *Edward Wilson* Justice, he sent Persons to observe who were there,

and

and accordingly fined many of them, and granted a Warrant for Diſtreſs, dated the 15th of the ſame Month, by which were taken

	l.	*s.*	*d.*
From the ſaid *Richard Atkinſon,* two Oxen, a Cow, and five other Beaſts, to the Value of	25	3	4
Thomas Preſton, of *Overforth,* two young Steers worth	5	0	0
James Fell, of *Sedgewick,* two Cows worth	7	0	0
Robert Waller, of *Hale,* a Cow worth	3	10	0
Thomas Camm, of *Cammſgill,* two Oxen worth	7	0	0
Oliver Leigh, of *Gatebeck,* three Heifers worth	6	10	0
Charles Story, of *Preſton-Patrick,* Goods worth	0	7	0
Richard Thompſon, of *Milnhouſes,* Braſs worth	0	10	0
William Walker, of *Milthorp,* Goods worth	1	0	0
Thomas Atkinſon, of the ſame, two Coats worth	1	0	0
Bridget Gregg, of the ſame, Flax and Candles worth	0	9	4
John Watſon, of the ſame, for his Wife	0	5	4
Edward Cragg, of *Ackonthwaite,* Goods worth	0	9	6
Jane Swainſon, a very poor Widow, a Bag of Potatoes provided for her Family, worth	0	0	10
Thomas Jackſon, of *Barton* in *Kendal,* Pewter worth	0	6	0
Chriſtopher Biſbrown, of *Arnſide,* Hemp-Yarn worth	0	5	7
	58	16	11

Several of the laſt named Perſons were fined on Account of a Preacher, who was ſaid in the Warrant to be fled, and his Habitation unknown : Whereas the ſaid Preacher was ſo far from flying, that he went to the Juſtice's Houſe, and left Word there that his Name was *Thomas Docwra,* and that he dwelt at *Swarthmore* near *Ulverſton* in *Lancaſhire,* and that he was of Ability to pay his own Fine, for which Reaſon he deſired it might not be impoſed on others.

Several other Perſons were alſo fined for being at the ſaid Meeting, *viz.* *Arthur Burrow,* of *Preſton-Patrick* ; *Richard Sill,* of *Warſe* ; *John Hudſon,* of *Hale* ; *Margaret Parke,* of *Woodhouſe* ; *James Harriſon,* of *Sedgewick* ; *Robert Hadwen,* of *Arnſide* ; *James Jackſon,* of the ſame ; *Alice Camm, Richard Skyring,* and *Mary Skyring,* of *Lupton* ; and *Simon Thompſon,* of *Endmore.*

ANNO 1684. On the 5th of the Month called *April,* a Sequeſtration for Tithes, granted againſt *John Dixon,* was put in Execution, by which they ſeized his Cattle, Houſhold Goods, and Apparel, to the Value of 20 *l.* But the ſaid *Dixon*'s Mother, one of the Prieſt's Hearers, made an Agreement with the Sequeſtrators, and took the Goods to herſelf, for 9 *l.* 16 *s.* which ſhe paid them.

In the ſame Month, the Sequeſtrators alſo came to the Houſe of *Reginald Holme,* and took away two Cows, a Steer, and a Mare : A few Days after, meeting him ſeveral Miles from Home, at a Publick-houſe where he had ſet up his Horſe, they went into the Stable, and took away his Horſe, Bridle, and Saddle : So that for an original Claim of 4 *l.* 13 *s.* for Tithe, they took away to the Value of 15 *l.*

From *Thomas Harriſon,* a very poor Man, for a Demand of 10 *s* for Tithes, they took away a Cow worth 3 *l.* which they ſold for 30 *s.*

Joſeph Gregg, of *Milthorp,* was proſecuted for Tithes, in the Biſhop's Court, by *Thomas Wright, Arthur Hudſon,* and other Tithe-farmers there, and was committed to *Appleby* Goal on the 26th of the Month called *May* 1682, where he was a Priſoner almoſt five Years : At length, *Thomas Wright,* the chief of his Proſecutors, being ſick, ſent for him, and ſignified his Uneaſineſs of Mind for detaining him ſo long in Priſon. The patient Innocence of this Sufferer had ſo far mollified the Heart of this Proſecutor, that he became an Interceſſor in his Behalf with the others concerned, and perſuaded them to diſcharge him : Accordingly they ſent a Writing under their Hands to the Sheriff and Juſtices

W E S T-
M O R-
L A N D.
1684.

Diftreffes for
Abfence from
the National
Worfhip.

who committed him, and they releafed him from his long Imprifonment about the Beginning of the Month called *March* 1686.

In this Year 1684, many fuffered Diftrefs of Goods for Fines of 12*d.* per *Sunday*, for Abfence from the National Worfhip, viz.

	l.	*s.*	*d.*
Taken from *Richard Atkinfon*, of *Farleton*, to the Value of	o	16	o
Thomas Prefton, of *Overforth*, Goods worth	o	9	o
Edward Cragg, of *Ackonthwait*, and *Bridget Gregg*, of *Milthorp*	o	6	o
James Harrifon and *James Fell*, both of *Sedgewick*	o	11	8
Thomas Camm, of *Cammfgill*, and *Margaret Thompfon* Widow	o	8	o
John Hudfon and *Robert Walker*, both. of *Hale*	o	19	6
William Jackfon and *Richard Barrow*, of *Arnfide*	1	13	7
Thomas Jackfon, of *Burton*, and *Thomas Huggonfon*	o	8	2
Richard Pye, of *Storth*, and *Thomas Williamfon*, of *Windermere*	1	13	o
George Williamfon, *William Williamfon*, *Martin Suart*, and *Miles Sawrey*, all of *Windermere*	4	12	10
Ifaac Dixfon, *George Dixon*, and *John Braithwaite*, of the fame	2	o	6
George Thompfon and *Elizabeth Blithe*, Goods worth	o	9	8
Thomas Wilfon and *Allen Wilfon*, Leather worth	o	18	o
Thomas Grave, *William Rawes*, *John Dixon*, and *John Rigge*, Wool worth	1	10	10
Dorothy Wilfon and *John Walker*, Pewter worth	o	16	o
Michael Wilfon and *Thomas Harrifon*, two Horfes worth	4	o	o
Reginald Holme, *John Holme*, *Jacob Holme*, and *John Thompfon*, Goods worth	o	18	o
Robert Barrow, *Richard Holme*, and *Robert Newby*, all of *Kendal*, Goods worth	o	14	o
	23	4	9

Imprifon-
ments.

Death of
E. Braith-
waite.

For the fame Caufe of abfenting from the National Form of Worfhip, *Chriftopher Bifbrown* and *Robert Harfden* were committed to Prifon : And for the like Caufe the Juftices alfo committed feveral married Women to Prifon, for the Act in that Cafe did not exprefsly authorize the Seizure of the Hufband's Goods for the Wife's Offence : Under this Pretext were imprifoned, *Jane*, the Wife of *Richard Atkinfon* ; *Agnes*, Wife of *Thomas Prefton* ; *Elizabeth*, Wife of *James Fell* ; *Dorothy*, Wife of *Robert Lorimer* ; *Alice*, Wife of *Richard Burrough* ; *Agnes*, Wife of *George Williamfon* ; *Margaret*, Wife of *William Williamfon* ; and alfo the Wife of *Thomas Williamfon* : Alfo for the fame Caufe, *Elizabeth Braithwaite*, a young Maiden about feventeen Years of Age, was committed to Prifon on the 6th of the Month called *July*, and remained there till fhe died on the 26th of *September* following, after about eleven Weeks Imprifonment. *Chriftopher Dixon*, a Servant, was alfo imprifoned for the fame Caufe.

For a Meeting at *Kendal*, in the Month called *July* this Year, was taken by Diftrefs,

Diftreffes for
Meeting.

	l.	*s.*	*d.*
From *Robert Barrow*, *Thomas Copeland*, and *Robert Newby*, Pewter to the Value of	1	6	6
Ifrael Newby, his working Tools worth	o	8	8
Carried over	1	15	2

	l.	*s.*	*d.*
Brought over	1	15	2
From *Henry Fisher* and *John Fell*, Pewter worth	0	18	0
George Taylor and *Thomas Wilson*, Goods worth	0	19	0
Bryan Lancaster had taken from him his Fine of	0	5	0
	3	17	2

We shall next insert the Copies of two Warrants for Distress, granted by Justice *Wilson*, viz.

A Copy of the first Warrant.

" EDWARD WILSON, *Esq; one of the King's Majesty's Justices of the*
" *Peace for the County of* Westmorland,

" *To all Constables, Churchwardens, and Overseers of the Poor within*
" *the said County, and more especially the Constables, Churchwardens,*
" *and Overseers of the Poor within* Beethom, Hale, Farleton,
" Overforth, *and* Milnethorp, *within the said County, and to every*
" *of them.*

" WHEREAS the several Persons hereafter named, every of them
" being of the Age of sixteen Years or upwards, and Subjects of this
" Realm, were the st Day of this Instant *October*, present at an Assembly,
" Conventicle, or Meeting, under Colour or Pretence of Exercise of Religion,
" in other Manner than according to the Liturgy and Practice of the Church
" of *England*, in the Dwelling-house of *John Hudson* in *Hale*, in the Parish of
" *Beethom* in the County of *Westmorland* aforesaid, Yeoman, contrary to an
" Act of Parliament intituled, *An Act to prevent and suppress seditious Con-*
" *venticles*, being by me, the said *Edward Wilson*, of the said several Offences
" duly convicted, and for their several Offences fined at the respective Sums
" on their Heads hereunder respectively set, as by a Record made thereof,
" under my Hand and Seal, doth and may more fully appear. These are
" therefore, in his Majesty's Name, to will and command you, and every of
" you, to demand the said several Sums, Fines, and Forfeitures of the said
" several Persons hereafter named respectively ; and in case they, or any of
" them, neglect or refuse to pay the same, that then of such you forthwith
" levy the same by Distress and Sale of the Offenders Goods and Chattels
" respectively, rendring to them the Overplus, if any be, viz.

" A Person being a Stranger, and his Name and Habitation not known,
" and being fled, and cannot be found, for that he did take upon him to
" preach or teach in the said Conventicle, has forfeited, and is fined in twenty
" Pounds.

" *John Hudson*, of *Hale* within the said County of *Westmorland*, Yeoman,
" for suffering such Conventicle, Meeting, or unlawful Assembly in his Dwell-
" ing-house, is fined in twenty Pounds. And the said *John Hudson* is farther
" fined, for being present at the said Conventicle, in ten Shillings for his second
" Offence.

" *Robert Waller*, of *Hale* within the said County of *Westmorland*, Yeoman,
" for being present at the said Conventicle, is fined in ten Shillings for his
" second Offence : *Robert Waller* is farther fined the Sum of ten Pounds to-
" ward the Sum of twenty Pounds, being the Forfeiture of the Stranger
" aforesaid, who took upon him to preach in the said Conventicle.

" *Richard Atkinson*, of *Farleton* within the said County, Yeoman, for being
" present at the said Conventicle, is fined in ten Shillings for his second Offence :
" *Richard Atkinson* is farther fined the Sum of ten Pounds toward the Sum of
" twenty

Copy of a Warrant for Distress.

WEST-
MOR-
LAND.
1684.

" twenty Pounds, being the Forfeiture of the Stranger aforesaid, who took
" upon him to preach in the said Conventicle.

" *Sarah Moore*, of *Hale* in the said County, for being present at the said
" Conventicle, is fined five Shillings.

" *Mary Flemming*, of *Hale* in the said County, for being present at the said
" Conventicle, is fined five Shillings.

" *John Preston*, of *Overforth* in the said County, Batchelor, for being present
" at the said Conventicle, is fined in five Shillings.

" *Thomas Atkinson*, of *Milnethorp* in the said County, for being present at
" the said Conventicle, is fined in ten Shillings for his second Offence.

" *Margaret*, the Wife of *Robert Weller* aforesaid, and *Jane*, the Wife of
" *Joseph Gregg*, of *Milnethorp* aforesaid, for being present at the said Conven-
" ticle, are fined five Shillings a-piece severally and respectively, which you are
" to levy upon their several and respective Husbands Goods and Chattels in
" Manner aforesaid. Which Fines and Sums of Money aforesaid, as you shall
" levy the same, you are hereby required forthwith to deliver unto me, that
" I may distribute the same according to the Act of Parliament aforesaid. And
" in Case you cannot, by reason of Poverty, levy all the said Fines as before
" directed, you are hereby required and authorized to levy such in Arrear by
" Distress and Sale of the Goods and Chattels of any other Offender or Of-
" fenders above-mentioned, provided you levy not above ten Pounds of any
" Person aforesaid for another's Offence : And hereof you are not to fail at
" your Perils. Given under my Hand and Seal at *Dallam* Tower, the 20th
" Day of *October*, *Anno rni. Dni.* Caroli secundi, *Dei gra.* Angliæ, Scotiæ,
" Franciæ, *et* Hiberniæ, *Regis, Fidei Defensoris*, &c. *Tricesimo sexto, Annoq;*
" *Dom.* 1684.

" EDWARD WILSON."

A Copy of the second Warrant.

" *Westmorland* fs.

" EDWARD WILSON, *Esq; one of the King's Majesty's Justices of the*
" *Peace for the County of* Westmorland.

" *To all Constables, Churchwardens, and Overseers of the Poor within*
" Beethom, Hale, Farleton, Preston-Patrick, Preston-Richard,
" Sedgewick, Lupton, Hutton, Roose, *and* Milnethorp, *within the*
" *said County, and to all and every of them.*

Copy of a se-
cond Warrant
for Distress.

" **W**HEREAS the several Persons hereafter named, every of them
" being of the Age of sixteen Years and upwards, and Subjects of this
" Realm, were the 19th Day of this Instant *October* present at an Assembly,
" Conventicle, or Meeting, under Colour or Pretence of Exercise of Religion,
" in other Manner than according to the Liturgy and Practice of the Church
" of *England*, in the Dwelling-house of *Richard Atkinson*, of *Farleton* within
" the Parish of *Beethom* in the County of *Westmorland* aforesaid, Yeoman, con-
" trary to an Act of Parliament, intituled, *An Act to prevent and suppress*
" *seditious Conventicles*, being by me, the said *Edward Wilson*, of the said
" several Offences duly convicted, and for their several Offences fined, and the
" respective Sums on their Heads respectively hereunder set, as by a Record
" made hereof, under my Hand and Seal, doth more at large appear. These
" are therefore, in his Majesty's Name, to will and command you, and every
" of you, to demand the said several Sums, Fines, and Forfeitures of
" the said several Persons hereafter named respectively ; and in case they,
" or any of them, neglect or refuse to pay the same, that then on such you
" forthwith

" forthwith levy the fame by Diftrefs and Sale of their Goods and Chattels
" refpectively, rendring them the Overplus, if any be.

" A Perfon being a Stranger, and his Name and Habitation unknown, and
" being fled, and cannot be found, for that he did take upon him to preach or
" teach in the faid Conventicle, has forfeited, and is fined twenty Pounds.

" *Richard Atkinfon*, of *Farleton* within the faid County of *Weftmorland*,
" Yeoman, for fuffering fuch Conventicle, Meeting, or unlawful Affembly in
" his Houfe, is fined in twenty Pounds : And the faid *Richard Atkinfon* is
" farther fined, for being prefent at the faid Conventicle, in ten Shillings, it
" being his fourth Offence.

" *James Fell*, of *Sedgewick* in the faid County of *Weftmorland*, Yeoman, for
" being prefent at the faid Conventicle, fined ten Shillings, it being his fecond
" Offence : And the faid *James Fell* is farther fined in the Sum of ten Pounds
" toward the Sum of twenty Pounds, being the Forfeiture of the Stranger, who
" took upon him to preach in the faid Conventicle.

" *Thomas Moore*, of *Newbiggin* in the faid County of *Weftmorland*, Houfe-
" Carpenter, for being prefent at the faid Conventicle, is fined in five Shillings :
" And the faid *Thomas Moore* is farther fined the Sum of two Pounds toward the
" Sum of twenty Pounds, being the Forfeiture of the faid Stranger, who took
" upon him to preach in the faid Conventicle.

" *Richard Story*, of *Prefton-Patrick* in the faid County of *Weftmorland*,
" Wool-Webfter, for being prefent at the faid Conventicle, is fined five
" Shillings.

" *William Herdfon*, of *Prefton-Patrick* in the faid County of *Weftmorland*,
" Woolendraper, for being prefent at the faid Conventicle, is fined in five
" Shillings.

" *John Audland*, of *Cammfgill* in the faid County, Batchelor, for being prefent
" at the faid Conventicle, is fined five Shillings.

" *Bryan Lancafter*, fined five Shillings for being at the faid Conventicle,
" and alfo eight Pounds toward the twenty Pounds, being the Forfeiture of the
" Stranger, who took upon him to preach there.

" *Charles Story*, of *Prefton-Patrick* in the faid County, Woolen-Webfter,
" for being prefent at the faid Conventicle, is fined in five Shillings.

" *Nicholas Thompfon*, of *Holmefkalls* in the faid County, for being prefent at
" the fame Conventicle, is fined five Shillings.

" *Arthur Burrough*, of *Prefton-Patrick* in the faid County, Woolen-Webfter,
" for being prefent at the faid Conventicle, is fined in ten Shillings for his
" fecond Offence.

" *Margaret Thompfon*, of *Prefton-Patrick* in the faid County, Widow, for being
" prefent at the faid Conventicle, is fined in ten Shillings for her fecond Offence.

" *Henry Skyring*, of *Lupton* in the faid County, Blackfmith, for being prefent
" at the faid Conventicle, is fined in five Shillings.

" *Simon Thompfon*, of *Prefton-Richard* in the faid County, Badger, for being
" prefent at the faid Conventicle, is fined ten Shillings for his third Offence.

" *James Harrifon*, of *Sedgewick* in the faid County, Linen-Webfter, for
" being prefent at the faid Conventicle, is fined in five Shillings.

" *Mary Pye*, Wife of *Richard Pye*, of *Storth*, for being prefent at the faid
" Conventicle, is fined in five Shillings.

" *Ifabel Hudfon*, Wife of *John Hudfon*, of *Hale* in the faid County, for being
" prefent at the faid Conventicle, is fined in ten Shillings for her fecond Offence.

" *Jane*, Wife of *Jofeph Gregg*, of *Milnethorp* in the faid County, Diftiller,
" is fined in ten Shillings for being prefent at the faid Conventicle, it being her
" third Offence.

" *Hannah*, the Maid Servant of the faid *Jofeph Gregg*, for being prefent at
" the faid Conventicle, is fined five Shillings.

" *Grace*, the Wife of *John Watfon*, of *Milnethorp* aforefaid, for being prefent
" at the faid Conventicle, is fined in ten Shillings, being her fecond Offence.

" *Mary*, the Wife of *Richard Pye* aforefaid, *Jane*, the Wife of *Jofeph*
" *Gregg* aforefaid, *Sibyl*, the Wife of *John Hudfon* aforefaid, and *Grace*, the

" Wife of *John Watson* aforesaid, for being present at the said Conventicle, are
" respectively fined in the several Sums before expressed at their Heads appear-
" ing, which you are to levy upon their respective Husbands Goods and Chattels
" in Manner aforesaid : All which Fines and Sums of Money aforesaid, as you
" shall levy the same, you are hereby forthwith to deliver unto me, that I may
" distribute the same according to the Act of Parliament aforesaid. And if,
" in case of Poverty, you cannot by Reason thereof levy all the said Fines as
" above directed, you are hereby required and authorized to levy such in Arrear
" by Distress and Sale of the Goods and Chattels of any other Offender above-
" mentioned, provided you levy not above ten Pounds on any Person aforesaid
" for another's Offence : And hereof fail not at your Perils. Given under my
" Hand and Seal at *Dallam* Tower, the 29th Day of *October, Anno rni. Regis*
" *Dni. nri.* Caroli secundi, *Dei Gra.* Angliæ, Scotiæ, Franciæ, *et* Hiberniæ,
" *Fidei Defensoris,* &c. *Tricesimo sexto, Annoq; Dom.* 1684.

" EDWARD WILSON."

By Virtue of the former of the said Warrants were taken

		l.	*s.*	*d.*
Distresses. From	*John Hudson,* Cattle and Corn, to the Value of	23	8	0
	Robert Waller, Cattle and Corn, to the Value of	11	4	0
	Richard Atkinson, five Beasts and other Goods, worth	13	10	0
	Jane Gregg, Pewter worth	0	5	0
		48	7	0

And by the latter Warrant were taken

	l.	*s.*	*d.*
From *Richard Atkinson,* Cattle and Corn, to the Value of	39	14	0
James Fell, seven Head of Cattle worth	14	0	0
Thomas Moore, Oats worth	2	5	6
Charles Story, Oats and Pewter worth	0	18	6
Bryan Lancaster, a Parcel of tanned Hides worth	11	0	0
Margaret Thompson Widow, Goods worth	1	12	0
William Herdson, a poor Labourer, a Pewter Dish and six Spoons, not worth the Fine, amounting to	0	3	0
Jane, Wife of *Joseph Gregg,* her Husband being then in Prison, Goods worth	0	12	0
Isabel, Wife of *John Hudson*	0	10	0
Henry Skyring, of *Lupton,* whose Fine was paid without his Knowledge or Consent	0	5	0
Simon Thompson, Goods worth	0	10	0
	71	10	0

Also by Warrants granted by Sir *Daniel Flemming* Justice, for Meetings held at the House of *William Rawes,* in *Langdale,* were taken

	l.	*s.*	*d.*
From *William Rawes,* Corn, Cattle, and Houshold Goods, worth	14	0	0
John Dixon, Beasts, Hay, and Wool, worth	20	12	0
Michael Wilson, Goods worth	0	12	6
Thomas Harrison, Wool worth	0	13	6
John Walker, four Oxen and an Iron Pot worth	16	8	0
James Harrison, Goods worth	1	0	0
Dorothy Wilson, and *Rebecca* her Daughter, Goods worth	1	14	0
John Rigg, Wool worth	1	6	6
	56	6	6

About

About this Time many of the People called *Quakers*, in this County, were
profecuted by Statutes made againft *Popifh* Recufants, a Lift of whofe Names is here fubjoined, *viz.*

John Abbott, Katharine Atkinson, Richard Atkinson, Robert Atkinson, Thomas Atkinson, Thomas Ayrey, Richard Ayrey, Peter Bateman, Miles Bateman, Mary Bateman, Alice Bateman, Jennet Barwick, Richard Barwick, Thomas Barwick, William Barwick, John Beck, Elizabeth Beck, Bernard Benson, Jane Benson, Richard Brinke, John Briggs, John Bolton, Arthur Burrow, Richard Burrow, Elizabeth Chambers, John Clark, Katharine Clark, James Clarkson, Richard Clarkson, John Cooper, Thomas Cooper, Thomas Claughton, Alice Cragg, Edward Cragg, George Crofsfield, Mabel Crofsfield, Stephen Crofsfield, Richard Crewdson, George Dennison, John Dickinson, Nicholas Denkin, William Ellery, Agnes Efcrigg, Michael Efkill, Cicely Fallowfield, Grace Fallowfield, James Fallowfield, Lancelot Fallowfield, Thomas Fallowfield, John Fawcett, Thomas Fawcett, William Fayrer, William Fothergill, Thomas Gardner, Ifabel Garnett, Jane Grave, Margaret Grave, Thomas Grave, Dorothy Gregg, Bridget Gregg, Edward Guy, Katharine Guy, William Hadwin, Ifaac Handly, Jane Harrison, Reginald Harrison, Richard Hayton, Elizabeth Holme, John Holme, Jane Holme, Reginald Holme, John Hebson, Bridget Holt, John Hudson, Ifabel Hudson, Robert Hutchinson, James Jackson, Sarah Jackson, Thomas Jackson, William Jackson, Thomas Langhorn, Francis Lawson, Thomas Lawson, Anne Laycock, Henry Laycock, Dorothy Lorimer, Margaret Mackew, John Middleton, Mariam Mitchell, John Nelson, Mary Nelson, Sarah Nelson, Jane Nicholson, Margaret Park, Agnes Pearson, John Pearson, Thomas Pearson, Elizabeth Powly, Edmund Powly, John Powly, Anthony Pindar, Agnes Prefton, John Prefton, Thomas Prefton, James Robertson, Anthony Robinson, Ifabel Salkeld, Thomas Savage, William Savage, Robert Shaw, John Shearman, Elizabeth Simpson, Martin Simpson, Mary Simpson, Robert Simpson, William Simpson, John Skaif, Ifabel Skaif, William Skaif, Nicholas Suart, Rowland Suart, Richard Stevenson, Rowland Stevenson, William Stevenson, Agnes Sutton, Edmund Sutton, John Sutton, Robert Teafdale, Agnes Thompson, George Thompson, Jane Thompson, John Thompson, Nicholas Thompson, Ifabel Thompson, Richard Thompson, Robert Thompson, Simon Thompson, Sarah Thompson, Thomas Thompson, John Tinkle, Agnes Toogood, William Toogood, George Walker, Roger Wakefield, Elizabeth Ward, Thomas Ward, Mary Wayman, George Wharton, Margaret Wharton, Elizabeth Whitehead, William Whitehead, Margaret Wilson, Rowland Wilson, Sarah Wilson, Robert Winter, Edward Winter, Thomas Wyburgh.

ANNO 1687. *James Fallowfield* and *Lancelot Fallowfield*, of *Great-Strickland*, fuffered Diftrefs of their Goods for refufing to pay toward the Repairs of the Steeple-houfe there.

ANNO 1690. We fhall clofe our Account of the Sufferings in this County with a Collection of the Values of Corn and other Things, taken out of the Fields from the Perfons under-named, for Tithes from the Year 1681 to the Year 1690 inclufive, *viz.*

	l.	*s.*	*d.*
From *Richard Atkinson*, of *Farleton*	25	7	3
Robert Atkinson, of *Middleton*	8	0	0
Thomas Atkinson, of *Goat-bufh*	2	5	0
John Audland	0	5	4
John Ayrey, of *Shapp*	2	7	10
Thomas Ayrey, of *Sellfide*	8	2	0
Widow *Ayrey*, of *Shapp*	1	6	0
James Baines, of *Strangerthwaite*	4	8	9
Jofeph Baines, of the fame	4	8	6
Jofeph Baines the Younger	0	7	6
William Baines, of *Strangerthwaite*	2	5	3
Richard Barwick, of *Shapp*	5	8	3
Thomas Barwick	8	1	6
William Barwick, of *Shapp*	3	10	7
John Beck, of *Hollins*	0	19	0
Carried over	77	2	9

		l.	*s.*	*d.*
Brought over		77	2	9
From	John Bownas, of *Kempham*	2	10	5
	Richard Burrough, of *Arnſide*	1	8	0
	Thomas Camm, of *Cammſgill*	20	18	2
	Elizabeth Chambers	0	13	4
	John Clark, of *Bampton*	3	4	5
	Thomas Cloudſdale, of *Weſt-Sleddale*	1	12	0
	William Coupland	0	4	0
	Edward Cragg, of *Ackonthwaite*	5	6	0
	John Cummings, of *Burton*	2	15	10
	George Denniſon, of *Manſergh*	6	6	0
	John Dickinſon, of *Beckhouſes*	5	17	8
	James Fallowfield, of *Great-Strickland*	5	7	4
	Lancelot Fallowfield, of the ſame	5	12	5
	James Fell, of *Sedgewick*	25	1	0
	Joſeph Gregg, of *Milthorp*	2	6	6
	Rowland Glover, of *Manſergh*	10	10	10
	James Harriſon, of *Sedgewick*	0	14	0
	Richard Hayton, of *Shapp*	2	7	2
	Elizabeth Hudſon Widow	0	4	6
	John Hudſon, of *Hale*	3	15	6
	William Hudſon	0	9	0
	Thomas Huggonſon, of *Sedgewick*	6	6	6
	Thomas Jackſon, of *Hale*	3	1	2
	Bryan Lancaſter, of *Kendal*	0	6	6
	Oliver Leighton, of *Preſton*	9	2	0
	Richard Lewis, of *Beckhouſes*	1	10	0
	Henry Lickburrow, of *Grayrigg*	7	4	0
	William Laycock	1	12	0
	Dorothy Middleton Widow	3	19	0
	Robert Middleton	1	6	8
	John Moore, of *Sunny-Bank*	6	19	0
	Thomas Moore, of *Newbiggen*	6	12	6
	Thomas Preſton, of *Overforth*	14	10	0
	Richard Pye, of *Storth*	0	1	0
	Robert Robinſon, of *Newby-Stones*	6	1	6
	William Savage, of *Clifton*	1	4	6
	Henry Skyring, of *Lupton*	8	8	0
	Richard Skyring, of *Preſton-Patrick*	4	18	10
	Barbara Story Widow	4	3	4
	Charles Story, of *Preſton*	8	5	0
	Rowland Suart, of *Shapp*	6	9	0
	Edmund Sutton, of *Moorhouſes*	4	17	4
	Edward Sutton, of *Lupton*	9	5	0
	John Sutton, of *Clifton*	17	3	10
	John Thirnbeck, of *Middleton*	11	7	3
	Anne Thompſon	0	9	10
	Margaret Thompſon Widow, of *Milnhouſes*	5	10	6
	Nicholas Thompſon, of *Croſslands*	0	10	0
	Richard Thompſon, of *Milnhouſes*	2	11	6
	Simon Thompſon, of *Endmore*	7	2	0
	Thomas Waſhington, of *Beckhouſes*	3	8	0
	William Whitehead, of *Waters*	5	9	6
	Edward Winter, of *Moreland*	0	13	4
	Robert Winter, of the ſame	4	13	0
	John Yeates, of *Burton*	0	8	0
		359	16	5

CHAP.

C H A P. IX.

C U M B E R L A N D.

ANNO 1653.

GEORGE FOX, for preaching the Truth in the great Worſhip-houſe at *Carliſle*, after the Prieſt had ended his Sermon, and for witneſſing a good Confeſſion before the Magiſtrates and People there, was impriſoned ſeven Weeks, ſometimes among Thieves and Murderers.

*G. Fox impri-
ſoned.*,

Robert Withers, for aſking the Prieſt of *Aketon* a religious Queſtion after Sermon, was impriſoned at *Carliſle* one Month ; as was *George Bewly* for accompanying him. *Robert Huntington*, for Preaching at *Carliſle*, was impriſoned three Months, and *James Noble*, for the ſame Cauſe, *nine Weeks*.

*Sundry others
impriſoned.*

Robert Withers, *Thomas Rawlinſon*, *John Stubbs*, and *Thomas Gwin*, for declaring againſt falſe Worſhip at the Steeple-houſe in *Coldbeck*, were inhumanly treated by the rude People, one of them being knocked down, and much of their Blood ſpilled on the Place.

John Martin, for teſtifying againſt the Prieſt of *Kirkbride*, whom he met in the Fields, and calling him by his proper Name, *viz. an Hireling*, was committed to Priſon.

ANNO 1654. *Thomas Stubbs* was concerned to go into the Steeple-houſe at *Deane*, where, when the Prieſt had done, he ſaid, *Thou daubeſt the People up with untempered Mortar* ; whereupon the Prieſt bid his Hearers *fight for the Goſpel* ; they fell violently upon *Stubbs* and ſome of his Friends, tore their Clothes, and beat them cruelly. The Prieſt's Son in particular ſorely bruiſed the Face of *Richard Richardſon*. After which two Juſtices ſent *Stubbs* to Priſon, but conſcious of the Wrong they did him, writ his *Mittimus* and *Diſchárge* both on one Paper ; this furniſhed the Goaler with a Claim for Fees, under Pretence of which he kept him fourteen Weeks in Priſon.

*T. Stubbs
abuſed.*

Peter Head, for teſtifying the Truth, in the ſame Place, was impriſoned fourteen Weeks in a cloſe Room among Felons in the Heat of Summer ; and *John Head*, for delivering ſome Queries to the Prieſt of *Deane* at his own Houſe, was impriſoned fourteen Weeks. *John Slee*, for reproving a Prieſt at *Griſdale*, was kept a cloſe Priſoner among Felons two Months. Alſo *Katharine Fell*, for aſking a Prieſt, *whether he did witneſs what he ſpake to the People*, was kept in Priſon nineteen Weeks, having a young Child ſucking at her Breaſt.

*Impriſonment
of P. Head
and others.*

Thomas Bewley and *Hugh Stamper*, ſtanding at the Seſſions in *Carliſle* with their Hats on, were by the Juſtices committed to Priſon without any legal Cauſe aſſigned. After a Month's Confinement they were diſcharged without paying Fees : But *Hugh Stamper* was afterward arreſted for Fees, and again impriſoned and detained there one and twenty Weeks.

ANNO 1655. *Matthew Carpe* and *Anthony Fell* were impriſoned for appearing at Seſſions with their Hats on, and detained three Weeks.

*Impriſonments
for ſundry
Cauſes.*

Matthew Robinſon and *John Dixon*, for refuſing to pay Tithes, were impriſoned at *Carliſle*, and afterward obliged to appear perſonally at *London*, above two Hundred and fifty Miles from their Habitations, to their great Expence and Trouble.

John Peacock and *John Stricket* Conſtables, refuſing to execute a Warrant of Diſtreſs for Tithes, were fined 1 *l.* 6 *s.* 8 *d.* and for Non-payment committed to Priſon.

CUMBER-
LAND.
1655.
*Cruel Ufage of
two Women.*

*Beating of
two Men.*

*Imprifon-
ments.*

*Diftrefs for
Tithes,* &c.

*Many Imprifon-
ments for not
Swearing.*

*Imprifonments
and Diftreffes.*

*Tithes reco-
vered at a Pa-
pift's Suit.*

Dorothy Waugh, for Preaching in the Streets of *Carlifle,* and *Anne Robinfon,* who accompanied her, were by the Mayor fent to Prifon, and fome Time after were led through the Street with each an Iron Inftrument of Torture, called a Bridle, on their Heads, to prevent their fpeaking to the People ; having been fo expofed to the Scorn and Derifion of the Rabble, they were turned out of the City.

John Weftray and *Thomas Scott* were cruelly beaten by the rude People, for teftifying againft the Doctrine of the Preacher at *Seck-Murder* Chapel.

ANNO 1657. The following Perfons were imprifoned at *Carlifle* for reproving the Priefts at feveral Times and Places, *viz. John Grave* twenty two Weeks, *George Bewley* fourteen Weeks, *John Burnyeat* twenty three Weeks, *Matthew Robinfon* twenty nine Weeks, *Anthony Tickle* twenty feven Weeks, and *George Wilfon.*

ANNO 1660. In this and the feveral foregoing Years had been taken from Perfons in this County by Diftrefs, for 156 *l.* 8 *s.* 7 *d.* demanded for Tithes, Goods worth 515 *l.* 1 *s.* 3 *d.* And for Demands of 3 *l.* 12 *s.* 3 *d.* for Steeple-houfe Rates and Clerk's Wages, Goods to the Value of 11 *l.* 13 *s.* 10 *d.*

In this Year alfo *Francis Hayton* and *William Rowland* were imprifoned for Tithes thirty two Weeks.

John Robinfon, for refufing to take an Oath at *Carlifle* Affizes, was fined 40 *s.* and had Goods taken from him to that Value.

In the fame Year *Thomas Stordy* was imprifoned nine Weeks for refufing to take the Oath of Allegiance ; and for the fame Caufe *James Adamfon* was kept clofe Prifoner feveral Weeks, during which Time, his Father, of the fame Name, coming to vifit him, was way-laid in his Return home, and by a Juftice of the Peace fent back to Prifon for refufing to Swear. For the fame Caufe alfo *Elizabeth Heath, Anne Bewley, Elizabeth Jackfon, Elizabeth Hazard, William Oglethorp, Anne* his Wife, *Ifabel Oglethorp,* and *Elizabeth Watfon,* fuffered twenty two Weeks Imprifonment : Alfo *Thomas Summers, William Summers, Humphry Twiddale,* and *Thomas Story,* were imprifoned fourteen Weeks, and * *William Lowthwait* one and thirty Weeks ; *Thomas Watfon, Richard Ribton, Chriftopher Manfer, Richard Banks,* and *Thomas Leathes,* nine Days ; *John Matthew* of *Brough,* feveral Weeks ; and *Robert Huntington, John Robinfon, Robert Matthew,* and *Margaret Martin,* twenty two Weeks, which laft four were taken up in *Carlifle* Market, being there about their lawful Occafions, and fent to Goal by the Mayor for refufing the Oath.

ANNO 1661. *John Nicholfon, Thomas Mark,* and *John Peacock,* on an Attachment out of the *Exchequer,* were committed to *Carlifle* Goal in the Month called *April* this Year, and detained there about three Years.

In this Year alfo *George Biglands* and *John Dobinfon* fuffered eight Weeks Imprifonment for refufing to Swear ; and for the fame Caufe *Chriftopher Manfer* had a Cow taken from him worth 2 *l.* 4 *s.* and *Chriftopher Birkett* a Cow worth 3 *l.*

ANNO 1662. In this Year *Adam Robinfon, William Bond,* and *John Richardfon,* fuffered about feven Months Imprifonment, having been arrefted for Tithes at the Suit of *Francis Howard* of *Corby,* a *Papift,* who afterward at the Affizes obtained Judgment againft them for treble Damages, upon which were taken from

	l.	*s.*	*d.*		*l.*	*s.*	*d.*
Adam Robinfon, for a Demand of	1	5	0	four Beafts worth	28	0	0
William Bond, for a Demand of	0	7	0	a Mare and Steer	3	15	0
John Richardfon, for a Demand of	1	12	0	Cattle worth	7	10	0
For Demands of	3	4	0	Goods worth	39	5	0

In

---

* *W. Lowthwait* had offended a Neighbouring Juftice's Servant by reproving him for profane Swearing ; whereupon the Juftice, to avenge his Man's Quarrel, tendred *William* the Oath, and fent him to Prifon.

In this Year alfo, for refufing to Swear at the Mannour Courts, were taken from

	l.	*s.*	*d.*		*l.*	*s.*	*d.*
Richard Thompfon, for a Fine of	3	6	8	a Cow worth	3	0	0
Francis Hayton, for a Fine of	0	3	4	Goods worth	0	8	0
Thomas Hunter, for a Fine of	3	6	8	Kine worth	6	0	0
For Fines of	6	16	8	Goods worth	9	8	0

Fines for not Swearing.

Thomas Stordy, being at *Carlifle* Affizes, went to vifit fome of his Friends there in Prifon, but was illegally detained by the Goaler, and the next Day, he, with *Stephen Pearfon*, then a Prifoner, was had to the Seffions-houfe, where the Oath of Allegiance was tendred them, which they refufing, were fent back to Goal among the Felons: Next Day they were indiated on the Statute of 3 K. *James*, found *guilty*, and had Sentence of *Premunire* paffed upon them; by which they were adjudged *to forfeit all their Lands, Goods, and Chattels, to be out of the King's Protettion, and to fuffer Imprifonment for Life*. Soon after the Sheriff feized their Cattle, Corn, and other Goods, and proclaimed a publick Sale of them; at which they were fold far beneath the Value, in regard very few cared to buy them. However they were at length difpofed of and carried away, without any Regard to the Prifoners or their Families, nor would the Sheriff, though earneftly defired, allow any thing to the poor Labourers, who had been employed in gathering in the Corn, and whom the Prifoners, thus plundered, were unable to pay. Under this hard Sentence *Thomas Stordy* and *Stephen Pearfon* continued clofe Prifoners feveral Years, enduring their great Sufferings with exemplary Patience and Conftancy, being fupported by the Teftimony of a good Confcience in their Obedience to the Precept of Chrift, *Swear not at all.*

Imprifonments for refufing the Oath.

Patience of the Sufferers.

John Grave of *Turpenhow*, *Thomas Watfon* of *Cockermouth*, and *John Robinfon* of *Brigham*, taken out of their own Houfes by Soldiers and carried to the Governour of *Carlifle*, were by him imprifoned, in the Depth of Winter, in a cold Place over one of the City Gates, where they were denied the Vifits of their Friends, and had their Food frequently kept from them, nor were they permitted to go out to eafe themfelves: After about ten Days Confinement there, the Oath was tendred them at a Meeting of the Juftices, and they were removed to the County Goal, where they lay thirty five Weeks. In the fame Year *John Slee* had two Steers worth 9 *l.* taken from him for a Fine of 5 *l.* for being at a Meeting; and on the 7th of the Month called *Auguft*, *Richard Ribton*, *William Ribton*, and *Thomas Afhley*, of *Great-Broughton*, *Chriftopher Shepherd* and *John Shepherd* of *Ribton*, *Chriftopher Palmer* and *William Hall* of *Little-Broughton*, *John Parker* of *Pop-Caftle*, and *Launcelot Wilfon* of *Tallontire*, were fummoned before the Juftices on an Information againft them for Meeting, and fent to Prifon till the Affizes, when they were indiated, and having pleaded *not guilty*, were recommitted till another Affizes, before which *Lancelot Wilfon* died in the Prifon, being a weakly Man, and unable to fuftain the Hardfhip of his Confinement. At the following Affizes the reft of them were difcharged. In this Year alfo *George Fletcher*, a Juftice of the Peace, fignalized himfelf by a violent Procedure at a Meeting at *Howhill* in *Sowerby* Parifh, into which he, with a Retinue armed with Swords and Piftols, rufhed in after an hoftile Manner, and finding a Perfon on his Knees, the Juftice ftruck him over the Head, and when he continued Praying, ordered him to be pulled down backward, and then caufed him, together with *John Slee*, *George Bewley*, *Mungo Bewley*, *Anthony Fell*, *John Banks*, and others of the Affembly, to be dragged down the Hill in a violent and cruel Manner, and afterward fent them to *Carlifle* Goal. At the next Seffions *John Slee* was fined 10 *l.* and the reft 5 *l.* each, for which Fines were taken from *John Slee*, three Kine, one Bull, and an Heifer, worth 13 *l.* from *George Bewley*, three Kine worth 8 *l.* and from *Mungo Bewley*, two Horfes worth 5 *l.* 2 *s.* 6 *d.* At the Time of making thefe Diftreffes *George Bewley* was remaining a Prifoner for the fame Fine.

Hard Imprifonments.

Many imprifoned for Meeting.

Death of L. Wilfon.

Violence of Juftice Fletcher.

Fines.

CUMBER-
LAND.
1663.

Long Imprison-
ments.
Seizures for
Tithes.

ANNO 1663. *Thomas Bewley*, after frequent Seizures of his Goods for Tithes, was this Year, on an *Exchequer* Procefs, committed to Prifon at *Car-lifle*, where he lay near three Years. In this Year alfo Seizures were made on *James Stanton* of *Weftdale*, to the Value of 27 *l.* and upwards, for a Demand of but 3 *l.* for Tithes ; and on *Thomas Bewley* the younger, to the Value of 11 *l.* for a Claim of 2 *l.* 18 *s.* for Tithes. And in the fame Year for Demands of 10 *l.* 4 *s.* 2 *d.* ¼ *d.* for Tithes, feveral others had Goods taken by Diftrefs, to the Value of 30 *l.* 1 *s.* 11 *d.* In this Year alfo fuffered by Diftrefs, for re-fufing to Swear, *Richard Fawcett* 1 *l.* 12 *s.* *Philip Burnyeat* 20 *s.* *Henry Allafon* 50 *s.* and *William Morrifon* 40 *s.* Alfo *Thomas Fell*, *John Fell*, *James Barnes*, and *John Tiffin*, were Sufferers by Diftrefs on the fame Account.

Exchequer
Procefs for
frivolous De-
mands.

ANNO 1664. *Richard Fawcett*, *John Gill*, *William Richardfon*, and *John Fearon*, were profecuted in the *Exchequer* by *George Fletcher*, for Tithes ; the Claim he made from fome of them was but 6 *d.* and from none of them above 1 *s.* for which Trifles fome of them were obliged by the Profecutor to appear feveral Times at *London*, two Hundred and fifty Miles from their Habitations : His Purpofe being not fo much to recover any Thing, as to perplex and har-rafs the poor Men, who at length were imprifoned at *Carlifle* for refufing to Swear to the Anfwers they gave into Court. For the fame Reafon alfo *William Bowman*, *William Morrifon*, and *John Fell*, were fent to Prifon. In this Year

Imprifonments
by Writs de
Excom. Cap.

likewife were imprifoned upon Writs *de Excommunicato capiendo*, after Profecu-tion in the Ecclefiaftical Court for Tithes, *Hugh Tickell*, *Anthony Tickell*, *John Wilfon*, *Anthony Wood*, *Chriftopher Scott*, *William Longftake*, *Thomas Stamper*, *Thomas Porter*, *John Pattinfon*, *Thomas Fell*, *Thomas Carleton*, *John Gibfon*, *William Adcock*, *Leonard Whitburne*, and *John Hetherington*.

Rigorous Ex-
action of
Fines.

In this and the foregoing Year, the generality of. the *Quakers* in this County, Men, Women, and Children, were fined for *Nonconformity* to the eftablifhed Worfhip, which Fines were rigoroufly exacted by Diftreffes made on. Parents for their Children, Mafters for their Servants, and even on fuch as being them-felves Conformifts, had Servants or others in their Families who were not. The Sums of Money levied for this Caufe in thefe two Years, amounted to 87 *l.* 17 *s.* 7 *d.* We alfo find that within thefe laft four Years, for Demands made for Steeple-houfe Rates and Clerk's Wages, amounting to 6 *l.* 13 *s.* Diftreffes were made to the Value of 18 *l.* 18 *s.* 3 *d.*

R. Banks
fined.

ANNO 1665. *Richard Banks*, fined for being at a religious Meeting, had two Cows taken away which coft him 9 *l.* 15 *s.*

ANNO 1667. In this Year a remarkable Cafe of the aforefaid *Richard Banks* occurring, we have extracted the fame from a *Narrative* thereof written by himfelf, *viz.*

The fuffering
Cafe of R.
Banks.

" IN the Year 1667, *Lancelot Simpfon* having purchafed that Eftate which I
"   farmed of him who was then. my Landlord, in the firft Place excom-
" municated me, becaufe I would not conform to their Church, he being then,
" and now is, a Proctor, refolving to make me fubmit, or elfe deftroy me
" in the Outward, which he hath very much laboured and endeavoured ever
" fince : So pretending that all I had was too little to fatisfy the Law, he
" one Day, I being from Home, came, and one *Thomas Stamper* with him,
" and nailed up the Garner-door, and went and turned out all my Threfhers,
" and nailed up the Barn-door, and afterward came in the Night Seafon, when
" the Snow lay thick on the Earth, and. we being all in Bed, got into the
" Stable and Byer, and turned out all my Horfes, and Cows with their
" young Calves, by reafon whereof fome perifhed, and others hardly efcaped
" with Life : He alfo fet his Men to pull down the Hedge from about the
" Hayftacks, and to keep his own Beafts at them, and to put mine from
" them. Nay farther, I had at that Time nine Score Sheep or thereabouts.
" He would fuffer no Man to buy them, but himfelf pretending a Title, and
" hindering others, I was forced to take a third Penny after a long Con-
" teft, and the Death of a third Part of them ; by all which I deeply fuffered.
                                                                                Then

" Then I, feeing his Cruelty, was forced to feek another Farm, which I got
" about twenty Miles off.————In a fhort Time after, the faid *Lancelot*
" *Simpfon* arrefted me with an *Excommunication* Writ, and it being found to be
" out of Date, he was at that Time prevented of his Purpofe ; and ftill his
" Cruelty lives againft me and my Wife, becaufe he cannot make us bow, as
" is evident by his many Fines againft us, and now laft of all by his appre-
" hending both me and my Wife, and carrying us rigidly away from our
" Children and Servants, I having at that very Time ten Men at Work,
" thefe cruel Fellows would fcarce let us fpeak to them. So we being carried
" away Prifoners, and ftraitly lookt to, as Thieves and Felons, in our Way
" to the Prifon met with *Lancelot Simpfon*, and after fome Difcourfe before
" many Witneffes, I afked him, *If I owed him any thing ? If he would fay*
" *that I owed him* 2 d. I would pay him 4 d. But he could not demand a Far-
" thing. And one Capt. *Leverook* fitting by, afked him, *For what he had ar-*
" *refted us ? L. S.* faid, *For Contempts of the Law.* The faid Captain afked
" him, *Which Way we might be freed.* He faid, *No Way without conforming*
" *and paying the Contempts,* viz. *the Fines, Court Charges, and his Fees.* When
" I defired the Favour of him but two Days to fet my Houfe in order, and
" then we would go to Prifon, he faid, *he could not give us two Hours :* Yet
" the Lord delivered us in fuch a Way, as our Enemies cannot find out to
" this Day : Bleffed be his Name for ever. Through all which cruel Dealing
" we have very greatly fuffered.————Befide the Hazard and Danger we are
" in, through the diligent renewing of his Writs again, unlefs fome timely and
" diligent Care be taken for the fpeedy preventing thereof.

" *Richard Banks.*"

After this Manner, by repeated Profecutions in the Ecclefiaftical Court, were
honeft Men frequently molefted, and *Excommunicated,* in Confequence of which,
Writs *de Excommunicato capiendo* were iffued for imprifoning them : This
appears by the foregoing Narrative to have been *Richard Banks*'s Cafe, who
yet doth not appear to have been actually imprifoned, though fo violently pur-
fued by one of the Officers of that Court ; however fuch repeated Attacks
could not fail of putting the Profecuted to great Trouble and Expence.

Confequence of Ecclefiaftical Procefs.

ANNO 1670. In this Year, for Meetings held at *Brough* in this County,
Diftrefs of Goods was made on feveral Perfons, to the Amount of 90 *l.* 14 *s.* 6 *d.*
Among thefe was *Robert Huntington,* from whom four Cows, and twenty five
Sheep were taken, and fold : A Concurrence of Difafters, which foon after
happened to the Buyers of them was much obferved : One *Simfon* of *Sowerby,*
who bought two of thofe Cows, died in a little Time, leaving the Cows to his
Father, who alfo died foon after him. One *White* of *Coldbeck,* bought another
of them through the Perfuafion of his Wife, who faid, *they might as well have*
her as another : In a fhort Time after, fhe and her Child were found drowned
in a Pond, where the Water was fcarce deep enough to cover her as fhe lay.
We think it but juft to lay before our Readers the Fact of fuch remarkable
Incidents, and leave them to form fuch a Judgment thereof, as from the
Nature of the Cafe, when maturely confidered, fhall refult,

Diftreffes.

Obfervable Accidents.

Remarkable alfo in this Year was the Cafe of *Thomas Stordy,* againft whom
a Warrant was granted for diftraining his Goods and Chattels for 20 *l.* 10 *s.* for
a Meeting at *Moorhoufe,* though himfelf was then in Prifon, and had been fo
near eight Years under Sentence of *Premunire* for not Swearing, and all his
Eftate had been feized for the King. But it pleafed God to * releafe him from
fo long Captivity, by Means of *Charles Howard* Earl of *Chefter,* through whofe
Interceffion alfo the King granted his Eftate back again to his Children.

Cafe of T. Stordy.

In

* Note, *Thomas Stordy* and *Stephen Pearfon* were fet at Liberty after about ten Years Imprifonment by the King's Letters Patent in 1672.

CUMBER-
LAND.
1670.

*Diſtreſſes for
Meetings.*

In the ſame Year, for Meetings at *Settura*, Goods were taken by Diſtreſs, to the Amount of 2 *l*. 2 *s*. 8 *d*. And for Meetings at *Uldaile*, to the Value of 8 *l*. 7 *s*. including the wearing Apparel and Bedclothes which were taken from *John Gardhouſe*, a very poor labouring Man. About the ſame Time *John Gill* of *Gray-Southen*, being with others in the Burying-place at *Eaglesfield*, read a *Paper* of *Chriſtian Advice*, written by *William Dewſberry* : For this he was fined 20 *l*. and being unable to pay it, the ſame was partly levied on *Richard Fawcett* and *John Fearon*, ſom whom, and others, for Meetings at *Pardſay*, were taken, Corn, Cattle, and other Goods, to the Value of 35 *l*. 11 *s*.

ANNO 1673. Taken from ſeveral Perſons for a Meeting at *Tuthill* in the Pariſh of *Coldbeck*, Goods worth 43 *l*. 19 *s*. 2 *d*.

Thomas Bewley of *Haltcliff-Hall*, aged about ſeventy eight, was proſecuted by *Arthur Savage* Prieſt, for 3 *l*. Preſcription Money, and had taken from him his Feather Bed, Bedclothes, and a Cupboard, worth 5 *l*. The Hardſhip of the poor old Man's Caſe ſo affected the Neighbourhood with Compaſſion, that when the Bayliff expoſed thoſe Goods to Sale, no Body would buy them at any Rate : Whereupon the Prieſt ſued the Bayliff, and made him pay both his Demand and his Coſts.

*Imprisonment
of* T. Bewley,
aged 79.

ANNO 1674. On the 1ſt of *November* this Year, the ſame Prieſt again proſecuted the ſaid *Thomas Bewley* for Tithe of Wool, Lambs, *&c.* and notwithſtanding his very great Age, ſent him to Priſon.

In this and the next preceding Year, were taken in this County for Tithes, in Corn and other Things, to the Value of 270 *l*. 13 *s*. 5 *d*.

Diſtreſſes.

ANNO 1675. In this Year were taken from *John Howe* of *Newtown*, and others, for a Meeting at his Houſe, Goods worth 57 *l*. 16 *s*.

*Many Proſecu-
tions for
Tithes.*

ANNO 1676. On the 20th of the Month called *January* this Year, *Thomas Bewley*, Son of old *Thomas Bewley* aforeſaid, and * *Alice Nicholſon* of *Woodhouſe*, Widow, were committed to Priſon on an *Exchequer* Proceſs, at the Suit of *Arthur Savage*, Prieſt of *Coldbeck* ; at which Time alſo *George Bewley*, an elder Son of the ſame ancient Man, was detained in Priſon by the ſame Prieſt, where he had then lain about two Years. In the ſame Year *John Strickett* of *Branthwait*, *William Scott* of *Greenrigg*, and *Iſabel Peacock* of *Whalpey*, a Widow, who had ſix Fatherleſs Children, were alſo committed to Priſon at the ſame Prieſt's Suit : As was likewiſe *Grace Stalker* Widow, at the Suit of *John Monkhouſe* for Tithes.

In this Year alſo, for a Meeting held at *Pardſey-Cragg*, were taken from *John Steel* and others, Goods worth 25 *l*. 1 *s*.

*Imprisonments
on Writs* de
Excom. Cap.

ANNO 1677. On the 30th of *September*, *John Jackſon* of *Kirklinton*, was impriſoned on a Writ *de Excommunicato capiendo*, at the Suit of *Robert Prieſtman* for *Predial* Tithes.

16 Perſons
ſent to Priſon.

ANNO 1679. In this Year ſixteen Perſons were taken by a Seſſions Warrant, and committed to Priſon, for Abſence from the National Worſhip, *viz.* *John Jackſon*, *William Graham*, *Chriſtopher Taylor*, *Chriſtopher Jackſon*, *Humphry Tweedal*, *Fergus Watſon*, *Andrew Taylor*, *Francis Gilleſpy*, *Thomas Vowe*, *George Graham* of *Rigg*, *Andrew Hetherington*, *Simon Armſtrong*, *James Clark*, *Henry Graham*, *George Graham* of *Blackhouſe*, and *John Scott*. And in the ſame Year *William Langcake*, *T. Oſtell*, *William Saul*, and *John Waite*, were impriſoned for Tithes at the Suit of *William Dalſton*.

*Amount of
Diſtreſſes for
Tithes.
Fines for
Meetings in
their Houſes.*

ANNO 1680. The Amount of the Tithes, taken in kind from this People in this County, in this and the four Years next foregoing, is 777 *l*. 5 *s*. 3 *d*.

In this Year alſo, for Meetings at their reſpective Houſes, were taken from *Thomas Drewry* of *Newland*'s *Row*, Goods worth 11 *l*. from *Henry Scollick* of *Newbiggen*, Horſes and Cattle worth 26 *l*. and from *Edward Tyſon* of *Bickerthwaite*, Goods worth 19 *s*. 7 *d*.

In

---

* This *Alice Nicholſon* was a poor Widow, with ſix Fatherleſs Children, whoſe Husband had died in Priſon at the ſame Prieſt's Suit.

In the fame Year *John Saul, Thomas Splatt, John Oftell,* and *John Barne,* fuffered Diftrefs of Goods for refufing to Swear when fummoned to ferve on Juries at the Mannour Courts : Alfo *John Graham* and *John Bell* were fined for the fame Caufe. Several others, dwelling at *Scotby,* were returned into the *Exchequer* for refufing to Swear, upon Convictions for Recufancy, on Statutes made againft *Papifts,* and fuffered Diftrefs of Goods on that Account, *viz.*

	l.	*s.*	*d.*
Elizabeth Bond, to the Value of	5	19	7
Thomas Dobinfon, to the Value of	6	0	0
John Richardfon, to the Value of	3	17	8
	15	17	3

Exchequer Proceffes.

Some of thofe Goods were fold at low Rates in *Carlifle* Market, but when the People underftood that they were the Spoils of Confcience, they refufed to buy any more of them.

ANNO 1681. In this Year *John Aglionby,* a Juftice of the Peace, was perfuaded by *Jeremy Nelfon,* Prieft of *Stanwick,* to iffue Warrants of Diftrefs on feveral Perfons for abfenting themfelves from the National Worfhip, by which Warrants Goods were taken to the Value of 8 *l.* 9*s.* One of them was *George Gray,* a Man very poor, from whom the Spoilers took five Sheep-fkins, which he had bought to clothe his Children, of whom he had feveral : One of the *Officers,* who made the Seizure, reprefented to the Prieft the Hardfhip of the poor Man's Cafe, and his great Charge of Children, but the Prieft's Anfwer to him was, *Let the Country maintain them.*

Diftrefs for Abfence from the publick Worfhip. Hard Cafe of a poor Man.

Churlifh Anfwer of a Prieft.

ANNO 1682. On the 20th of the Month called *April* this Year, the following Perfons were continuing Prifoners for Tithe, at the Suit of *Arthur Savage,* Prieft of *Caldbeck, viz. Thomas Bewley* and *Alice Nicholfon,* who had then been Prifoners five Years and three Months, *William Scott* five Years and four Months, *George Stalker* four Years and four Months, and *Grace Stalker* five Years and ten Months. Alfo *John Sowerby,* who had been Prifoner three Years and feven Months at the Suit of *Allan Smallwood,* Prieft of *Grayftock,* and *John Todhunter,* who had been imprifoned three Years and two Months, at the Suit of the fame Prieft. Alfo *William Langcake, William Saul,* and *John Waite,* imprifoned three Years and three Weeks, at the Suit of *William Dalfton* Tithe-farmer. Likewife *William-Holme,* imprifoned above a Year on a Writ *de Excommunicato capiendo,* at the Suit of *William Stanley* of *Dalgarth,* Impropriator, died a Prifoner on the 2d of *September* this Year. *Hugh Tickell* and *Thomas Birkhead* were Prifoners by Attachments out of the *Exchequer,* at the Suit of *Richard Lowry,* Prieft of *Croffthwaite.* In this Year were difcharged out of Prifon *Randolph Bulman,* committed on a Writ *de Excommunicato capiendo,* at the Suit of *Thomas Blemer,* Farmer of the Bifhop's Tithe : Alfo *John Slee,* who had been committed at the Suit of *Allan Smallwood* ; and *George Bewley,* who had lain in Prifon more than five Years, at the Suit of *Arthur Savage,* Prieft of *Caldbeck.*

Long Imprifonments for Tithes.

W. Holme died Prifoner.

Some releafed.

In *November* this Year, *John Holme* was committed to Prifon at the Suit of *Lancelot Simpfon* Impropriator : Alfo *Thomas Robinfon, Matthew Stordy,* and *Thomas Bone,* were imprifoned after Excommunication, at the Suit of *Jeremy Nelfon* Prieft : *Arthur Cordell* was alfo imprifoned fix Weeks, at the Suit of *Rowland Nichols* a Prieft.

Imprifonments.

ANNO 1683. On the 13th of the Month called *February* this Year, feveral Informers came to a Meeting at *Pardfey Cragg,* and found *Peter Fearon* preaching : They applied to Juftice *Fletcher,* who fined him 20*l.* and ordered the fame to be levied on himfelf and feveral others prefent, although the faid *Peter* defired him to charge the Whole on himfelf, he being of fufficient Ability, but the Juftice would not. In a fhort Time after were taken by Diftrefs for the faid Fine,

Fines for
Meeting at
Pardsey-
Cragg,

From		*l.*	*s.*	*d.*
	Peter Fearon, Goods worth	5	5	0
	Allan Peele, an Horse worth	3	0	0
	John Banks, Goods worth	7	4	0
	John Tiffin, two Cows worth	5	10	0
	John Fallowfield, Goods worth	7	0	0
		27	19	0

When thefe Goods were expofed to Sale, and Buyers of them could not be found, the Juftice ordered his own Servants to purchafe fome of them, which they did at a very low Price, and the Officers, to fupply the Defect, made another Seizure on fome of the Perfons concerned.

and at Crofs-field.
For a Meeting at *Crofsfield* in the Parifh of *Cleater,* were taken from *John Nicholfon* two Oxen worth 8*l,* and from *Thomas Sharp* of St. *Bee*'s Parifh, two Oxen worth 6*l.* 6*s.*

Chriftopeer Story of *Righead,* for permitting a Meeting at his Houfe, had taken from him by a Warrant granted by Juftice *Aglionby,* two Horfes worth 5*l.* 10*s.*

Prifoners for Tithes.
ANNO 1684. In the Month called *May* this Year, *Thomas Stordy, William Johnfon, John Robinfon, Japhet Allafon, Jofeph Steel, John Banks,* and *John Bewley* of *Gatefkail,* were Prifoners in *Carlifle* Goal: And in the fame Year *Richard Ribton, Jonathan Bewman,* and *Thomas Hall,* all of *Broughton,* were imprifoned for refufing to pay fmall Tithes, at the Suit of *Richard Tickel,* Prieft of *Bridekirk.* Alfo in the Month called *January* this Year, *Chriftopher Fearon, Richard Head, John Robinfon, Thomas Robinfon,* and *Anne Steel* Widow, all of *Meffer,* and *Luke Steel* of *Merfgill,* were committed to *Carlifle* Goal by an *Exchequer* Writ for Tithes, at the Suit of *George Fletcher* of *Hutton.* About

Death of T. Stordy.
the latter End of the Month of *December, Thomas Stordy* died a Prifoner, having continued ftedfaft through manifold Sufferings to the End of his Pilgrimage.

Taken this Year for Fines on the Conventicle Act,

Fines for Meeting.

From		*l.*	*s.*	*d.*
	William Graham of *Riggfoot,* Corn worth	0	5	6
	Chriftopher Taylor of *Hetherfide,* Rye worth	0	15	0
	Chriftopher Story of *Righead,* Sheep worth	1	8	0
	Henry Graham, Oats worth	0	15	0
		3	3	6

A Womens Meeting.
On the 17th of the Month called *February* this Year, was a Meeting of Women at *Pardfey-Cragg,* to which three Juftices came, and demanded of them *What they met there for?* One of the Women anfwered, *To take Care of the Poor:* Which was indeed the Occafion of their Meeting. One of the Juftices afked, *Whether there were no Beggars among them?* To which they anfwered *No.* He replied, *That is well.* Neverthelefs the Juftices turned them out of the Houfe, and fined fome of them as being at an unlawful Affembly: For which Fines, *Elizabeth Tolfon* and *Mary Wilfon* fuffered Diftrefs of Goods to the Value of 12*s.*

Diftreffes for not Swearing.
Thomas Scott of *Oufebridge-End,* for refufing to take an Oath at the Mannour Court, fuffered Diftrefs of Brafs and Pewter to the Value of 4*l.* 8*s.* and *John Roger* of *Water-End,* had for the fame Caufe his Pewter taken away, to the Value of 8*s.* Alfo *John Caipe* of *Uldall,* for not procuring a Perfon to fwear that his Wife was buried in Woolen, though divers were ready to atteft it, had his Goods taken by Diftrefs to the Value of 2*l.* 10*s.*

W. Adcock fined.
ANNO 1685. *William Adcock* of *Sunderland,* was fined at a Mannour Court for refufing to Swear, and had taken from him Goods worth 15*s.*

Chriftopher

Chriſtopher Taylor, Andrew Taylor, William Graham, Henry Graham, George Blair, Andrew Graham, Philip Haſſard, Richard Latimer, Andrew Hetheringtor, Simon Armſtrong and *Chriſtopher Story,* for being at a Meeting, were indicted at the Aſſizes as Rioters, and for not traverſing that Indictment, ſent to Priſon.

ANNO 1687. On the 8th of the Month called *March* this Year, *Elizabeth Watſon* of *Highmore,* Widow, died a Priſoner for Tithes, at the Suit of *George Fletcher* Impropriator.

ANNO 1688. In this Year were remaining Priſoners in *Carliſle* Goal, at the Suit of *George Fletcher* Impropriator, *Japhet Allaſon, Luke Steel, John Seenhouſe* ſen. *John Seenhouſe* jun. *Joſeph Steel, Chriſtopher Fearon, Anne Steel, John Banks,* and *William Wright* ; and at the Suit of *John Lowther* of *Lowther* Impropriator, *Thomas Oſtel, Mary Saul* Widow, *William Glaiſter, Thomas Drapp, Anthony Skelton, William Bouch, Arthur Skelton, John Biglands,* and *Thomas Wilkinſon.*

ANNO 1689. The Generality of the People called *Quakers,* impriſoned in this County, were ſet at Liberty by Means of an Act of Grace granted by King *William* and Queen *Mary* after their Acceſſion to the Crown.

ANNO 1690. By the Accounts of Tithes taken from the ſaid People in this County, from 1681 to 1690, it appears, that the Value of Corn and other Things taken in Kind, amounted within thoſe ten Years, to the Sum of 2215 *l.* 15 *s.* 9 *d.* And that in three of thoſe Years the Sums taken from them for Steeple-houſe Rates and Clerks Wages, amounted to 3 *l.* 13 *s.* 6 *d.*

CUMBER-
LAND.
1685.

12 *Indicted as Rioters.*
Death of E. Watſon.

Account of Priſoners.

Releaſe of Priſoners.

Summary of Tithes taken in kind.

Court Scene.
Drawing by Geoffrey Makins, courtesy of Margaret Fell: Mother of Quakerism.

Quaker women and men being marched to prison by an armed guard.
Drawing by Robert Spence, courtesy of Friends House Library, London.

C H A P. XIII.

D U R H A M *and* N O R T H U M B E R L A N D.

A N N O 1658.

JOHN RICHMOND fuffered Diftrefs of his Cattle to the Value of 40 *l.* for 8 *l.* demanded for Tithes. Alfo *William Richmond* and *Thomas Richmond* had their Cattle diftrained for Tithes to a great Value. About this Time *Margaret Ramfey,* for giving a Godly Exhortation to the People, after the Prieft had ended his Sermon, was imprifoned at *Durham*; as was *George Humble,* an aged Man, who, feeing fome of his Friends put in the Stocks, reproved the Juftice who had commanded it: The Juftice, offended at the Reproof he deferved, fent the honeft old Man to Goal for giving it, where, after about ten Months Confinement, he died.

Diftrefs of Goods.

G. Humble died in Prifon.

ANNO 1660. On the 11th of *November,* a Party of Soldiers, commanded by Captain *Bellafife,* came to a Meeting at *Simon Townfend*'s Houfe in *Norton,* and took thence * *Stephen Crifp* of *Colchefter* in *Effex, Humphry Norton* of *Newtown, William Fofter* of *Carleton, George Brough* of *Norton, Thomas Jackfon* of *Arfham-Grange* in *Yorkfhire,* and *Francis Roundtree* of *Stockley* in the fame County: A Juftice of the Peace ordered them to appear at the next Quarter Seffions, which they did, and, for refufing to take the Oaths of Allegiance and Supremacy, were fent to Prifon; as were alfo at the fame Time for the fame Caufe, *William Maddifon* of *Billingham, Marmaduke Storr* of *Yorkfhire,* and *John Richmond* of *Heighington,* who had been forcibly taken out of their Inn at *Durham*; and three Days after *John Richardfon, George Thompfon,* and *Chriftopher Hodgfon,* taken out of a Friend's Houfe; and on the 24th *George Richardfon, Philip Richardfon, Thomas Redhead,* and *Ralph Loftis,* all of *Shotten,* Hufbandmen, *Robert Leighton* and *Thomas Paxton,* of *Effington,* Hufbandmen, who were taken from their Work by an Order of the Juftices, were fent to Prifon; as were in the next Month *Chriftopher Crofby, William Jekyl,* and *John Ufham,* all of *Stockton.*

S. Crifp and others imprifoned.

About the fame Time alfo were fent to Prifon for refufing the Oaths, *John Heighington, Robert Fifher,* and *William Wilfon,* all of *Durham*; *John Langftaff* of *Bifhops-Aukland,* and *Emanuel Grice* of the fame.

In the Month called *January, William Hodgfon* and *Francis Hodgfon,* both of *Cockerton, John Robinfon* Weaver, *Thomas Nefhome* of *Pyborne,* and *John Robinfon* of *Ulnaby,* Farmer, were taken by Soldiers from a Meeting at the Houfe of *John Richmond* in *Heighington,* and by fome Juftices of the Peace committed to Prifon.

In the next Month, *Thomas Spark, Thomas Williamfon, Hugh Hutchinfon, Thomas Shield* of *Wooley, Francis Shield* fen. *Francis Shield* jun. *Hugh Shield, John Brown, Richard Shield, Thomas Rowell, Hugh Rowell, Hugh Rodam, Anthony Watfon, Robert Watfon, Samuel Farlam, Cuthbert Rodam, Thomas Whitfield, Thomas Williamfon, Thomas Henlyfide, Hugh White, Cuthbert Fetherftone, John Shield* jun.

Profecutions a the Promotion of Papifts.

* *Stephen* C*rifp,* and *Thomas Turner* fent to Prifon about the fame Time, were confined in a feparate Place from the other Prifoners, who in the next Month were above an Hundred.

DURHAM,
&c.
1660.

William Lea Yeoman, and *John Shield* Fuller, all of *Allendale*, were taken by *William Errington* and others, known *Papifts*, and carried to *Hexome*, where they were kept feveral Days, fome of them feveral Weeks, in a nafty ftinking Dungeon, and afterward fent to *Morpeth* Goal. About the fame Time the faid *Errington* and other *Papifts* took out of a Meeting at *Holeraw*, and fent to *Hexome* and *Morpeth* Goals the following Perfons, viz. *John Hunter* of *Benfield-fide*, *Cuthbert Hopper* of *Dikenook*, *William Hopper* of *Iviftone*, *Ralph Hopper* of the fame, *William Burrell*, *Andrew Raw*, *Anthony Richardfon*, *Chriftopher Vickers*, *John Brown*, *John Ellifon*, *George Ellifon*, and *Richard Snawball*, all of *Derwent*, Hufbandmen, *Robert Dickenfon* of *Iviftone* Labourer, *Thomas Layburne* of *Derwent-Coat*, Wright, *Thomas Baker* and *Henry Baker* of *Knitchley*, Hufbandmen : All thefe were continued Prifoners near five Months. Soon after *George Hornfby* and *Thomas Hornfby* Yeomen, and *Nicholas Pickering* Wright, of *Lenchefter*, *Michael Ornefby*, *Gilbert Taylor* and *Thomas Jackfon* of *Wilton*, *John Woodnas*, *Thomas Johnfon* and *Chriftopher Johnfon* of *Walnuke*, were taken from a Meeting and fent to the Common Goal at *Durham*, where they continued fix Months.

The Ufage of fuch of the aforefaid Prifoners, as were in *Durham* Goal, is reprefented in a Letter from one of them to his Friends in *London*, dated the 19th of the Twelfth Month 1660, out of which the following Extract is taken *verbatim*, viz.

Extract of a Letter relating the Ufage of the Prifoners.

" *Beloved Friends,*

" **Y**OUR refrefhing Lines came to my Hand, which I communicated
" unto my Fellow-prifoners, whereby the Life of the Righteous was
" much cherifhed, and the living tender Plant of God's Renown watered as
" with the refrefhing Springs of the former and latter Rain. O, *Dear Friends*,
" our Hearts are fealed in fweet Fellowfhip with you, in the ever-blefled Cove-
" nant of Peace, Truth, and Righteoufnefs, where the earning Bowels of our
" Love and Unity breath toward you in the hidden Life of the Lord *Jefus*,
" (who is our Head, Judge, and only Law-giver) which cannot be feparated
" by the Toffings of the Floods, nor fwelling Noife of the raging Tempeft,
" having our Souls anchored upon the unmoveable Rock of Ages and Gene-
" rations, where we find the ftill and fecret Movings of his ever-blefled Spirit,
" lifting up a Standard againft *Amalek* and all his Accomplices.

" *Dear Friends*, as touching the manner of our Sufferings here at this Place ;
" here are ninety and odd in Prifon, very near an Hundred, moft committed
" for refufing to take the Oath of Allegiance, fome being taken out of their
" Meetings, and fome out of their Houfes and from their Employments, and
" for refufing to Swear committed to Prifon. We met with a very avaricious
" inhuman Goaler, who, becaufe we could not agree to his unreafonable De-
" mand in paying 2 s. 6 d. per Week every Man for our Beds, threw twenty
" of us into a ftinking Dungeon, where we could not all lie down at once ;
" and put thirteen of us into another, where we remained five Days ; but
" the High Sheriff underftanding it, manifefted a large meafure of Chriftian
" Compaffion towards us, and caufed us to be removed to the Houfe of
" Correction, where we have had moderate Ufage, and the reft were all
" removed into a cold Room, where the Grand Jury wonted to fit, where
" the Goaler ftill continued much Harfhnefs, in refpect they would not be-
" come a Prey to his Covetoufnefs, very hardly fuffering any to come in to
" them, faving twice a Day that his Man unlocked the Doors, and of late
" would not fuffer them to exonerate Nature."

Diftreffes.

For Abfence from the National Worfhip, *John Moore*, *Hugh Teafdale*, *William Vayfey* of *Alftone*, and *Francis Shield* of *Burnfoot*, had their Goods taken away by Diftrefs to the Value of 3 *l.* 2 *s.*

Imprifonments in Tinmouth Caftle.

ANNO 1661. On the 10th of the Month called *Auguft*, *John Blakeling* of *Drawell* near *Sedberg* in *Yorkfhire*, Yeoman ; *Thomas Jackfon*, *Robert Fowler* of *Burlington*, *Samuel Nelheft* of *Whitby* in *Yorkfhire*, Mariners ; *John Stockley*, *Thomas*

Thomas Allinson, *William Hart*, *John Dove*, and *William Dove* of *Whitby*, Yeomen ; *Mary Dove* jun. of the fame, Spinfter ; *William Truthwaite* of *Bowden* ; *Robert Linton*, *Thomas Chandler*, *Thomas Merriman*, *Lancelot Wardell* Merchant, *Thomas Smith* Labourer, *Richard Wilson* and *Margaret* his Wife, *George Carr* Salt-Merchant, *Sarah Knowles*, *Dorothy Dawson*, *Joane Sanderson*, Spinfters, *William Maud* Merchant, *George Linton*, *John Harrison*, all of *Sunderland* or *Shields*, *Susanna Truthwaite* Spinfter, and *Laurence Heslam* of *Whitby* in *Yorkshire*, Mariner, were taken at a Meeting at *Robert Linton*'s in *South-Shields* by Major *Graham*, then Deputy-Governour of *Tinmouth* Caftle, and caft into nafty Holes there, where they lay a full Month, and then he turned them out, having, fo far as appeared to them, neither Order, Authority, nor Warrant for any Part of his Proceding.

In this Year alfo *Thomas Williamson*, cited to a Court, and appearing with his Hat on, was fined 5*l.* and for Non-payment fent to *Morpeth* Goal, where he lay three Months.

ANNO 1662. In the Month called *June* this Year, *William Fofter* of *Carleton*, was fent to Prifon by Order of Seffions, for fuffering Meetings at his Houfe. On the 3d of the Month called *Auguft*, *Henry Grainger*, *Chriftopher Pickering*, *Francis Temple*, and *George Dickson*, all of *Raby*, Yeomen ; *George Gundry* Milliner, *John Atkinson* Mafon, of *Stanethrop*, and *James White* of *Hope-well* near *Pierce-Bridge*, were taken by Soldiers from a Meeting at *Henry Draper*'s Houfe in *Headlam*, and committed by a Juftice to *Durham* Goal for nine Weeks. At next Seffions they were indicted, and *James White*, *Henry Grainger*, and *Chriftopher Pickering*, were fined 10*l.* each, for which Diftreffes were made on their Goods to the Value of 37*l.* 3*s.* 4*d.* *John Greenwell*, for Meeting, was fined by the Bifhop of *Durham* 40*s.* and for the fecond Offence 10*l.* for which Fines four Kine were taken from him worth 16*l.* Alfo *Richard Hopper*, for 10*l.* Fine, had Goods feized to the Value of 13*l.* In the fame Year *John Moore* of *Wellgill*, for 12*s.* demanded for Tithe, fuffered Diftrefs of Goods to the Amount of 3*l.* 10*s.* In this Year alfo *William Mare*, *Nicholas Pickering*, and *Thomas Toole*, were imprifoned for Tithes ; the two former remained Prifoners about eight Years.

Fines for Meeting.

Long Imprifon-ments.

ANNO 1663. In this Year *Hugh Hutchinson*, *Cuthbert Fetherftone*, *Thomas Williamson*, and *John Moore* of *Hazlewell* in *Allendale*, were committed to *Morpeth* Goal on Writs *de Excommunicato capiendo*, for not paying Tithes : The *firft* of them was continued Prifoner ten Years and four Months ; the *next two* above ten Years ; and *John Moore* upwards of fix Years, who, during his Imprifonment, had his Goods taken by Diftrefs to the Value of 9*s.* for being abfent from the publick Worfhip. About the fame Time *William Hodgson* of *Cockerton* was fent to Prifon by an *Exchequer* Writ for Tithes, and continued there eight Months. In the fame Year *Thomas Toole*, then in Prifon, had 40*l.* worth of Goods taken from him for a Claim of 7*l.* for Tithes, befides Corn worth 4*l.* 10*s.* His Profecutor alfo ftopt in a Neighbour's Hand a Debt of 10*l.* due to the faid *Thomas Toole*. In *October* this Year, *Chriftopher Crofby* was fent to Prifon by an Order of Seffions, on the third Conviction upon the firft Statute for Tranfportation ; and *Richard Errington*, taken from a Meeting at the Houfe of *Simon Townfend* in *Norton*, was committed to Prifon during the King's Pleafure.

Imprifonments on Writs de Excom. Cap.

ANNO 1664. *William Truthwaite* of *Weft-Bowden*, for a Demand of 3*l.* 6*s.* 8*d.* for Tithes, had Goods taken away worth 7*l.*

Diftreffes.

On the 26th of the Month called *April*, *Ralph Pattifon*, *Roger Hudson*, *John Blakeftone*, *Thomas Chipchafe*, and *Simon Townfend*, all of *Norton*, Yeomen ; *George Brough* of the fame, Farmer ; *Robert Walker* and *Thomas Toole* of *Coopan*, Farmers ; *Richard Errington* of *Gretham*, *John Ufhaw*, *William Jekyll*, and *Mark Waps*, of *Stockton*, and *Margaret Adamthwait* of *Rofendale* in *Weftmorland*, Spinfter, were taken at a Meeting in *Norton*, and ordered to appear at Seffions, whence they were all fent to Prifon for refufing to take the Oaths.

Imprifonments for refufing to Swear.

In

In the Month called *August* this Year, *Peter Mason*, *Robert Taylor*, *Henry Emerson*, *Ralph Hodgson*, *Thomas Johnson*, and *Henry Mason*, were committed to the House of Correction for six Months, on the Act for Banishment ; as were *John Mason* and *Anne Taylor* for three Months. On the same Act were committed in *September*, *Richard Errington* and *John Rawlin* ; in *October*, *John Blakestone* and *Christopher Crosby* ; in *November*, *William Hutton* jun. *Richard Thompson*, *Ambrose Thompson*, and *Thomas Skafe* an Apprentice.

ANNO 1665. Many were committed to Prison on the Act for Banishment, *viz.* In the Month called *May*, *Thomas Shield* ; in the Month called *August*, *Roger Hudson*, *Thomas Chipchase*, *Ralph Pattison*, *Thomas Yoole*, *Robert Walker*, *Mark Waps*, *George Brough*, *Patrick Wallis*, and *Rowland Wheldon* ; in *September*, *Sarah Brough*, *Elizabeth Middleton*, *Thomas Yoole*, and *John Ushaw*.

At the Quarter Sessions in *October*, *Richard Errington* and *John Ushaw* received Sentence of Banishment to *Barbadoes*, and to continue in the House of Correction till an Opportunity of shipping them. During their close Confinement *Richard Errington* was taken sick, and his Friends were denied the Favour of removing him, so that the poor Man, after about two and twenty Months close Restraint, died a Prisoner for worshipping God according to his Conscience. *John Ushaw* was detained in Prison about three Years, probably till the Expiration of that Act. In this Year also were committed to *Durham* Goal on the same Act, *Richard Whitehead*, *George Jackson*, and *Henry Bowran*, for twenty one Days, and *John Bowran* for twenty Weeks : *Nicholas Pickering*, *George Ornesby*, *Thomas Ornesby*, *Ralph Hopper*, *William Hopper*, *Cuthbert Leighton*, *Andrew Raw*, *Anthony Richardson*, *John Brown*, and *William Green*, for six Weeks. In the same Year *Anthony Wilkinson*, *John Ellison*, and *Richard Snawball*, were committed to *Morpeth* Goal, where they continued seven Years. *Thomas Rowell* of *Woodhead*, for suffering a Meeting at his House, had three Cows taken from him worth 6*l*.

In this Year also, *Thomas Spark* and *Elizabeth Shield* were committed to *Morpeth* Goal, and kept there three Years : During their Imprisonment their Prosecutor took from him Corn worth 13 *l*. and from her to the Value of 9 *l*. *Ralph Fetherstone* and *John Brown* were also imprisoned for not paying Tithes.

ANNO 1666. At a Sessions held on the 20th of the Month called *April*, *Sarah Brough* received Sentence of Banishment to *Jamaica :* And at the same Sessions *Patrick Williamson* was committed to Prison for ten days. At *Durham* Assizes in the Month called *August*, *Thomas Yoole* and *Roger Hudson* were sentenced to be transported to *Barbadoes*. In the same Month, *James White*, *John Robinson*, *John Trotter*, *John Wilkinson*, *Thomas Robinson*, and *William Robinson*, taken from a Meeting at the said *John Robinson*'s House in *Alnaby* ; and *Peter Mason*, *Constance Baker*, and *Thomas Johnson*, taken at a Meeting in the said *Peter Mason*'s House at *Branspeth*, were, by Warrant from the Bishop of *Durham* and other Justices, sent to Prison for two Months ; the said *Constance Baker* having with her a Sucking-child. At the Sessions in *October*, *Edward Lampson* of *Bishops-Aukland*, *William Heavyside*, *Anthony Hodgson*, and *Emanuel Grice*, were sentenced for Transportation to *Barbadoes*. About this Time also *William Hutton*, *William Peacock*, *Edward Alwaine*, *John Graystone*, *John Robinson*, *Thomas Lawson*, *John Richmond*, *Henry Lox*, *James Hall*, *John Crawford*, *Christopher Richmond* and *William Trotter*, were taken from their Houses by some of the Trained Bands, and by Order of the Bishop, and Justice *Tempest*, committed, some of them to the Marshal's Custody, and others to the County Goal ; whither also soon after *George Bilson* was sent from a Meeting at *Thomas Wrightson*'s at *Norgill* : At which Meeting were likewise taken, *George Jackson*, *Henry Smith*, *George Appleby*, *John Bolran*, *Andrew Appleby*, *Thomas Wrightson*, *Francis Wrightson*, *Christopher Goodson*, *George Raine*, *Thomas Milbourn*, *Thomas Myers*, *William Hutton* jun. *Richard Thompson*, *James Raine*, *Dorothy Kestlop*, *Jane Wilson*, and *George Kipling*, who were committed by Justice *Robinson* of *Barnard*'s *Castle*, to the House of Correction at *Richmond*.

ANNO

ANNO 1668. *Simon Townsend* was Prisoner for Tithes in *October* this Year, having then been confined seven Years at the Suit of *Thomas Davison* Vicar of *Norton.*

ANNO 1670. *Mark Stones* of *Stockton,* for a Demand of 5s. for Tithes, had Goods taken from him worth 15s. In this Year also, *William Hodgson* was close Prisoner for Tithes, at the Suit of *William Ward* of *Newcastle,* Impropriator. *George Wilson* was also a Prisoner for Tithes four Years and eight Months.

After the Passing of the Conventicle Act this Year, many suffered Distress of Goods for themselves and others being at Meetings, *viz.*

	l.	*s.*	*d.*	
John Crawford of *Blackwell,* Yeoman	40	0	0	*Many Distresses.*
James Wastel of *Haughton,* Currier	30	5	0	
Thomas Pyborne and *Anthony Claxton*	6	6	0	

Pyborne's Case was somewhat singular, for when *Miles Gerry,* Constable of *Nesham,* had the Warrant sent him, he refused to execute it, and for that Refusal his own Goods were taken away to the Value of *Pyborne's* Fine, which was 6l. *Pyborne,* unwilling that his Neighbour should lose so much by favouring him, paid the Money and released the Constable's Goods.

At STOCKTON were taken from

	l.	*s.*	*d.*
Christopher Crosby, four Cows worth	18	0	0
Richard Watson, Richard Tindal, William Gores, Mark Waps, Robert Corney, and *Thomas Rawlins*	20	17	0
Robert Boulton	20	0	0
George Williamson, Roger Trotter, John Robinson, George Gundry, and *John Langstaff*	11	4	6
At NORTON, from			
Thomas Chipchase, Simon Townsend, and *John Blakestone*	3	19	5
At WOLVERSTONE, from			
Robert Young, for himself and Wife	0	14	0
At CARLETON, from			
William Foster, Yeoman	4	0	0
At COWPAN, from			
Thomas Yoole and *Robert Walker*	5	13	4
At DARLINGTON, from			
Laurence Appleby, Edward Fisher and *Cuthbert Thompson*	20	0	6
At HOPEWELL, from			
James White	1	15	0
	182	14	9

It was observable, that one *Thomas Dawson,* Overseer of *Norton,* having kept some Brass Utensils, Part of these Distresses, in his House above a Year, being visited with Sickness, was the Night before he died under so much Trouble of Mind, that he could not be satisfied till the said Brass was removed out of his House. It was also remarkable, that when a Warrant for levying 7l. on *John Langstaff's* Goods was brought to *John Brown,* Constable of *Condon,* he refused to serve the same, rather suffering a Distress on his own Goods to the Value of 3l.

ANNO 1671. In this Year were taken from *William Hodgson* and *John Robinson* of *Cockerton,* for Tithes, Goods worth 3l. 10s. The said *William Hodgson* being then in Prison.

ANNO 1672. By the King's Letters Patent were released out of *Durham* Goal, *John Langstaffe, Humphry Norton, Joseph Heling, Francis Temple, John Hunter,*

DURHAM,   *Hunter, Thomas Yoole, John Ushaw, Roger Hudson, Edward Lampson, Anthony*
&c.   *Hodgson, Thomas Gower,* and *Emanuel Grice.*
1673.   ANNO 1673.   Taken for Tithes this Year,

Tithes, &c.

		l.	s.	d.
From	*John Robinson* of *Cockerton,* and *Laurence Appleby,* Corn worth	6	5	0
	James Wastel, to the Value of	30	0	0
	John Langstaffe of *Whitley,* Corn worth	36	0	0
	Elizabeth Hopper, for 5 s. demanded, a Mare worth	4	0	0
		76	5	0

Thomas Wood of *Cleadon,* was imprisoned nine Months for 4 s. 5 d. for repairing the Steeple-house there.   And *Margaret Haddock* suffered Distress of Goods for Wages of the Parish-Clerk at *Sunderland.*

Imprisonments.   ANNO 1674.   *Anthony Richardson* of *Holcrom,* was committed to *Morpeth* Goal, at the Suit of *Isaac Bassier,* for Tithes.   Also *George Kipling* of *Balderfdale* was imprisoned in the Common Goal at *York,* on a Process in the *Exchequer* for Tithes, at the Suit of *Peter Ingram* Priest at *Rombald-Kirk.*

On the 14th of the Month called *February,* Complaint being made to *Henry Coverly,* a Justice of the Peace, of a Meeting at *Croft-bridge-end* in *Harworth* Parish, he granted a Warrant, by which Distresses were made on the Goods

Distresses for Meeting.

		l.	s.	d.
Of	*John Bolron, Robert Wilson, Robert Trueman,* and *Cuthbert Thompson,* to the Value of	21	3	0
	Laurence Appleby, Edward Fisher, Richard Trotter, and *John Robinson*	12	11	5
	Thomas Pyborne and *Christopher Appleby*	27	0	0
	John Robinson and *Matthew Dent*	3	11	0
		64	5	5

ANNO 1675.   For a Meeting at *Margaret Crawford's,* in *Darlington,* on the 4th of the Month called *May,* were taken

Distresses for Meeting.

		l.	s.	d.
From	*Margaret Crawford* and *Laurence Appleby,* four Cows worth	22	0	0
	John Robinson of *Ulnaby,* twenty two Sheep worth	14	0	0
	Cuthbert Thompson, William Dobson, and *Christopher Hodgson*	2	4	0
	Edward Fisher, Laurence Appleby, Robert Wilson, and *Robert Trueman*	4	19	0
		43	3	0

For Meetings, held this Year at *Norton,* by Warrants granted by *George Morland* Justice, Distresses were made on the Goods

Distress for Meetings.

		l.	s.	d.
Of	*John Blakestone, Ambrose Wright, Robert Chipchase, Richard Watson,* —— *Young,* and *William Foster,* to the Value of	30	8	0
	Thomas Yoole, William Geers, John Ushaw, John Richmond, William Harrison, and *Patrick Wallis*	12	12	0
	Thomas Chipchase, Simon Townsend, John Chipchase, and *Robert Walker*	9	1	0
	William Maddison, William Jekyll, Mark Waps, and *Christopher Crosby*	14	2	8
		66	3	8

ANNO

ANNO 1676. For Meetings at the fame Place, were taken

		l.	*s.*	*d.*
From *Thomas Chipchafe, Mark Waps, John Blakeftone, John Forfter, Robert Heron,* and *George Swainton,* Goods worth		23	13	10
Chriftopher Crofby, Mark Staines, William Fofter, Robert Hartburn, and *Richard Wheldon*		22	6	0
		45	19	10

Diftreffes for Meeting.

Richard Watfon, for Preaching in a Meeting at *Darlington,* had fix Cows taken from him, worth 30*l.*

ANNO 1678. Fines were this Year impofed on many Perfons for Meetings at *Stockton* and *Norton,* and for *Richard Watfon's* Preaching there, which when he underftood, he went to *George Morland* the Juftice, defiring him to recall thofe Warrants, and grant one againft himfelf only, who had fufficient Effects to anfwer the fame; but the Juftice refufed: And on the 9th of *November* Diftreffes were made

	l.	*s.*	*d.*
On *Simon Townfend, John Blakeftone, Chriftopher Crofby, William Harrifon, William Fofter, Robert Pattifon, Thomas Chipchafe, James Peacock,* and *Cuthbert Hunter,* to the Value of	69	10	0
Edward Fleatham of *Yarme* in the County of *York* Merchant, *Benjamin Lindley,* and *John Langftaff*	31	10	0
	101	0	0

Diftreffes on others for R. Watfon's Preaching

The faid *Edward Fleatham* was convicted in his Abfence, without any Summons, by a Certificate from Juftice *Morland* to *James Pennyman,* a Juftice in *Yorkfhire,* as Owner of one of the Meeting-houfes; he appealed to the Quarter Seffions, but obtained no Redrefs. In like manner Diftreffes were made

Conviction of an abfent Perfon.

	l.	*s.*	*d.*
On *James Peacock, William Smith, Robert Heron, Zachary Heron, Giles Calvert,* and *Eleanor Wheldon,* to the Value of	28	12	0
Daniel Toes, William Jekyll, Cuthbert Hunter, William Harrifon, Richard Watfon, and *Thomas Chipchafe*	35	2	8
William Smith, William Laurence, Robert Hartburne, John Ufhaw, James Peacock, and *Robert Corney.*	12	10	0
	76	4	8

Other Diftreffes.

Thefe laft named eighteeen were convicted in their Abfence, without any Summons to anfwer their Accufers, on whofe Information, whether true or falfe, they were convicted unheard, and generally ignorant of the Sums charged, the Officers refufing to fhew their Warrants; which being complained of to one of the Juftices, he confeffed, that he had commanded them not to fhew their Warrants. Thus the arbitrary Proceedings of *inferior Officers* were encouraged by thofe who fhould have checked them.

Arbitrary Proceeding.

About the fame Time *Thomas Gathorne, Robert Fowel, William Wake,* and *Richard Halliman,* Informers, or fome of them, acquainted Juftice *Morland* of a Meeting at *Darlington,* who iffued his Warrant, by which were taken

	l.	*s.*	*d.*
From *Edward Fifher, Margaret Crawford, Robert Trueman, John Trueman,* and *Robert Appleby,* Goods worth	21	15	9
Carried over	21	15	9

Diftreffes for Meeting.

DURAAM,
&c.
1678.

	l.	*s*	*d.*
Brought over	21	15	9
Joshua Middleton, Michael Collins, Cuthbert Thompson, *John Shaw, Thomas Nickson, William Dobson,* and *Frances Comfit,* to the Value of	5	5	6
	27	1	3

Hard Cafe of a poor Widow.   This *Frances Comfit,* a poor Widow, near eighty Years of Age, was cruelly ufed by the diftraining Officers : They turned her out of her Houfe after eight at Night, and kept her out of her Bed in extream frofty Weather. At another Time *Fofter,* the Conftable of *Darlington,* with a Watchman, came to her Houfe about Midnight, called to her to let them in to look for *Jefuits,* which fhe, fearing that they were drunk and would abufe her, refufed : Upon which they got Stones, and after about an Hour's Difturbance, broke the Lock, and burft the Door open, to the grievous Terror of the poor ancient Woman.

We are next to relate the grievous Cafe of *Roger Hudfon,* who was committed to Prifon by the following *Mittimus,* viz.

" *Dunelm* ſs.

Commitment of R. Hudfon.   " WHEREAS the right Worfhipful *Richard Lloyd,* Knight and Dr. of " Laws, Vicar general and Official of the right Reverend Father in " God, *Nathaniel,* by Divine Providence Lord Bifhop of *Durham,* lawfully " conftituted, by a Certificate under the Seal of his Office aforefaid, hath in- " formed us his Majefty's Juftices of the Peace, and *Quorum* hereunder named, " that *Roger Hudfon,* in the County and Diocefe of *Durham,* Yeoman, was " duly cited to appear before him, to anfwer *Thomas Davifon* Clerk, Mafter of " Arts, Vicar of the Parifh and Parifh-Church of *Norton* aforefaid, in a cer- " tain Caufe of Tithes and other Ecclefiaftical Rights, and upon his appear- " ing was judicially required to appear before him as aforefaid, at a certain " Time and Place likewife affigned to him, to take and receive a Libel in " the faid Caufe, at the Suit of the faid *Thomas Davifon* Clerk, and for his " Contempt in not appearing accordingly, he, the faid *Roger Hudfon,* was by " him pronounced *contumacious :* In fuch Contumacy he yet ftands, not caring " to obey the Procefs, Proceedings, Decrees and Sentences of the Ecclefiafti- " cal Judge : Whereupon the faid Official hath requefted us to fend forth our " Warrants for the attaching of the faid *Roger Hudfon,* and to proceed againft " him according to the Power committed to us, by a Statute made to that " Purpofe in the 27th Year of the Reign of *Henry the Eighth,* late King of " *England.* Thefe are therefore in his Majefty's Name, ftrictly to charge and " command you to attach the Body of the faid *Roger Hudfon,* and bring him " before us to find fufficient Sureties bounden by Recognizance to yield due " Obedience to the Procefs, Proceedings, Decrees, and Sentences of the faid " Official in the Caufe aforefaid, according to the Tenour of the faid Statute : " And if the faid *Roger Hudfon* fhall refufe or neglect fo to do, that then you " convey him to his Majefty's Goal at *Durham,* there to be kept without Bail " or Mainprize untill he fhall enter into Recognizance as aforefaid. Given at " *Durham* under our Hands and Seals the 11th Day of *March, Anno rni Ca-* " *roli fecundi nunc Regis Angliæ,* &c. *Tricefimo, Annoq; Dom.* 1678.

To the Bayliffs, Conftables, and other his Majefty's Officers in the County Palatine of Durham, *more efpe- cially to the Conftables of* Norton, *and to every or any of them.*

" JOSEPH STOKEL.

" JOHN MORLAND."

Thus

Thus committed, the poor Man was closely confined eleven Weeks, in which Time, for want of Air, he fell sick, and applying to the Goaler for a little Liberty, he alledged, that he durst not grant it for fear of the Vicar, who threatened him with the Loss of his Place : However, when the Goaler saw him extreamly weak, he, moved with Compassion, gave him some Liberty, and he quickly began to recover. But the Vicar complained against the Goaler at the next Assizes, when he was reprimanded by the Bench, and, as it was reported, fined 20*l.* After which the Goaler kept him very close, and he soon fell sick again ; upon which, *Robert Selby,* a Physician of *Durham,* applied to the Under Sheriff, but not prevailing, he wrote to the *Vicar,* representing the Prisoner's Case, and that it was probable a little fresh Air might preserve his Life, but received from him this Answer :

" *Sir,*

" I HOPE I am, and desire to continue a tender-hearted Man : Yet I
" would not have you or others judge me a *soft Fool,* and one easily to be
" wheedled out of his right Reason and Senses, by little phantastick Bugbears.
" If *Roger Hudson* were not able to pay (though a *Turk)* I know what I have
" to say ; but if either you or he pretend Conscience for Non-payment of just
" Debts or Dues, you must pardon me if I have as little Credit for, and give
" as little Respect to that *Coynage* and *Cozenage,* as to one that picks a Purse,
" or cuts a Throat by the same Pretence."

This Letter shews the Disposition of its Writer, and how little he regarded the Life of his *Christian Neighbour,* whose Conscience opposed his Interest. The poor Sufferer, after above five Months Imprisonment, died a Victim to this Prosecutor's Vengeance. Being dead, he was buried in Woolen, as the Law directed, but his Sister having omitted to make Affidavit thereof till a Day or two after the Time limited by the Act, the Vicar got a Warrant from the Justices to make Distress for 5*l.* the Penalty of the Law in that Case ; half of which fell to the Share of the Informer.

ANNO 1680. Upon an Information of a Meeting held at *Durham,* Warrants were granted by *John Sudbury* Dean, *Dennis Greenvil* Archdeacon, *Cuthbert Hutcheson* Mayor, *John Morland, Ralph Davison,* and *Isaac Bassire,* Justices ; by which were taken

Side notes: DURHAM, &c. 1678.

R. Rudson *died Prisoner.*

The *Vicar an Informer.*

Distresses for Meeting.

		l.	*s.*	*d.*
From *Robert Fisher,* at whose House the Meeting was, two Mares, six Oxen, and three Kine, worth	}	32	0	0
Martin Nicholson Grocer, Goods worth		76	0	0
Robert Hetherington, William Hetherington, Robert Wallis, and *William Hickson,* Goods worth	}	19	10	6
Richard Hall, Richard Hopper, James Hall, and *George Hall,* to the Value of	}	50	5	0
		177	15	6

And for another Meeting at the same Place, on the 29th of the Month called *June,* were taken from *Martin Nicholson, George Hall, James Hall,* and *Robert Doubleday,* Goods worth 45*l.*

About the same Time *John Ande* and *James Dickson,* Constables of *Market Audland,* became Informers, and procured Warrants from *Robert Eden* and *Cuthbert Caire* Justices, to make Distress for several Meetings, by which they took

		l.	*s.*	*d.*
From *Zachariah Murthwaite* and *William Spencely,* Goods worth	}	16	7	0
Anthony Hodgson and *Edward Tonstall,* to the Value of		27	10	0

	l.	*s.*	*d.*
Brought over	43	17	0
John Trotter, James Trotter, and *James White*	31	7	1
John Dodson and *Charles Watson,* Goods worth	6	5	0
	81	9	1

For a Meeting at *Jane Vickers's,* in *Raby,* were taken from *George Dickson, Henry Grainger, William Grainger, William Pickering, Jane Vickers,* and *Katharine Temple,* Goods to the Value of 20 *l.* 5 *s.*

For a Meeting at *Henry Grainger's,* on the 17th of *October,* were taken from *William Elstobb* and *Ralph Hodgson,* Goods worth 10 *l.*

For a Meeting at *Norton,* were taken from *Richard Watson, William Harrison, George Hall, Robert Hartburne, Christopher Crosby, Cuthbert Hunter,* and *William Smith,* Goods worth 109 *l.* 14 *s.* 4 *d.*

For a Meeting at *Darlington,* on the 31st of *October,* were taken

		l.	*s.*	*d.*
From	*John Robinson, Michael Collins, Edward Fisher, Robert Trueman,* and *Richard Trotter,* Goods worth	24	9	9
	Eleanor Weldon, Robert Corney, Robert Hartburne, Laurence Strickland, Anne King, and *Cuthbert Thompson*	3	18	6
	John Trueman, William Harrison, Giles Calvert, and *William Laurence,*	11	18	0
		40	6	3

Distresses for Absence from the publick Worship.

Many of the before-named Persons and others had also their Goods taken by Distress, for Fines of 12 *d.* per Day, for Absence from the National Worship, to the Value of 12 *l.* 13 *s.* 6 *d.* Some of whom were *Margaret Foster, George Burden, Jane Richardson, James Anderson, Anthony Robinson, Christopher King, Thomas Paxton, Philip Richardson,* and *William Maud.*

Hard Case of E. Tonstall, and R. Watson.

Hard was the Case of *Edward Tonstall* of *Bishops-Aukland,* who, with two others, presented to the Justices, at their Quarter Sessions at *Durham,* an Account of the Sufferings of their Friends at that Time in that County, but instead of obtaining Redress, the Justices, at the Bishop's Motion, tendred him the *Oath of Allegiance,* and for refusing to take it, he, who sollicited for the Liberty of his Friends, was himself sent to Prison. Nor was the Case of *Richard Watson* of *Norton* less severe, who was sent to Goal by an Order of Sessions, specifying no particular Cause for his Commitment ; it was as follows,

" *In plenâ Sessione pacis tent apud* Dunelm *in* Com. Dunelm, *decimo*
" *quinto die Januarii, Anno rni Caroli secundi nunc Angliæ,*
" &c. 30º.

Order of Sessions for Commitment of R. Watson.

" FORASMUCH as Information is given unto this Court upon Oath, that
" *Richard Watson,* of *Norton* in this County, Yeoman, hath lately spoken
" divers Words tending to the Breach of the Peace of this Kingdom, and the
" Disturbance of the Government. These are therefore in his Majesty's Name
" to will and require you, that forthwith upon Receipt hereof, you appre-
" hend the Body of the said *Richard Watson,* and bring him before *George
" Morland* Esq; one of his Majesty's Justices of the Peace for this County,
" then and there to answer to such Matters and Things as on his Majesty's Be-
" half shall be objected against him : And in the mean Time shall be of the
" good Behaviour toward our Sovereign Lord the King, and all his Liege
" People. Which if he shall refuse or neglect to do, that then you do carry
" him to the Common Goal at *Durham,* there to remain till he shall willingly
" do

' do the fame. Herein you are not to fail at your Perils. Given in the open   DURHAM,
' Seffions abovefaid.   &c.
   1678.

To the *Bayliffs, Conftables, and other*   P. Cur.
   his Majefty's Officers for this Coun-
   ty, and efpecially to the Conftables
   of Norton.
   " *Exam. p.* Fra. Crofby, *Dep. Cler. Pacis.* Com. Dunelm."

After five Weeks Imprifonment he was brought to the Quarter Seffions, where   *Releafe of*
the Chairman was faid to blufh at the extrajudicial manner of his Commit-   R. Watfon.
ment, and, after a Charge not to go to any more Meetings, difmift him without Fees.
   ANNO 1681. *William Peart* was a Prifoner at *Durham* for Tithes, at the   *Imprifonments*
Suit of *Luke Mawburne* Prieft, where he had been then confined about two   *for Tithes.*
Years. *John Wilkinfon* alfo was imprifoned for Tithes, at the Suit of *Edward*
Moorcroft Prieft.
   Richard Hall, fined 10*l.* for Meeting, had eight Beafts taken from him
worth 20*l.* *Patrick Livingftone,* preaching at *Gatefhead* Meeting, was ftruck   *Imprifonment*
violently on the Shoulders with a Stick by *George Simfon,* who, without any   *of P. Living-*
Warrant, charged *Patrick* to go with him, but he refufed. Next Day the   *ftone.*
Juftices-*Baffire* and *Moreland,* fent him to Prifon till next Seffions.
   In the Month called *January, John Turnball* and *Thomas Wake,* taken from   *More Imprifon-*
a Meeting at *Embleton,* were, by Order of *Henry Ogle* and *Thomas Collingwood*   *ments.*
Juftices, fent to Prifon at *Newcaftle.* Alfo *John Watfon* and *Hannah Davifon,*
committed by the fame Juftices, continued in Prifon above three Months.
   In *October* this Year, *Michael Collins, Laurence Appleby, Ellinor Tompfon,* and
Jofhua Middleton, fuffered by Diftrefs, for religious Meetings, to the Value
of 32*l.* 18*s.*
   Taken alfo for Meetings,

		l.	s.	d.
From	*John Airey, Mofes Fifher, James White, Lionel Hether-* *ington,* and *Chriftopher Bickers,* Goods worth	45	10	7
	Bartholomew Turner, John Carneath, Mark Staines, *George Hall,* and *Chriftopher Crofby*	61	12	7
	William Harrifon, Cuthbert Hunter, Richard Watfon, *William Geers, William Smith,* and *Thomas Chip-* *chafe.*	68	0	0
	John Wood, William Fenwick, Richard Hall, William *Hetherington, Robert Wallas, Robert Hafwell, Tho-* *mas Hafwell,* and *Robert Hetherington*	62	17	0
		238	0	2

In making thefe Diftreffes it was ufual, with *William Adamfon* and *Richard*   *Illegal Acts*
Harperly, Conftables of *Stockton,* to take away Goods without producing any   *of fome Con-*
Warrant. When they had taken what themfelves declared fufficient, they   *ftables.*
would come again for more. They feized a Man's Cow, and when he told
them he was not at the Meeting, they look'd in their Lift, and not finding his
Name, left the Cow. They would fometime make Seizures at Midnight.
Having forcibly entered a Shop, and fome Neighbours ftanding by who obferved their Doings, they caufed them to be bound over to the Seffions as Ob-
ftructers of Juftice. Thus the Spoilers exceeded the Bounds of Law with Im-
punity, and it was dangerous to contradict them.
   In this Year the Officers of *Barnard's-Caftle,* by Warrants for twelve Fines,
for Abfence from the National Worfhip, took

   From

DURHAM,
&c.
1681.

Fines for
Abfence from
the National
Worfhip.

	l.	*s.*	*d.*
From *Richard Tomfon, Chriftopher Eyons, Ellinor Bolton, Mary Hutton, John Bolron, Peter Allafon, Edmund Robinfon, John Walker, George Wilfon, William Wilfon, Roger Wilfon, Matthew Hutchefon, Henry Bowran,* and *George Wilfon,* Goods worth	13	9	4

For the fame Caufe the Officers of *Lartington* took

	l.	*s.*	*d.*
From *Francis Wrightfon, Thomas Wrightfon, John Turner, Charles Key, Chriftopher Key, Chriftopher Goodfon, Michael Wrightfon,* and *Thomas Smith,* Goods worth	7	13	8

The Officers of *Bowes* made Diftrefs on the Goods

	l.	*s.*	*d.*
Of *Henry Wennington, William Coats, Thomas Day,* and *William Alder,* to the Value of	5	4	0

Diftreffes.

By like Warrants the Officers of *Reeby* and *Stainthorp* took

	l.	*s.*	*d.*
From *Cuthbert Brainbridge, Henry Grainger, William Pickering, Jane Vickers, George Dickfon, Ralph Mafon, John Heighington* jun. *John Wilkinfon, William Heighington,* and *Martin Nicholfon,* Goods worth	6	12	10

| | 32 | 19 | 10 |

Sum of Diftreffes.

| The Sums taken this Year, for Meetings and Abfence from the National Worfhip, amounted to | 323 | 18 | 0 |

ANNO 1682. *Robert Wallis* of *Durham* was imprifoned for refufing to pay a Fine impofed on him for Abfence from the National Worfhip.

In this Year alfo were imprifoned *James Halliday, Robert Hill, Thomas Wilkinfon, John Airey,* and *Patrick Livingfton,* who had been taken out of their religious Affemblies for Worfhip.

Emanuel Grice, after about fix Years Imprifonment for Tithes, was releafed by means of the fudden Death of his Profecutor, *Richard Ball* an Impropriator.

On the 9th of the Month called *June, James Wood* was committed to Prifon at the Suit of *Thomas Davifon,* Prieft of *Norton,* for 9 s. 8 d. for Tithes.

E. Fifher *died Prifoner.*

Edward Fifher and *Robert Trueman* had been clofe confined in *Durham* Goal above thirteen Months for Tithe, at the Suit of *Elizabeth Marfh,* Widow to the Prieft of *Haughton,* when *Edward Fifher* fell fick and died there on the 31ft of the Month called *May* this Year. His Death being reprefented to the Widow, fhe relented, and freely difcharged *Trueman* about four Months after.

There were imprifoned this Year for refufing the Oath of Allegiance, *Thomas Fearon, Edward Tonftall, Mark Staines, William Gafcoyn,* and *George Rook :* Alfo *Ralph Nicholfon, Martin Nicholfon, Robert Hetherington, John Hetherington,* and *Robert Wallis,* which laft five had Sentence of *Premunire* paft upon them.

In this Year many Diftreffes were made for Meetings, *viz.* taken

	l.	*s.*	*d.*
From *Martin Nicholfon, Anthony Hodgfon, William Spencer,* and *John Dodgfon,* Goods worth	69	0	0
James Vickers, Zachary Murthwaite, Sarah Hickby, John Dodgfon, James Watfon, Emanuel Grice, William Spencely, and *James Trotter,* to the Value of	81	0	8
Anne Arundel, Sarah Kirkby, William Spencer, Henry Trotter, John Allafon, William Appleby, and *Richard Middleton*	33	6	11

| | 183 | 7 | 7 |

For

For Meetings at or near *Raby* were taken

	l.	*s.*	*d.*
From *Henry Grainger, William Pickering, Cuthbert Bambridge, Jane Vickers,* and *Thomas Johnfon,* to the Value of	63	8	0

And for Meetings at *Darlington,*

	l.	*s.*	*d.*
From *William Singleton, William Dobfon, Robert Trueman, Jofeph Fifher, Chriftopher Appleby, Frances Conceit, Thomas Hodgfon,* and *George Williamfon,* Cattle and Goods.	65	14	0
Jofhua Middleton, Laurence Appleby, Ralph Morgan, John Robinfon, Cuthbert Hodgfon, John Trueman, and *William Lynas,* Cattle and other Goods to the Value of	92	4	6
	221	6	6

Taken alfo this Year at or near *Newcaftle,* for Abfence from the National Worfhip,

	l.	*s.*	*d.*
From *Thomas Rumford, Andrew Neale, Francis Fofter, John Heighington* jun. *John Wilkinfon, Ralph Mafon, Martin Nicholfon,* and *William Heighington,* Goods worth	4	13	2

The Sums taken this Year for Meetings and Abfence from the National Worfhip, amounted to	409	7	3

In *December* this Year, fome of the Sufferers prefented to the Juftices a State of their Cafe, intituled

" *A Reprefentation of the Sufferings of the People of God called*
" QUAKERS *in* Durham. *A Copy of which is as follows, viz.*

" *To the Juftices at* Quarter Seffions, 4th and 5th *Days of the*
" *Tenth Month* 1682.

" WE the People of God in Scorn called *Quakers,* living peaceably in
" the Fear of God, have undergone the Severity of the Law made to
" fupprefs feditious Conventicles, to the Lofs of many Hundred Pounds,
" almoft every Year fince the Act took Date, whereby many honeft and in-
" duftrious Families have been cruelly oppreffed, and deeply impoverifhed ;
" having the Teftimony of a good Confcience in the Sight of God, that we
" are free from and clear of all feditious Cenventicles, which we deny as con-
" trary to the Spirit of *Chrift Jefus,* and the Faith we have received of him,
" neither have the Informers feen any fuch Thing among us. And we are not
" without a Witnefs in the Confciences of Men, among whom we have had
" our Converfation, that we are a People of no dangerous Principles or evil
" Practices, our Meetings being only to worfhip God according to the Com-
" mand of *Chrift Jefus,* and Practice of the primitive *Chriftians,* or to provide
" for the Fatherlefs, Widows, and Poor, with other Chriftian Duties, which
" the Chriftian Religion requires.

" We are fenfible that the late Act extended againft us (befide the Encou-
" ragement of Self-ended Informers to fwear almoft any thing againft us in
" our Abfence for their Intereft, whereby many grievous Oppreffions have
" befallen us) in many other Particulars alfo exceeds the Severity of other
" Laws of this Realm, yet we have fuffered many Extremities beyond the Se-
" verity of this Act, whereof the following Account may give fome In-
" ftances, which becaufe they are frefh, and in your Power to redrefs, we fhall
" only acquaint you with at prefent. Thofe many which are long fince tranf-
" acted, not coming fo properly under your Confideration now, farther than

A Reprefentation to the Juftices.

" being

DURHAM,
&c.
1682.

" being certified that many such have been these twelve Years, and you hereby
" made sensible thereof may be the more inclinable to redress these at present,
" and in Christian Wisdom to prevent any more for the future, that Oppres-
" sion may cease which the Righteous lie under, for which the God of Heaven
" is grieved ; with whom that you may find Mercy in the great Day of Ac-
" count, is the Christian Desire of

" Your Peaceful Friends and Neighbours

Emanuel Grice	*Anthony Hodgson*
James Trotter	*Jane Vickers*
Zachary Murthwaite	*Sarah Kirby.*
John Wilson	

Lawless Acts
of Informers.

To this. Representation some *particular suffering Cases* were annexed, of
which the *lawless* Acts of hungry Informers about this Time afforded many
Instances : Some of them were so daring as to seize Goods without any Warrant or regular Conviction : Two of them, *Watson* and *Rickerby*, took away
two Horses in the Night, intending to sell them to Persons appointed to meet
them at *Ferry-hill* the next Morning, having promised them two of the best
Horses the *Quakers* had : The Owner, pursuing the Spoilers, stopt the Horses
before they were sold, and the Informers could not produce any Warrant or
Authority for taking them. Complaint of this was made to the Bishop, who
said, *they might be prosecuted for Felony*, and spake to the Sheriff about it, who
examined one of the Informers, and he confessed their taking the Horses without any lawful Authority. The Sheriff reproved them, and ordered them to
return the Horses, which they did, and to ask the Owner's Pardon, which they
never did, nor did they refrain from repeating their lawless Practices : For at
another Time, two of them, *Dickson* and *Rickerby* came to the House of *Jane
Vickers* at *Raby*, where some of her Friends were eating : She asked the Informers to eat with them some Honey and Butter : They did eat and drink, and
talked very familiarly, but went away and gave Information of a Conventicle
at her House, where they had only seen Persons eating and drinking what
themselves partook of : For this the hospitable Woman was fined 15*l*. and had
her Cattle and Sheep taken away to the Value of 20*l*.

After the Informers had levied more than sufficient Distress on the Cattle of
Christopher Appleby, they ordered the Constable to go again to his House with
them, where they made a Seizure of his Beef, Cheese, and Houshold-Stuff :
While they were thus pillaging the poor Man of his Family's Provision, Sir
William Clayton, a Justice of the Peace, coming by, advised the Constable to
forbear, and to represent to the Justices, that there was nothing farther to be
levied without depriving the Family of Food and Lodging. By this Means
those ravenous Creatures at that Time were disappointed of their Prey.

From *Frances Conceit*, a poor Widow about eighty Years of Age, who had
been maintained by the Charity of her Friends for ten Years past ; *Ratcliff*
and *Boyse*, two Informers, took away most of her Apparel and Linen, with
the Trunk they were in. When the Informers at another Time had sworn
falsly against *Anne Arundell* for a Meeting she was not at, she appealed to the
Quarter Sessions, where she plainly proved their Information false, and recovered
her Goods at an Expence greater than her Fine. But the Justices were usually
tender of the Informer's Reputation, whom they regarded as the King's *Evidence*, and whose Mistakes, however careless or wilful, they were disposed as
much as possible to overlook.

ANNO 1683. For meeting together to worship God were taken by Distress this Year,

Fines for
Meeting.

	l.	*s.*	*d.*
From *Robert Trueman, Anne King, William Dobson, Laurence Appleby, Ursula Fisher,* and *Ellinor Tompson*, all of *Darlington*, Corn and Goods to the Value of	56	8	8
Carried over	56	8	8

	l.	s.	d.	DURHAM, &c. 1683.
Brought over	56	8	8	
From *Thomas Yalloley, Christopher Appleby, Thomas Hodgson, Anne Robinson, William Norton, Robert Hartburne, James Wood,* and *Christopher Crosby,* Goods worth	45	12	3	
John Airey, Christopher Bickers, Francis Foster, Alexander Neale, George Lowry, Lionel Hetherington, Martin Nicholson, William Hetherington, Thomas Johnson, and *Robert Hetherington,* to the Value of	63	0	3	
Sarah Kirby, Zachary Murthwaite, Henry Grainger, Robert Hartburne, William Laurence, Margaret Walker, and *Anne Chipchase,* Goods to the Value of	31	3	7	
	196	4	9	

Abuses and Imprison-ments.

In this Year, by an Order of *John Morland, Isaac Bassire, John Duck,* and *Miles Stapleton* Justices, thirty two Persons were taken from the Quarterly-Meeting at *Durham,* and committed to Prison ; but through the Favour of the Bishop and the High Sheriff were released again in a few Days. Also *Anthony Robinson* and *Margery Fan,* taken at a Meeting, were committed to Prison by *James Burden* Mayor of *Stockton* ; who also sent to Goal *William Jekyll* and *Christopher Crosby,* two elderly Men, after he had suffered them to be abused in his Presence, and one of them dragged in the Dirt fifty or sixty Yards. He also committed *Thomas Chipchase, Robert Pattison,* and *George Hall,* to Prison from a Meeting at *Norton.* *Hugh White* of *Berkley* was imprisoned on a Writ *de Excommunicato capiendo.*

Death of T. Branting-ham.

ANNO 1684. About the Month called *June* this Year, *Thomas Brantingham* died a Prisoner for Tithes in *Durham* Goal.

For being at religious Meetings Distresses were made this Year on the Goods

	l.	s.	d.
Of *Samuel Freeman, Francis Foster, Robert Wallis, Henry Hunter, Lionel Hetherington, Robert Askew, Robert Fletcher, William Hewett, William Fenwick, Thomas Johnson, Ralph Hodgson,* and *William Testob,* to the Value of	52	17	6
Henry Grainger, William Pickering, Martin Nicholson, and *Thomas Ornesby,* to the Value of	36	10	0
John Hunter, twenty Oxen and other Kine, three Horses and eleven Sheep, worth	51	4	0
William Giers, Christopher Crosby, Zachary Murthwaite, Sarah Kirkby, and *Robert Trueman,* Goods worth	19	16	0
William Dobson, Thomas Pyeborne, Christopher Appleby, Laurence Strickland, and *Robert Trueman*	7	11	0
	167	18	6

Oppression of the Poor.

Of these Sufferers, though many of them were Men of Substance, others were poor : One of them, *William Hewett,* was a poor Labourer, from whom the Informers took most of his wearing Apparel ; after which he still continuing constant in going to Meetings, the Justices, *Bassire* and *Jenkins,* sent him to the House of Correction. Another of them, *Thomas Pyborne,* was so poor, that when the Informers brake into his House, and seized all his Houshold Goods, the Constable, moved with Compassion to the Man and his Family of young Children, gave the Informers 20 *s.* to desist from the Attempt. A third, *Laurence Strickland,* was reduced, for want of Bedding, to much Hardship, having nothing of necessary Bedclothes left for him and his Family to cover themselves. A fourth, *Robert Trueman,* having been several

Times

Times diftrained on, at laft had the poor Remainder of his Goods taken away worth but 20 s.   Thefe Men, though *poor* in this World, were *rich* in Faith, patient in Affliction, and unmoveable in the Stedfaftnefs of performing their religious Duties.

On the 3d of *November, Ellinor Grainger, Elizabeth Wilfon, Anne Card, William Hewett, William Heron, John Rumford, Henry Middleton,* and *William Hodgfon,* taken at a Meeting the Day before, were by the Juftices, *Baffire* and *Jenkins,* committed to the Houfe of Correction in *Durham* to be kept to hard Labour, and were detained there about ten Weeks, till the Seffions, at which they were difmift with Threats, and charged to come at no more Conventicles. *George Swallow* was alfo imprifoned about the fame Time.   There were alfo about that Time in Prifon, *Lionel Johnfon, Ifaac Robinfon, Samuel Freeman, Robert Afkew,* and *Philip Simfon.*

Excommunications.

On the 24th of the Month called *January, John Young* and *John Willoughby,* both of *North-Shields,* were committed to *Morpeth* Goal by a Writ *de Excommunicato capiendo.*

Diftreffes.

About the fame Time *William Singleton, Laurence Appleby,* and *Jofhua Middleton,* had their Goods taken by Diftrefs, for their religious affembling to worfhip God, to the Value of 12 *l.* 6 *s.*

Hardened Informers.

Remarkable was the Infolence of *Boyfe* and *Ratcliffe,* drunken Informers, who coming to the Houfe of *Robert Trueman,* when only his Wife, Maid, and a little Child were within, fplit the Door with a Smith's Hammer, and with one of the Splinters hurt the Maid who was coming to open it, and finding little in the Houfe (for they had before taken away almoft all the Goods) abufed the Woman, calling her *Whore,* and affrighted the Child: One of the Informers, like an hardned Reprobate, fwearing, that *he car'd not what he did, for,* faid he, *I am as bad as I can be.*

In this Year were taken by Diftrefs, for Abfence from the National Worfhip,

	l.	*s.*	*d.*

Diftreffes.

From *Mary Corn, Chriftopher Crofby, Thomas Ornefby, William Pickering, Martin Nicholfon, Mary Hutton, George Oates,* and *Francis Fofter,* Goods to the Value of } 30   8   0

Impudence of Informers.

About this Time *James Dickfon, John Hudfpath,* and *Lancelot Rowel,* Informers, behaved with an Impudence fcarce to be parallell'd.   They came to the Houfe of *Thomas Hedly* of *Hedly-hill,* with a Warrant demanding a Fine of 5 *l.*   The Man being weak, and terrified by their Threats, gave them 20 *s.* and they blotted his Name out of the Warrant.   In like manner they extorted from *Chriftopher Vickers* 20 *s.* threatning to diftrain for a Meeting he had not been at. So arbitrary were thofe Informers, that they fet themfelves above the Juftices, and affumed a Power of altering their Warrants by putting in or out whom they pleafed.   They were fo prefumptuous, as to undertake to indemnify Perfons, and gave a kind of negative Licence to go to Meetings.   They gave a Bond for a 100 *l.* to one *Thomas Hunter,* not a *Quaker,* conditioned for their not difturbing, but keeping harmlefs feveral of his Relations for being at any Meeting in this County.   The like Bonds they gave to others who were not *Quakers,* and contracted for Sums of Money to leave People out of their Informations.

In this Year were taken from *Chriftopher Vickers,* a Mare, four young Beafts, five Sheep, and other Goods, worth 12 *l.* 11 *s.* 6 *d.*

Sum of this Year's Diftreffes. Grofs Abufe of Authority.

The whole of the Diftreffes this Year, for Meetings and Abfence from the National Worfhip, amounted to 222 *l.* 14 *s.*

We fhall clofe the Account of this Year with an Inftance of much Paffion and Abufe of Authority exercifed by the Juftices *Baffire* and *Jenkins,* on *John Hedley* a Servant to *Chriftopher Bickers* a Grocer in *Gatefhead.*   Hedley obferving the Officers coming to make a Seizure of his Mafter's Goods, put a Bar crofs the lower Part of the Shop-door, which was fhut before.   The Conftable feeing this, leapt over the Door, faying, *Sirrah, do you intend to knock me on*

the

the Head with the Bar, though there was not the leaſt Colour or Appearance of any ſuch Deſign : However, the Conſtable hurried him away to the Juſtices then in Town at a Tavern. They required *Hedley* to kneel down on his bare Knees and beg Pardon : He refuſed, alledging, *that he had not committed any Offence.* Upon this *one* of the Juſtices took him faſt by the Hair on one Side of his Head, and the *other* on the other Side, and ſo pulled him up and down the Room, calling him *Dog, Whelp,* and ſuch like Names as their Anger ſuggeſted, bidding him *kneel down or they would have him ſcourged :* But he not ſubmitting to their reaſonleſs Requirings, Juſtice *Jenkins* with his own Hands ſtript him, and ordered an Officer immediately to whip him through the Street to his Maſter's Shop : Which was done, the People generally exclaiming againſt the Illegality and Barbarity of their Doings. No Wonder that Informers exceeded the Bounds of Law, when the Juſtices gave them ſuch Examples.

ANNO 1685. *William Peart* of *Craik* in *Yorkſhire*, but in the Dioceſe of *Durham*, was committed to Priſon by Warrant from *Marmaduke Allaſon,* Mayor of *Durham*, and another Juſtice, grounded on a Certificate of Contumacy out of the Eccleſiaſtical Court, at the Suit of *Luke Mawburne* Prieſt, who had formerly kept him a long Time in Goal. While he lay in Priſon the Prieſt's Agents took Hay and Corn off his Ground in what Quantities they pleaſed.

By Warrant from *John Morland* of *Durham*, a Juſtice of the Peace, upon the Informations of *Richard Noble, John Curry,* and others of *Biſhop's-Aukland,* ſeveral Perſons had their Goods taken by Diſtreſs, for being preſent at religious Meetings, *viz.*

		l.	s.	d.	
Edward Tonſtall, * *John Walton,* and *James White*, to the Value of		13	9	4	*Diſtreſſes*
Zachary Murthwaite, Margaret Spencely, James Trotter, Emanuel Grice, and *William Pickering,* to the Value of		14	1	0	
Taken alſo from *George Williamſon, Laurence Appleby,* and *Joſeph Fiſher,* Cattle and Goods worth		22	0	0	
		49	10	4	

The Informers having a Warrant againſt *Ralph Hodgſon*, the Conſtable they would have given it to refuſed to execute it, alledging that the Place was out of the Verge of his Office. Upon this the Informers got a Warrant againſt him for Neglect of Duty, and made him pay 5*l.* which he recovered again upon *Ralph Hodgſon's* Goods.

The Sum of the Diſtreſſes this Year amounted to 54*l.* 10*s.* 4*d.*

ANNO 1686. *John Walton* of *Biſhop's-Aukland* had taken from him, for Abſence from the National Worſhip, an Horſe worth 6*l.*

At the Aſſizes this Year, thoſe who remained in Priſon were generally diſcharged by the King's Proclamation ; among whom was *Thomas Sparks,* who had been impriſoned about thirteen Years on a Writ *de Excommunicato capiendo :* But *Hugh Williamſon* died in Priſon about a Month before.

ANNO 1687. Taken from ſeveral Perſons in *Durham* and *Northumberland,* Tithes in Kind amounting to 12*l.* 19*s.* 8*d.*

ANNO 1688. At *Sunderland*, on the 20th of *December* between eight and ten at Night, *William Shepherdſon, William Hincks,* and *Gerrard Sidgewick,* Maſters and Mariners, *Edward Robinſon* and *John Mickſon* Fitters, all of that Town, broke two Locks, entred the Meeting-houſe, the Copyhold Eſtate of *William Maud,* pulled out a Form and went away. About one of the Clock the ſame Night they returned with a Rabble of Boys, and the baſer Sort of the People, and broke open the Houſe again, pulled up and burnt the Floors, Doors,

* The ſaid *John Walton* was impriſoned, for that he, being Conſtable, refuſed to act in making Diſtreſſes on the Goods of his Friends who were fined for their Meetings.

DURHAM, &c. 1688.

Doors, and Windows, Seats, and Roof of the Houfe, totally demolifhing it before eight next Morning : About which Time *Shepherdfon* marched in the Front of the Rabble with his Sword by his Side, when they broke the Windows of feveral Houfes of the People called *Quakers* as they paffed the Streets.

Tithes.

William Maud brought an Action of Trefpafs againft *Hincks* and others for demolifhing his Houfe, and made legal Proof of 49*l*. Damages : But the Jury gave him but 20*s*. upon which he proceeded no farther, but fat down with his Cofts of Law added to the Damage of his Houfe.

Poll-Act.

ANNO 1689. In this and the next preceding Year, feveral Perfons had Corn taken out of their Fields for Tithe, to the Value of 30*l*. 6*s*. 6*d*.

Tithes.

ANNO 1690. *Robert Wardell*, for refufing to pay 20*s*. affeffed on him as a Preacher by the Poll-Act, fuffered Diftrefs of Goods to the Value of 1*l*. 8*s*. 6*d*. In this Year alfo feveral Perfons had their Corn taken for Tithes, to the Amount of 43*l*. 6*s*. 3*d*.

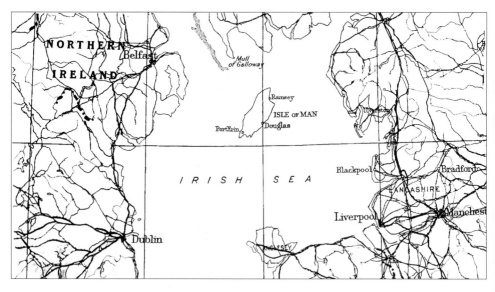

Map of the isle of Man.

C H A P. XX.

I S L E *of* M A N.

A N N O 1656.

THE Magiftrates of this Place, being early prepoffeffed with an Averfion to the *Quakers* and their Doctrine, which the Preachers of thofe Times, whofe Intereft it thwarted, had induftrioufly mifrepre-fented, made Laws againft them at their firft coming thither, one of which was for banifhing all of that Perfwafion, whether Natives or others : Accordingly *Katharine Evans* was taken out of her Bed by Night, and fent away. *James Lancafter* was alfo expelled the Ifland, for no other Reafon than his being a *Quaker*. *Peter Cofnock*, his Son, and feveral others, were clapt up in Prifon at *Caftle-Peel*, by Order of *William Chriften* a Magiftrate there ; from thence they were removed to *Douglas* and banifhed. They applied to the Lord *Fairfax*, Governour of the Ifland, for Leave to return, but he would not grant it, though fome of them were born there. At length, upon Appli-cation to the Parliament, fuch as were Inhabitants of the Place were permitted to go Home again.

Banifhment of divers from the Ifland.

ANNO 1657. *William Callow* was detained eight Weeks in Prifon, for publickly reproving a Prieft, whom he heard abufing the *Quakers* in his Sermon to the People. The fame *William Callow* and his Wife fuffered a Month's Im-prifonment, for admitting a Meeting at their Houfe. Several Perfons were taken out of a Meeting on the Firft-day of the Week, and fet in the Stocks four Hours in the Market-place : Others were fined, of whom were *William Callow*, *John Chriften*, and *Evan Kerufh* ; from the two Former ten Bufhels of Oats were taken by Diftrefs, which were laid in * *William Chriften*'s Barn : On the next Firft-day, after Sermon, the Prieft gave publick Notice for the Poor of the Parifh to go to the Barn and take fome Corn which the Governour had ordered to be given them : Some poor People of his own Hearers anfwered, *That it had been more Charity to have given his own Goods to the Poor than other Mens, and that they would receive none of it.* However fome of the Poor went to the Place with the Prieft and Soldiers, and *W. Callow* went alfo. The Prieft feveral Times called to the Poor to hold their Bags, but none of them would. At this the Prieft grew angry, and lookingly fternly on *W. Callow*, calls to the People, *Why don't you take the Corn ? Is there any one here that has ought to do with this Corn, or faith, that it may not be given to the Poor ?* This he did on purpofe to provoke *William* to fay fomething, but could not. The Poor ftood ftill a while, and then withdrew one by one, leaving the Corn with the Prieft and Soldiers. On the following Firft-day the Parfon again publifhed the Diftribution of the Corn as before ; fignifying how much the Governour was difpleafed that they had not taken it ; for Fear of the Gover-nour and the Prieft, fome poor People went again to the Place, but only one among them (named *Coole*) would take any, and he vauntingly faid to the Reft, *You are fo proud you will not take it : I have got this, and there will be more of his Goods taken before this be eaten, and then I'll get more.* But fo it was,

Some impri-foned.

Others fet in the Stocks.

The Poor re-fufe to take Corn of W. Callow's.

---

* This *W. Chriften* was a Deputy under the Lord *Fairfax*, but falling afterward under his Difpleafure for fome Mifdemeanour, was fhot to Death on the Ifland. In his laft Speech he mentioned with much Regret what he had done to the *Quakers*.

ISLE of
MAN.
1657.

Obfervation.

that before he had eaten what he took, he was taken away by Death. His fudden *Exit* was interpreted by the other Poor as a Judgment upon him ; and they rejoiced that they had kept themfelves clear. The reft of the Corn lay till it was fpoiled, for no Body would take it, and then it was faid to be caft into the Streets to the Horfes and Swine. From this Inftance we may juftly obferve, that the Innocence and Patience of Sufferers in the Caufe of Religion, carries with it a Force of Conviction on the Confciences of the People, which the Arts of defigning and interefted Men cannot eafily eradicate.

Imprifonment of W. Callow *and others.*

ANNO 1659. *William Callow* and feveral others, for 2 *d.* each, demanded by the Prieft for Bread and Wine, which it was well known they had not received, were imprifoned by a Warrant from * *James Challoner* the Governour ; from whom alfo in *September* this Year the Prieft procured another Warrant for the Imprifonment of *William Callow* and *Evan Chriften* for refufing to pay Tithes. One Morning early, as foon as they came on Shore, having been all Night in the Wet and Cold at Sea, (for they were Fifhermen) they were hurried to Prifon in their wet Clothes, and detained feveral Days in the Midft of their Herring-Fifhery, the moft advantageous Seafon for their Bufinefs :

Remarkable Draught of Fifhes.

This, however defigned by their Adverfary, was not prejudicial to them, for the next Night after they were releafed, they caught as many Fifh as they were able to bring on Shore ; fo that they could do no lefs than gratefully acknowledge a peculiar Providence attending them.

Imprifonment for frivolous Claims of Tithes.

ANNO 1660. *William Callow, Evan Chriften,* and others, were again fent to Prifon by the Prieft's Procurement, fome for Tithes of Corn, fome for 2 *d.* each for Bread and Wine, others for Tithe of Fifh, not worth 1 *d.* for which trivial Demands they were kept in Prifon fixteen Days,

Difmal Confinement of W. Callow, *and* E. Chriften *in a Dungeon.*

ANNO 1662. The faid *William Callow* and *Evan Chriften,* for refufing to pay, the Former 16 *d.* and the Latter 2 *d.* demanded by the Prieft for *Bread and Wine for the Sacrament,* were committed to a Prifon called St. *Germain's* in *Caftle-Peel,* and were clofe lockt up in a Dungeon (under a Yard where dead Corps were buried) without Fire, Candle, or Bedding, having only Straw to lie on, and a Stone for their Pillow : Here they lay fixteen Days, till fome of their Neighbours, of mere Pity, unknown to them, paid the Money, otherwife they might have perifhed there, their rigid Perfecutors, two Priefts, of whom one was the Complainant, and the other, being a Judge of the Bifhop's Court, granted the Warrant for their Commitment, appearing by their Actions to value the Lives of two honeft innocent Men at lefs than 18 *d.* In the Month called *July,* the fame Perfons, and fome others, were imprifoned ten Days for Abfence from the publick Worfhip : And in *September,* they two, and fix others, were taken out of a Meeting and carried to *Caftle-Ruffien,* where they

8 Confined in an high Tower.

were confined in an high Tower, without Fire or Candle, in the cold Winter, fifteen Weeks ; only *William Callow,* after a Month's Imprifonment, appealing to the Earl of *Derby,* was permitted to go to *London,* where he at length obtained the Earl's Warrant for the Difcharge of himfelf and the Reft.

Imprifonments.

ANNO 1663. The faid *William Callow* and *Evan Chriften,* with the faid *Evan's* Father, eighty Years of Age, were committed to *Peel-Caftle* for Abfence from the Parifh-Church, but after about fixteen Days Confinement were releafed by Order of the Bifhop, who then came to the Ifland to be fworn.

ANNO 1664. In this Year two Priefts, Judges of the Bifhop's Court, iffued an Order for imprifoning the *Quakers,* viz.

Order of two Priefts for imprifoning Quakers.

" WE have received late Orders from our reverend Ordinary to admonifh
" the *Quakers* to conform and come to Church, or be committed
" until they fubmit to Law ; and forafmuch as they refufe, after feveral Charges
and

---

* This Governour *Challoner* had been one of the Long Parliament, and upon the King's Return was fent for to *London,* in order, as it was thought, to be tried among the Regicides : The Day he fhould have gone, he took fomething called Phyfick, which killed him in a fhort Time. He had been a violent Perfecutor, and was heard to fay a little before his Death, that *he would quickly rid the Ifland of* Quakers.

" and Publications in the Parifh-Church, but continue their Meetings and Refrac-
" torinefs to all Government of the Church, and are therefore cenfured to be
" committed into St. *Germain*'s Prifon, and there let them remain till Orders
" given to the contrary, and for fo doing this fhall be your Difcharge.

" *Robert Parr.*"
" *John Harrifon.*"

" *P. S.* If they refufe to be committed by you, call for the Affiftance of a
" Soldier from Captain *Afcough.* Let the Sumner put this in Execution
" immediately."

By this Order the faid *William Callow, Evan Chriften*, and fome others, were
again committed to Prifon on the 22d of the Month called *May* this Year.
A few Days after their Commitment *William Callow*'s Wife fell fick of a *Fever*,
and was thought to be at the point of Death. Interceffion was made by fome
Neighbours to the Bifhop, that he, then Prifoner fixteen Miles from Home,
might have Leave to go vifit his Wife, which Liberty was with much Difficulty granted him for two Days only.

She was fcarce well recovered, when, on the 18th of *October*, the Apparitor
or Sumner, came to her, and the reft of the Women called *Quakers* on the
Ifland, with an Order from the Bifhop to carry them all to Prifon, they being,
as he faid, all of them, both Men and Women, excommunicated ; of which
Excommunication they knew nothing till he told them. As he was conveying
them to Prifon, *William Callow*'s Wife was found unable either to walk or ride,
wherefore the Sumner, having reprefented her Cafe to the Bifhop, was ordered
to let her be carried Home again. The other five, namely, *Jane Chriften,*
Jane Kennell, Anne Chriften, Mary Callow, and *Mary Chriften,* (one of whom
was feventy four, and another fixty feven Years of Age ; a *third* was a poor
ferving Man's Wife, having three Children, one of whom, fucking at her
Breaft, fhe took with her to Prifon ; a *fourth* was the Wife of one not called a
Quaker, having a large Family and many Children ; and the *fifth* was a Servant of *William Callow*, whom they took away from her fick Miftrefs) were
carried to *Caftle-Peel*, to the Place called St. *Germain*'s Prifon, and put into the
aforefaid difmal Dungeon under the Burying-Ground, where the Men alfo were :
When the Sumner had brought them to the deepeft Part of the Dungeon, he
took off his Hat, and formally pronounced what he called the *Bifhop's Curfe*,
to this Effect, *viz.* " I do here before the Standers by, deliver you up into
" St. *Germain*'s Prifon by the Law of my Lord the Bifhop and his Clergy,
" you being caft out of the Church by Excommunication, and I do take Wit-
" nefs that I do deliver you over from the Power of the Bifhop and his Law,
" to be and continue the Earl of *Derby*'s Prifoners." What he meant by this
the Prifoners knew not, there being none prefent but himfelf and them : Having fo faid he left them, and they lay there many Months, enduring the Hard-
fhips of a clofe and unhealthy Confinement, the *cruel* Mercies of the *Bifhop* and
his *Clergy*.

ANNO 1665. On the 15th of the Month called *June, Henry Nowell*, the
Deputy-Governour, came to the Caftle, and read to the Prifoners an Order from
the Earl of *Derby*, that *they muft be forthwith tranfported into fome other Land.*
On the 29th of the fame Month *Thomas Harrifon* and *John Woods*, two Priefts,
came to the Prifoners and told them, they were come by the Deputy-Governour's Order, *to admonifh them to conform to the Church*, otherwife *they muft be*
banifhed forthwith.

On the 5th of *September* the Commander of the Caftle received an Order to
fend all his *Quaker* Prifoners to *Douglas*, which was done on the 7th ; they
were kept there guarded by Soldiers till the 14th, and then put on board a Ship,
whereof *Thomas Brittain* was Mafter. As the Prifoners entred on one Side the
Ship,

*Sumner's Or-
der to carry
all the Women
to Prifon.*

*5 Women com-
mitted to St.
Germain's
Prifon.*

*The Sumner's
Speech in the
Dungeon.*

*Prifoners put
on Ship-board.*

ISLE of
MAN.
1665.

*Seamen refuse
to carry them.*

Ship, the Seamen went out on the other into the Boat, telling the Master, that *they were not hired to carry People out of their native Country against their Wills, neither would they go with him if he carried them,* and so went on Shore, leaving him only a Boy or two. The Master seeing his Men resolute, and himself unable to proceed on his Voyage without them, conferred with the Soldiers, and set the Prisoners on Shore again, which being done, the Seamen returned to the Ship, and set Sail.

About three Days after, several Vessels came into the Road, but all refused to carry the Prisoners. The Soldiers would have forced them on board the Ship of *Anthony Nicholson,* a *Whitehaven* Man, but he stoutly opposed it, saying, *he would carry no Prisoners, except they would send a Guard of Soldiers, and Money to maintain both the Prisoners and them, and also signify in Writing the Crime laid to their Charge* ; adding, that *if they were such dangerous Persons as were unworthy to live in their own Country, he would not trust them on Board, left perhaps they should overpower him and take away his Vessel.* This he spoke

*4 Prisoners at
Midnight put
on board two
Vessels against
the Will of
the Masters.*

*Carried to
Dublin.*

ironically. However, on the 18th of *September* about Midnight, four of the Prisoners, *viz. William Callow, Evan Christen, Jane Christen,* and *Mary Callow,* were * hurried out of their Beds (not having Time allowed them to put on their Clothes, some of which were left behind) and by Force two of them were put on board *Nicholson's* Ship, and the other two on board *William Crossthwaite's,* another Man of *Whitehaven,* against the Will of the Masters, from one of whom the Officer detained his Sails, and would not let him go off without the Prisoners. So they sailed to *Dublin* in *Ireland,* where neither Prisoners nor Seamen were suffered to land, till one of the Masters, *William Crossthwaite,* was examined by the Mayor, who demanded his Order or Warrant for bringing the Prisoners without their Consent, to which he answered, *that he had no Warrant, but was compelled to take them on Board by one* Quail, *an Officer, who took away his Sails, and would not let him put off without them, and that his Vessel was in Danger of breaking.* Upon which the Mayor gave him the following Order, *viz.*

" *Sir,*

*Order of the
Mayor of
Dublin for
carrying them
back.*

" YOU are hereby required to take back in your own Vessel, the four
" Prisoners called *Quakers,* which you brought against their voluntary
" Consent out of the *Isle* of *Man,* and them to put on Shore on the said Island,
" there to follow their necessary Occasions, of which you may not fail at
" your Peril. Dated the 27th of *September* 1665.

To William Crossthwaite, *Master of the
Ship* Elizabeth *of* Whitehaven.

*Landed at
Whitehaven.*

Pursuant to this Order he brought them back, but either being, or pretending to be, put by the Island through contrary Winds, he carried them to *Whitehaven* in *Cumberland,* and there put them on Shore with this Certificate, *viz.*

*The Master's
Certificate.*

" THESE are to certify whom it may concern, but especially the
" Officers of the *Isle* of *Man,* that I *William Crossthwaite,* Master of the
" Ship called the *Elizabeth,* of *Whitehaven,* was, by Order of the Mayor of
" the City of *Dublin,* ordered to carry back the under-named Persons into
" the *Isle* of *Man,* at my own proper Costs and Charges, they being sent
" out of the said Island against their voluntary Consent, and that the said
" Persons were ordered to return into my Vessel, or else to be imprisoned :
" Furthermore, my Sails were taken from my Yards, until I would promise
" to

---

* They purposed also to have sent away another Woman of seventy four Years of Age, but left her, being too weak to remove, lying, as they thought, at the point of Death, on a Bed of Straw.

" to bring them back again, to wit, *William Callow, Evan Chriften, Jane*
" *Chriften,* and *Mary Callow.*

Whitehaven, *the 7th of*
Oćtober 1665.   " WILLIAM CROSSTHWAITE."

Attefted by   *Robert Greafons, George Robinfon,*   }   Mariners.
              William Stockdell, John Rodery.   }

The Prifoners having given Information to a Juftice of the Peace of their
prefent Condition and Circumftances, he made the following Order, *viz.*

" Cumberland *fs.*

" JOHN LAMPLUGH *Efq; one of his Majefty's Juftices of the Peace*
" *and* Quorum *for the faid County: To the Conftables of*
" Prefton, *and others of the Officers of* Whitehaven, *Greeting.*

" **F**ORASMUCH as Information is given unto me, that *William Crofs-*   Order of a
" *thwaite* of *Whitehaven,* Mafter of the Ship called the *Elizabeth,* hath   Juftice for
" lately brought over out of the *Ifle* of *Man, William Callow, Evan Chriften,*   carrying them
" *Jane Chriften,* and *Mary Callow,* Inhabitants of the faid Ifland, who are   Ifland.
" faid to be *Quakers,* without any Order or legal Proceedings appearing for
" his fo bringing them into this County ; and fince it may endanger the Peace
" of the faid County, to permit the faid Perfons to continue here. Thefe
" are therefore in his Majefty's Name to command you, that you caufe the
" faid *William Callow, Evan Chriften, Jane Chriften,* and *Mary Callow,* to
" be put on board the faid Ship of the faid *William Croffthwaite,* and he to
" carry them upon the next Opportunity back again to the faid *Ifle of Man.*
" And hereof you are not to fail. Given under my Hand and Seal the 4th
" Day of *November, Anno regni Regis Caroli fecundi* 17° *Annoq; Dom.* 1665.

" JOHN LAMPLUGH."

On the 12th of *December,* Croffthwaite took them on Board again, but in-   They are car-
ftead of carrying them to the Ifland, carried them again to *Dublin* ; but was   ried again to
not fuffered to land there, till he had given Security to convey them to the   Dublin.
Ifland on his Return : After which Security given they landed, and on the   Thence back
25th of the fame Month came on Board again : But he, contrary to his En-   again to
gagement, returned with them to *Whitehaven.* Thus were thefe innocent People   Whitehaven.
harraffed and toffed up and down in the cold Winter Seafon. Being landed   tendance of
again in *England,* the two Men went to the Earl of *Derby,* and while they were   the two Men
employed in fruitlefs Sollicitations to him and the Bifhop, *Croffthwaite* carried   on the Earl
the two Women back to the Ifland, where they were again fhut up in Prifon.   and Bifhop.
A few Days after his Veffel was driven on Shore by a violent Storm, and fome   Women car-
Paffengers, with almoft all his Goods, were loft.   ried back to
ANNO 1666. *William Callow* and *Evan Chriften,* after long Attendance   the Ifland.
on the Earl of *Derby,* were by Meffage from him directed to attend the   Veffel caft
Bifhop, then at *Windfor,* when he fhould come down to *Knowlfey-Hall* in *Lan-*   away.
cafhire : He went thither fome Time after, and there they got Admittance   They are di-
both to the *Bifhop* and the *Dean* of the Ifland, on the 1ft of the Month called   rected by the
June this Year, and had a long Conference with each of them in the Prefence   Earl to the
of the *Countefs* of *Derby* and others, which Conferences we here fubjoin, *viz.*   Bifhop.

    1. A DISCOURSE between the *Bifhop* of the *Ifle* of *Man,* and *William*   A Difcourfe
        Callow and *Evan Chriften,* two banifhed *Quakers.*   between the
                                                                Bifhop and
Bifhop. *What have you to fay to me ?*   banifhed Men.

Anfw. We have to fay to thee to let thee know, that we are perfecuted and banifhed from Place to Place for Confcience-fake, and moft of it is long of thee.

Bifhop. I did not banifh you : I left you faft enough when I came out of the Ifland.

Anfw. Yet notwithftanding we know that our Banifhment *hath been long of thee,* or elfe the *Earl* would be loth to ufe us there worfe than his Tenants in this Country.

Bifhop. You are not banifht, but you banifh your felves.

Anfw. Nay, we do not banifh our felves, neither have we done any Thing worthy of Banifhment, but are by you contrary to Law perfecuted.

Bifhop. I have no more to do with you, nor to fay to you, but what I told you before, that if I can perfuade my Lord to the contrary, you fhall not go again to the Ifland.

Anfw. Indeed we do expect no better from the Spirit of Perfecution in any whomfoever : But thou art contrary to the Spirit of Chrift, who faid, *Do unto all Men as you would be done unto,* and *love thy Enemies,* and not to perfecute any.

Bifhop. You are not at all perfecuted, but you perfecute your felves, and you are the Caufes of the Ruin of your own Families, and their Blood fhall be upon your own Heads.

Anfw. We are not guilty of our own Blood, nor yet of the Blood of our Families, but our Blood and theirs too fhall be upon your Heads by whom we are perfecuted.

Bifhop. You are not perfecuted, but banifhed becaufe you do not come to the Church.

Anfw. When did Chrift or his Apoftles banifh any for not coming to hear them, as you do.

Bifhop. Yes, many.

Anfw. Prove it, for I cannot remember that I ever read of any.

Bifhop. Did not Paul *caft them out that were diforderly in the Church ?*

Anfw. But he did not banifh or imprifon them that were without, if they did not come in, as thou haft caufed to be done to us.

Bifhop. I did not banifh you neither, but excommunicate you, as he did ; and I have no more to fay to you.

Anfw. But neither Chrift, nor his Apoftles, did force them that were without to come in, or elfe be banifhed or compelled, as thou haft done to us.

Bifhop. Yea, Chrift bade his Servants *go and compell them to come in.*

Anfw. That was a Parable concerning a certain Man that had bidden many to a Feaft, who began to make their Excufes, one of his Land, another of his Wife, another of his Oxen : Mark what he faid, *They fhall not tafte of my Supper.* He did not fay, *Banifh them and perfecute them.*

Bifhop. You are not perfecuted, but punifhed becaufe you do not come to the Church, nor obey the Law, but are in Rebellion.

Anfw. We are not in Rebellion, but they that act againft the Spirit of Chrift in their Confciences are in the Rebellion.

Bifhop. But why will not you come to the Church ?

Anfw. We do not own your Church to be the true Church.

Bifhop. Why, what have you to fay againft it ?

Anfw. It is but an Houfe of Lime, Wood, and Stone, and therefore not a true Church, for *the Church is in God.*

Bifhop. We matter not what you call the Place ; the Congregation that meet in it is the Church.

Anfw. They that meet in the Name of the Lord, and in his Power to worfhip him in Spirit and in Truth, we own : But they that meet to worfhip with the Body, and to make a Confeffion with their Lips of other Men's Lines made ready to their Hands ; and as foon as they have done, they fight and quarrel, cheat and deceive one another, thefe are not the true Church of Chrift.

Bifhop. How fhall I know that you have the Spirit of God ?

Anfw. Thou

Anſw. Thou mayſt try us ; for every Tree is known by its Fruits, and an evil Tree cannot bear good Fruits, nor a good Tree evil Fruits.

Biſhop. *Let me ſee the Spirit of God.*

Anſw. Bleſſed are the Pure in Heart, they ſhall ſee God : But they that are not led by the Spirit of God, they are none of his.

Biſhop. *All Men have not the Spirit of God.*

Anſw. Yes, the Grace of God hath appeared unto all Men to profit withal, by which Salvation is witneſſed.

Biſhop. *Then Thieves may ſay, they have the Spirit of God, and cry out for Liberty of Conſcience, as you do.*

Anſw. That which reproves the Thief for ſtealing other Men's Goods is of God ; but that which leads them to ſteal other Men's Goods, (contrary to that of God in their Conſciences) is of the Devil, which Spirit we deny, and is in the Perſecutor.

Biſhop. *Had* Simon Magus *the Spirit of God ?*

Anſw. What was that in *Simon Magus* which did let him ſee his Errors, when he deſired the Apoſtles to pray to the Lord, that what he had ſaid might not be laid to his Charge?

Biſhop. *Had* Judas *the Spirit of God ?*

Anſw. The Meaſure of God's Spirit, which was in *Judas,* condemned him for betraying innocent Blood, or elſe he had not brought back again the thirty Pieces of Silver.

Biſhop. *Let me have the Liberty of my Conſcience.*

Anſw. We do not ſay any Thing againſt the Liberty of any Man's Conſcience, while they do not act againſt that of God in their Conſciences, which reproves them for Sin and Evil in them.

Biſhop. *Then my Conſcience tells me, that I muſt puniſh you, and that I do well in puniſhing you.*

Anſw. Then the Scripture is fulfilled upon thee, which ſaith, *He that killeth you ſhall think he doth God good Service* ; for that which would perſecute Men for Conſcience-ſake is not of God, but an evil Spirit, which rules in the evil Conſciences of the Children of Diſobedience. And Chriſt ſaid, *The Devil ſhall caſt ſome of you into Priſon :* And therefore the perſecuting Spirit ought not to have its Liberty, for Chriſt *came not to deſtroy Men's Lives, but to ſave them :* And therefore he ought to be ſet at Liberty in every Man's Conſcience, to lead them from Sin and Tranſgreſſion into Righteouſneſs, whereby they may be ſaved.

Biſhop. *I thought ſo : You would have the Liberty of your own, but you would not that I ſhould have the Liberty of my Conſcience.*

Anſw. Yea, we would that all Men might have the Liberty of a tender Conſcience, to obey that of God in a pure Conſcience, which makes manifeſt Sin, and reproves Evil, but that which would perſecute Men for Conſcience-ſake towards God, ought not to have its Liberty.

Biſhop. *But if you might have your Liberty,* you would corrupt *all your Neighbours about you.*

Anſw. Nay, we would not corrupt them, they are corrupted enough : Swearers, Liars, Whoremongers, are all corrupted.

Biſhop. *But you would be bad Examples to them to follow your Ways.*

Anſw. They have ſeventeen Prieſts among them to be Examples to them, if they be good and as they ought to be ; and what need they fear us, who are but two Men, if we had been as thou haſt ſaid. The People are their Hearers, and ought to follow the beſt Examples, whether it be us or them, or at leaſt that of God in their Conſciences, which reproves them for Sin and Evil, which we would have all Men to be guided by.

Biſhop. *The Devil is cunning : He will not appear in his own Shape to deceive People.*

Anſw. He appears in the Sheep's Clothing, which is the Words of the Prophets, Chriſt, and the Apoſtles, to deceive People while they put into
their

their Mouths; but if any will not put into their Mouths, then the Wolve's Nature appears in them, and they will bite with their Teeth at them, and caft them into Prifon, and perfecute or banifh them.

Bifhop.   *I thought you would have been better for the Punifhment, but you are rather worfe.*

Anfw.   We did think, that thou mightft have been in a better Mind, to confider what thou hadft done to us, and to our Families and Children, and to have given us thy Order to return to the Ifland again to them; but it feems thou art worfe indeed.

Bifhop.   *This is all your Difcourfe, both in the Ifland and here, but you will neither give Reafon nor take Reafon : I have nothing to fay to you, nor to do with you, neither will I confent that you fhall go to the Ifland again, if I can help it.*

Anfw.   We know our Duty.

Bifhop.   *What is that ?*

Anfw.   The Lord God of Heaven and Earth preferve and keep our Families in his Fear and Wifdom, and if we fhould not fee their Faces as in the Outward Appearance, it is for our faithful Teftimony to the Lord.   Therefore we can freely give them up into his Hands : And the Lord God of his Mercy forgive you our Perfecutors.

Bifhop.   *Pray not for us, pray for your felves.*

Anfw.   We are bound in Confcience to pray for our Perfecutors, and to blefs them that curfe us, and though thou wouldft have curfed us in thy Excommunication, we pray for thee, and deny thy Curfe.

Bifhop.   *I fee you neither give Reafon, nor take Reafon, I have nothing to fay to you : Go your Ways to Mr.* Fletcher, *and fee what he will fay to you.*

Anfw.   Thou art the Man we have waited fo long for, and feeing thou art refolved to perfuade the Earl againft us, what fhould we go to him for ?

Bifhop.   *He is the* Dean *of the Ifland, and it concerns him as well as me, and if you can fatisfy him, I'll be fatisfied.*

Then the Bifhop's Man directed him to the *Dean* in his Chamber.

2.   A DISCOURSE between the *Dean* of the *Ifle* of *Man,* and the faid *banifhed Perfons.*

Dean.   *Come in, Friends, what would you have from me ?*

Bifhop's Man.   They would have their Liberty.

Dean.   *So I fee they have, and much more they might have if they would be obedient to the Law.*

Anfw.   We are obedient to the Law, and for our Obedience to the Law, we are here perfecuted.

Dean.   *If you are obedient to the Law, what are you here for ?*

Anfw.   We are perfecuted for Confcience-fake by the Priefts, and now banifhed (contrary to the Law of the Nation) from our Wives, Children, Families, and Eftates.

Dean.   *Why fo ?*

Anfw.   Becaufe for Confcience-fake we cannot bow to their Way of Worfhip.

Dean.   *Oh, then you are not perfecuted, but punifhed becaufe you are not obedient to the Law.*

Anfw.   We are not difobedient to the Law, but are obedient to the Law of God and Man for the Lord's Sake.

Dean.   *Then your Peace is made, I'll affure you.*

Anfw.   Yea, we know that our Peace is made with God in Chrift.

Dean.   *But you muft obey the Law of the Land where you live.*

Anfw.   Whether we muft obey the Law of God, or the Law of the Land, judge thou.

Dean.   *Is not our Law the Law of God ?*

Anfw.   I deny that.

Dean.   *Then go your Ways : If you deny that, I have no more to fay to you.*

Anfw.   The

Anfw. The Law of God is *Light*, and teaches People to love Enemies, and to do unto all Men as they would be done unto ; but your Law is cruel, by which you perfecute the innocent People of God, who have not done you, nor any Body elfe any Harm, quite contrary to the Law of God, which faith, *Love Enemies.*

Dean. *You are not perfecuted, but punifhed becaufe you do not obey the Law.*

Anfw. We do obey the Law, and contrary to any juft Law are we perfecuted by you for Confcience-fake.

Dean. *You are not perfecuted for Confcience-fake, but punifhed for your Difobedience to the outward Law.*

Anfw. How far hath the outward Law Power over a Man ?

Dean. *The outward Law hath not Power but over the outward Man.*

Anfw. Then you ought not to perfecute us by your outward Law, for our Obedience to the Law of the inward Man, the Light of Chrift in a pure Confcience, which the outward Law hath nothing to do with, as thy felf haft faid.

Dean. *No more it has not.*

Anfw. Then we ought to be free ; for when we were fent for to Prifon, we obeyed and went, and we were banifhed ; fo we cannot be accufed of difobeying the outward Law : Notwithftanding all this we are ftill Sufferers, and that for our Confcience towards God.

Dean. *We meddle not with your Confcience at all : God forbid we fhould : But you muft obey the outward Law, and you may keep your Confcience to your felves.*

Anfw. Haft thou not read, that a Candle is not lighted to be put under a Bufhel ; and what befel to him that hid his Talent in the Earth.

Dean. *We do not defire you to put your felves under any Thing : Keep your Confcience to your felves ; but you muft obey the higher Power.*

Anfw. The higher Power we own, and for our Obedience to the higher Power, who is the Light and Life of Men, we are perfecuted.

Dean. *'I tell you it is not Perfecution, therefore call it not fo. ; but you are punifhed becaufe you will not be obedient to the outward Law, as the Apoftle commanded.*

Anfw. The Apoftle himfelf withftood the Powers that then were in the World, as much as any of the Apoftles did, that is to fay, in what they commanded that was contrary to God's Law.

Dean. *The Apoftle did not refift the outward Law.*

Anfw. For what then was he perfecuted ?

Dean. *Becaufe he was a Chriftian.*

Anfw. So are we perfecuted, becaufe we are Chriftians, who witnefs Chrift the Light to be fufficient to be our Teacher now, as he did then, for if he would have denied Chrift to be the Light of the World, he fhould not have been perfecuted, neither fhould we, if we would deny him to be our Light, which we intend not to do.

Dean. *You know not what you fay, nor what Perfecution is, therefore call it not fo.*

Anfw. Then you ought to let us alone, if you think that we know not what we fay, and pray to the Lord for the Converfion of us, for Perfecution hardeneth the Hearts of fuch People.

Dean. *But we would have you fubmit to the higher Power, as the Apoftle commanded.*

Anfw. The Apoftle faid, *Let every Soul be fubject to the higher Power, for Confcience-fake,* and that we own, and for our Obedience to the higher Power, which is the Power of God, we are perfecuted, as the Apoftle was for his Obedience to the fame Power.

Dean. *The Apoftle was not perfecuted for his difobeying the outward Law or Power, neither did he refift the outward Law as you do, but becaufe he was a Chriftian, was he perfecuted.*

Anſw. So are we by you perſecuted becauſe we are Chriſtians, *viz.* we conſeſs Chriſt manifeſt in us now, as he did confeſs in him then ; and it was becauſe the Apoſtle would not conform to the *Jews* Way of Worſhip, who were his Perſecutors, that he was perſecuted.

Dean. But they were dark, wicked, and Unbelievers.

Anſw. So are all Perſecutors in Darkneſs now, as they were then : We are now perſecuted by you who pretend your ſelves to be Chriſtians : So both they and you are found in one Spirit, perſecuting the Innocent for their good Conſcience, and their Obedience to the higher Power.

Dean. You do not obey the higher Power in Church and State ; the Law which we have here in England, *and you have in the* Iſle *of* Man.

Anſw. Yea, we are obedient to the higher Power both of Church and State, for the Church is in God, who is the Power, State, and Stay of all the true Churches built upon Chriſt, the Corner Stone, whom the wiſe Builders of the World did reject, who daubed with untempered Mortar, as you do now, who were the Perſecutors in all Ages, and upon which Stone the Perſecutors in all Ages have been broken to pieces, that ever fought againſt it.

N. B. Toward the End of the Conference, the *Counteſs* and alſo the *Biſhop* came into the *Dean's* Apartment.

Counteſs of *Derby. What is it then that you do hold to be the higher Power.*

Anſw. The Power of God, which crucified *Paul* to the World, and the World to him.

Counteſs. *It is true.*

Biſhop. What will you ſay of St. *James*, who ſays, *We muſt obey the King.* Will you make the King GOD.

Anſw. We do own the King's Power over the outward Man, but I hope you will allow the Power of God, who is King of Kings, to be above the King's Power.

Counteſs. It is true : The Power of God is above the King's Power.

Anſw. We own both, and for our Obedience to the Power of God, the higher Power, we are perſecuted, and do ſtand here this Day under Perſecution, deſiring an Order for our Return to our native Country.

*They return to
ſee their Families, but
are not ſuffered to land.*

Thus the Conferences ended, but the Sufferers obtained no Redreſs, nor could the Biſhop be prevailed upon to admit their Return, and through his Influence the Earl alſo was hardened againſt them. So they went into *Cumberland*, and then being determined at any Riſque to viſit their diſtreſſed Families, they took Shipping again for the Iſland, but before they could get on Shore, the Maſter of the Veſſel, *Pickering*, was ordered not to ſuffer them to land, ſo they were detained on board till the 1ſt of *September*, when the Maſter ſent a Petition to the Biſhop, requeſting that they might go on Shore till he was ready to return, and then, if required, he would carry them back to *England*, whereunto the Biſhop anſwered thus,

" **I** AM content that the *Quakers* mentioned be ſecured on Shore, till the
" Return of the Veſſel, upon Security given by the Owner of the Veſſel,
" and by the *Quakers*, for their Return upon his Departure from the Iſland.

" ISAAC *Soder* and *Man.*"

*Set on Shore
by the Biſhop's
Leave.
Put again on
Board.*

Upon this they were ſet on Shore, and continued at Home about a Month, till the Veſſel being ready to ſail, a Soldier was ſent to fetch them to *Ramſey*, where they were kept till the 1ſt of *October*, and then put on Board by two Soldiers, *William Callow's* Wife and Relations taking their Leave of him with Tears. The Maſter of the Veſſel alſo wept, compaſſionating their Condition, and ſaid to *William's* Wife, *Fear not, your Huſband is an honeſt Man : We will live and die together, and he ſhall want for nothing that I have or can do for him :* So he put to Sea, but the Wind proving contrary, brought them back

to *Douglas* in the Iſland, where they lay two or three Days, during which Time one *Qualtrop* an Attorney took Poſſeſſion of their Eſtates, and made an

Inventory of all they had, both real and perſonal, by Virtue of the following
Order, *viz.*

" *The* 27*th of* July, 1666.

" I N Purſuance of my Honourable Lord's Order, that the Eſtates, as well
" real as perſonal, of the ſeveral Perſons within this Iſle, who ſtand con-
" victed for embracing and following the *Heretical Doctrine* of the Sect com-
" monly called *Quakers*, are forfeited, and do accrue and belong to his Lord-
" ſhip : You are according to your ſaid Order to repair to the ſaid reſpective
" Perſons, now in Poſſeſſion of any ſuch Eſtate, Goods, or Chattels, and take
" Security from them for the true Payment of the Yearly Rent reſerved upon
" every ſuch Eſtate, and alſo to take good Security to render a true and
" perfect Account to his Lordſhip, his Heirs and Aſſigns, of the Yearly
" Profits of ſuch Eſtate or Eſtates, at any Time or Times, when the ſame
" ſhall be required.

Order for ſuch Seizure.

To Mr. Qualtrop *his Lordſhip's Attorney.*

" ISAAC *Soder* and *Man*
" HENRY NOWELL
" RICHARD STEVENSON
" JOHN CHRISTEN
" RICHARD TYLELERLY."

On the 5th of *October* they ſet ſail again, and next Day arrived at *Newhaven*, from whence *W. Callow* went into *Lancaſhire*, and made Application
again to the Earl, but found no Relief ; wherefore he repreſented his Caſe to the
Duke of *York*, and to Prince *Rupert*, and obtained from the Prince his Letter
to the Earl of *Derby*, *viz.*

Landed at Newhaven.

W. Callow *returns to London.*

Whitehall, *the* 18*th of* December, 1666.

" *My Lord,*

" T H E R E is one *William Callow*, an ancient Tenant of your Lordſhip,
" in the *Iſle* of *Man*, is now, it ſeems, turned *Quaker*, and for that
" Reaſon baniſht the Country : I am deſired by another of that Profeſſion,
" whom I knew to be a faithful and Loyal Subject to his Majeſty in the Time of
" the late War, to intreat with you for the ſaid *Callow* ; he aſſuring me, that
" he is a quiet, inoffenſive Perſon in every Thing, ſave in the Matter of his
" Religion, and though I would not be an Advocate for any dangerous un-
" peaceable Perſon, yet in ſuch an Inſtance I am induced to give your Lord-
" ſhip this Trouble, the Man himſelf appearing to me not likely to be dan-
" gerous, and alſo expreſſing with as much Reſpect and Reverence toward
" your Lordſhip, as his Profeſſion will give him leave : If there be no more
" in it than being a *Quaker*, I do preſume your Lordſhip may be inclined to
" reſtore him and his Family to their ancient Poſſeſſions, and that you may
" pleaſe to do ſo, is the Reaſon I give your Lordſhip this Trouble, who am

A Letter from Prince Rupert to the Earl of Derby.

" *Your Lordſhip's faithful Friend and Servant*

" RUPERT."

To this Letter of the *Prince* the Earl returned this Anſwer, *viz.*

" *May it pleaſe your Highneſs,*

" I H A D the Honour to receive a Letter from your Highneſs, by the
" Hands of a *Manks Quaker*, wherein your Highneſs is pleaſed to inti-
" mate your Command to me, that he ſhould be permitted to return to the
" *Iſle* of *Man*, from whence he ſtands baniſhed (with others becauſe they are
" *Quakers*) by the Laws of that Place : I make bold to inform your High-
" neſs,

The Earl's *Anſwer.*

" nefs, that there is now in the Ifland not one * *Quaker* or diffenting Perfon
" of any Perfuafion from the Church of *England*, and I humbly conceive your
" Highnefs, for that one Man's Concern, would not have that Place endan-
" gered to be infected with *Schifm* or *Herefy*, which it might be liable to, if
" *Quakers* fhould be permitted to refide there.   Having given your Highnefs
" this Account, I fhall now detain your Highnefs no longer from your more
" ferious Affairs.   I fhall only add that I am

" *Your Highnefs's moft humble Servant*

" D E R B Y."

While *William Callow* was thus bufied at *London* in folliciting for Liberty
to return Home, he received a Letter from his Wife, dated the 19th of the
Eleventh Month 1666, relating that fhe, and her Sifter *Jane Chriften*, *Mary
Callow*, and his Daughter *Anne Callow*, were Prifoners in *Caftle-Peel*, where
they had been five or fix Weeks, and that all their Eftates, real and perfonal,
were feized ; that *William*'s Father faid, *he would fell the Land*, and that the
Servants were about to go away and leave the Houfe, and that, fhe heard,
the Attorney would fhortly come and take away the Goods ; that both

*The impri-
foned Women
being with
Child peti-
tion the Bi-
fhop for Leave
to go Home.*
fhe and *Jane Chriften* were with Child, and that they had writ to the Bifhop
for Leave to return to their Houfes till the Spring, and then return to Prifon,
they not having wherewith to fubfift there in Winter, nor Neceffaries for Perfons in their Condition, but that the Bifhop had returned a fhort and rough
Anfwer thus,

Caftle-Town, *the 15th of* December 1666.

*The Bifhop's
rough Anfwer.*
" I F upon Releafement they put in Security to promife to come to the Ser-
" vice, and conform to the Order of the Church, and all fuch as are
" excommunicated to acknowledge their Schifms, and receive Abfolution, I
" fhall fo far prefume upon my † Lord's Favour as to grant them Liberty,
" otherwife I have no Power to meddle with them, they being my Lord's
" Prifoners, and if they mifcarry in their Health or Lives, it is wholly im-
" putable to their own wilful Difobedience, and they muft be accounted Mur-
" derers of themfelves, and this is all I can fay to them.

" I s a a c *Soder and Man*."

ANNO 1667.   Both the *Earl* and *Bifhop* continuing thus inflexible, *William
Callow*, moved with the hard Eftate of his Wife and Family, refolved to go
again to the Ifland.   His Motives for fo doing, and his Ufage there, are expreffed in the following Paper of his own writing, directed

" *To the* Earl *of* D E R B Y.

*W. Callow's
Letter to the
Earl of Der-
by.*
" H AV I N G formerly fhewed unto thee my Condition of Imprifonment
" and Banifhment from thy Ifland (about three Years and three Months
" at Times) from my Wife and fmall Children, for Confcience-fake, and
" though often with thee, could not have thy Order for my Return into the
" Ifland again : Therefore being in the North of *England*, and hearing that
" my Wife was in Prifon, and had been a long Time in the Winter Seafon of
" Froft and Snow, and by Reafon of the Cold, and fhe being with Child and
" likely to die, I was perfuaded to adventure to fee her, although it fhould
" coft me my Life, and the fame Day that I came Home, (when I found my
" Wife in a weak Condition) I was fent for to Prifon by Order from the
" Bifhop,

* This was a Miftake, there being three Women *Quakers* then in Prifon on the Ifland.
† The Earl of *Derby*.

" Bifhop, and after feven Days was put on board a *Scotch* Veffel, and fent to
" *England.* And now I appeal unto that of God in thee, who will let thee fee
" and know the Eftate of my weak Family, who by Reafon of my Banifh-
" ment, and my Wife's Imprifonment, (our Eftates being feized on for thee)
" are much deftroyed, and fhe and the Children likely to fuffer for Want,
" well knowing that it is in thy Power to relieve us, and to reftore me to
" them, that I may be helpful for their Relief; for if I have done any Thing
" worthy of Bonds or Imprifonment, let me fuffer in my own Country, that
" we may fuffer Want all together, if it muft be fo, I with them, and they
" with me, but rather that I might be helpful to them. Thefe Things being
" but reafonable, and it being in thy Power to grant thefe my Requefts, I
" hope thou wilt not always harden thy Heart, as *Pharaoh* did againft the
" Children of *Ifrael,* and would not let them go to their own Land, which
" the Lord had given them, until the Lord by his Plagues and Judgments did
" force him to let them go : Though (for all my hard Ufage) I do not defire
" that that fhould come upon thee, but knowing that the Lord is juft, and
" will in his own Time hear the Cry of his Elect, and of the Widows,
" Fatherlefs, and Orphans : And if that be the Faft which the Lord hath
" chofen, to loofe the Bands of Wickednefs, to undo the heavy Burdens, and
" let the Oppreffed go free, and to break every Yoke : And if it be ac-
" ceptable to the Lord to vifit the Widows in their Diftrefs, furely he will
" not take it well from thee, or thofe who make them Widows and Father-
" lefs. So left any Thing otherwife than what is good fhould come upon
" thee, thou mayft in Time before it be too late prevent it, by granting our
" reafonable Requeft, by eafing us that are oppreffed under thee : So no more
" but that I wait for thy Anfwer, who am a Well-wifher to thee in Soul and
" Body, even thy everlafting Welfare.

The 9th of the Seventh
Month 1667.   " WILLIAM CALLOW."

The *Scotch* Veffel in which he was fent away fet him on Shore at *Liverpool* *The Earl re-*
in *Lancafhire,* whence he went to the Earl of *Derby*'s Houfe, and laid his Cafe *jects him and*
before him, but the *Earl* turned the deaf Ear to his Requefts, and told him, *his Letter.*
If he would not conform, he fhould not go to poifon his Ifland. He would at the
fame Time have given to the *Earl* the aforefaid Paper of his State, but he
refufed to receive it.

ANNO 1668. The cruel Ufage and Banifhment of the four Women *Women's Ba-*
Quakers, who were remaining on the Ifland, is expreffed in the following *nifhment again*
Letter written by *Evan Chriften* to *William Callow,* who was then at *London, viz.* *expreffed in*

" *My dear Brother,*

" IN the Covenant of Light and Life doth my Soul entirely falute thee, and *Evan Chrif-*
" thefe are to inform thee of the fad Paffages that our Friends have been *ten's Letter*
" put in to the *Ifle* of *Man,* and what Perfecution they have fuffered by the *to William*
" Bifhop and Soldiers there. *Firft,* Thy Wife being fick, and lying in Bed, *Callow.*
" *Hugh Cloven* and *Mungo Hatley,* two Soldiers, came with an Order from the
" Bifhop to thy Houfe, to bring thy Wife to Prifon, and all the reft of our
" Friends, and if in cafe they would not willingly go at their Demands, to
" call to Captain *Afcough,* being the Captain of the Parifh, that he fhould
" raife the Parifh to affift the Soldiers to bring two fickly Women out of their
" Beds, with two more, to Prifon, and they alfo faid, that their Order was
" from the Bifhop to take them with them to Prifon, though they fhould die
" by the Way : And coming firft to thy Houfe, thy Wife being in Bed,
" fweating and very weak, *Hugh Cloven* took hold of her by the Arm, and
" *Mungo Hatley* took her by the other Arm, and attempted to pull her out
" of the Bed, whereupon the Children all cried out, and feveral Parifhioners,
" that came with the Soldiers to affift them, alfo wept exceedingly to behold
" their Cruelty towards her, however at that Time they were ftopt in the

" Proceedings, and fo went to *Ramfey*, and the next Day came again to thy
" Houfe, and took thy Wife inhumanly from thy Houfe to Prifon, and my
" Mother alfo, who is between feventy and eighty Years of Age, who was
" not able to go two Miles from her Houfe this two Years or more, and
" they had taken all the Goods that fhe had long fince. Then the faid
" Soldiers came to *Jane Chriflen*'s Houfe, although her Hufband be a con-
" formable Man, and did the like to her, and fhe faid to them, *What fhall
" I do with my fucking Child ?* The Soldiers anfwered, *We care not if the
" Dogs eat him.* So they took my Mother and thy Wife, and her youngeft
" Child about ten Months old, and *Mary Callow*, all thefe they carried to
" *Ramfey* that Day, and the next Day to *Kirk-Michael*, and the third Day to
" *Peel Caftle* Prifon, which was, as we account it, fixteen Miles. So being
" there one Night, the Conftable of the Caftle came next Day with an Order
" from the Bifhop to fend them back again to *Ramfey*, which accordingly was
" done by the fame Soldiers, who delivered them to Captain *Afcough*, where
" they were detained feveral Weeks, till *George Pickering*'s Veffel was ready,
" and *Alice Coward* being there before them to be banifhed with them, although
" her Hufband was and is a conformable Man, the faid *Afcough* fearched her,
" and took from her 40 *s.* in Money, and gave her 10 *s.* back : And when
" the Veffel was ready, Captain *Afcough* brought them to the Boat, and the
" Children being with them weeping, thy Wife would have taken her Children
" with her, but the faid Captain took them by Violence from her, and alfo
" faid, that the Bifhop had given Orders to take their Clothes from them if
" they would not pay their Fees ; and fo the Boat being afhore, he forced
" them all on Board, and put to Sea, and fo left the four Children weeping
" and mourning on the Sea-fhore, only let thy Wife take her youngeft
" Child with her, and left the other four without Father or Mother ; and
" alfo banifhed *Jane Chriflen* and her youngeft Child, and left her other
" five Children behind her ; alfo banifhed my Mother of the Age aforefaid,
" and *Mary Callow*, and on the 13th of the Second Month (called *April*) 1668,
" they landed at *Whitehaven*, and fo with the Remembrance of our dear Love
" to thee in that which changes not, I reft

" *Thy truly loving Brother*

" EVAN CHRISTEN."

Soon after the Banifhment of thefe Women, the Bifhop caufed a Publication
to be made in every Steeple-houfe in *Garfefden*, three feveral Firft-days, that
whofoever would come and compound for *William Callow*'s Eftate, he and his
Commiffioners would give them an Affurance of it for ever.

The banifhed Perfons having continued a confiderable Time in *England*, the
Juftices of the Peace in *Cumberland* iffued a Warrant for fending them back to
the *Ifle* of *Man*, a Copy of which is as follows, *viz.*

" *Cumberland* fs.

" WHEREAS Information is given unto us, that *William Callow* and
" *Anne* his Wife, and *Margaret* his Daughter, *Jane Chriflen* and *Evan*
" her Son, *Alice Coward* and *Katharine* her Daughter, and *Mary Callow*, all
" Inhabitants of the *Ifle* of *Man*, have been lately brought over into this
" County, whereby they being brought over from their Eftates, they may
" be a Charge to the fame, and it not appearing, that there hath been
" any legal Proceeding againft them or any of them to prohibit them from
" their faid Habitations : Thefe are in his Majefty's Name therefore to require
" you and every of you, that you fee the Parties above-named put on Board
" and fhipped, to be reconveyed to the faid Ifland, where their Habitations
" are as abovefaid, in fome *Manks* Veffel or other by the firft Opportunity, and
" alfo that you give Notice to the Mafters and Owners of the Veffels belonging

" longing to the Port of *Newhaven*, that they for the future forbear to bring
" any such Paſſengers over, for which they cannot give a good Account of
" their legal Paſſage into the ſaid County, and hereof you are not to fail, as
" you and every of you will anſwer the Contrary at your Peril.   Given under
" our Hands and Seals the 15th of *March*, in the 21ſt Year of the Reign of
" our Sovereign Lord King *Charles the Second*, &c. 1668.

To all and every the Conſtables   " JOHN LAMPLUGH.
  of the Pariſh of St. Bees,
  and eſpecially the Conſtables   " EDWARD STANDLY."
  of Whitehaven.   *Theſe.*

ANNO 1669. Purſuant to the aforeſaid Warrant, on the 13th of the   *Landed again*
Month called *May*, *William Callow* and his Wife, with *Jane Chriſten*, and their   *at Douglas.*
two young Children returned, and were landed about ten next Morning at
Douglaſs in the Iſland.   Soon after their Landing a Cuſtom-houſe Officer,
with a Soldier, came and ſearched them for Letters and Books, and then
taking the Owner of the Veſſel with them, went to the *Governour* about ſix
Miles diſtant, and returned in the Night with the following Order, *viz.*

"   FORASMUCH as there hath been a legal Proceeding againſt   *Order to the*
"   *William Callow* and *Alice* his Wife, and *Jane Chriſten*, all of the fac-   *Shipmaſter*
"   tious Sect called *Quakers*, for their Continuance beyond the Seas out of this   *again to tranſ-*
"   Iſland, according to my Honourable Lord's Order, which for a Seaſon   *port them.*
"   hath been effected, but lately being given to underſtand, that one *John*
"   *Chriſtian* of *Ramſey* hath brought the ſaid Perſons into this Iſle : I do
"   therefore ſtrictly require you that the ſaid Perſons be put on Board by you,
"   and the Aſſiſtance of Conſtable *Quail*, in the Boat or Ship of the ſaid *John*
"   *Chriſtian*, and there to continue until he doth again tranſport the ſaid Per-
"   ſons out of this Iſle again to ſome other Country, according to former
"   Order made to that End. Mr. Water-Bayliff *Cannel* and his Cuſtomers,
"   are to take great Care that they ſuffer no ſuch Perſons to be landed for the
"   future : Alſo while theſe Perſons do reſide in the Iſle, no Perſon or Perſons
"   is to be admitted to talk with them, or in any wiſe to come in their Company.

To Water-Bayliff *Cannell, and*
  all Officers and Soldiers to   " HENRY NOWELL."
  give Aſſiſtance to ſee this Or-
  der put in Execution.

In Conſequence of this Order, they took *William Callow*, his Wife, and   *Taken out of*
Siſter, out of their Beds, and put them on board the Ship again in ſuch an   *their Beds and*
Hurry, that the Women were obliged to take their Children naked in their   *hurried on*
Aprons, crying through the Streets in the Night : Being put on Board, a   *Shipboard.*
Watch was appointed to keep them there, and when *Jane Chriſten*'s Huſband,
and other of their Relations, came next Day to ſee them, they were driven
away and not ſuffered to ſpeak to them. About Sun-ſet the Veſſel ſet ſail, and
arrived on the 18th of the ſame Month at *Dublin*, where they continued till   *Arrived at*
the 24th, when the Lord-Mayor of that City made the following Order, *viz.*   *Dublin.*

"   WHEREAS Complaint is made before and by ſome of the Al-   *Order of the*
"   dermen of this City, and others Inhabitants of this City, that there   *Mayor of*
"   hath been landed here ſeveral Perſons brought into this City out of the   *Dublin to*
"   *Iſle* of *Man*, viz. *William Callow* and *Anne* his Wife, and *Jane Chriſten*, all   *carry them*
"   Inhabitants of the ſaid Iſland, without their own Conſents, contrary to the   *again to the*
"   Law and the Privilege of the Subjects, without any legal Proceeding   *Iſland.*
"   againſt them ; and foraſmuch as the ſaid Perſons ought rather to live in
"   the ſaid Iſland upon their own Eſtates than to be burthenſome to his
                                            " Majeſty's

ISLE of
MAN.
1669.

" Majesty's Subjects here, and that if they committed Crimes worthy of Ba-
" nishment, they ought not to be continued here in this Kingdom, unless by
" legal and special Order. These are therefore in his Majesty's Name to will
" and require you forthwith to put on Board all and every the said Persons back
" for the aforesaid Island, either on board the Ship called the *Trinity* of *Ram-*
" *sey*, or some other Vessel bound for the said Island, the Master whereof is
" hereby required to carry them over, and not to bring them back into this
" Kingdom without their own Consents as aforesaid, and hereof you may not
" fail. Dated in the City of *Dublin* the 24th Day of *May* 1669.

To all or any of the Constables in
the City of Dublin, *or the*
Liberties thereof.

" John Forrest,

" Mayor of *Dublin.*"

Hard Passage.

According to this Order, on the 13th of the Month called *June*, they took
Shipping again for the Island on board a Vessel prest to carry them, whereof
John Christian was Master. The Wind being contrary they were five Days at
Sea, during which Time the Women suffered much for Want of Provisions
and Necessaries, *William Callow*'s Wife being with Child, and near the Time
of her Delivery: At length being come near the Island, the Master put the
Women on Shore in his Boat, and the Vessel put in the next Day, being the
18th, at *Ramsey*. The Bishop and Governour being informed of their Arri-
val, ordered a Watch to prevent *William Callow*'s landing, and on the 25th
sent Soldiers to carry the Women again on Board. Accordingly the Soldiers
that Night took *Jane Christen* by Violence from her Husband and Children,
and put her on Board, and then, taking the Master of the Vessel with them,

The Ship-
master's Com-
passion, and

The Bishop's
Cruelty.

went to the Governour at *Castle-Peel*. The Master represented to the Governour and the Bishop, the weak Condition of the Women, and what they had
suffered at Sea, and the Danger which the hurrying them on Board again must
needs expose them to; but the Bishop, unmoved at their distressed Case, sent
by a Messenger an Order to raise the Parish People to carry *William Callow*'s
Wife to *Ramsey*, and put her on Shipboard: The Messenger returning told
the Bishop, that he found her in a weak Condition, and for ought they knew
in Labour: The Bishop nevertheless repeated his Order, and sent Soldiers
again to the House with a strict Charge to take and put her on Shipboard:
The Soldiers took nine or ten Persons, Men and Women, with them, left
she should be delivered, or miscarry by the Way, and coming to the Bedside,
the Soldiers bade her get up and go with them, swearing that they had Orders
from the Bishop, if she would not go to carry her in a Cart, or cross an
Horse's Back, adding, that if she would say she was in Labour, the Bishop
ordered them to leave her at Home a Day or two, and then put her on Board.

Unchristian
Barbarity.

The Woman answered, *She was not well, and knew not her Hour.* So they
took her Children out of Bed from her, and then scarce giving her Time to
put her Clothes on, hurried her away to *Ramsey*. Three of the Neighbours,
who refused to assist in this Inhumanity, were by the Bishop's Order sent to
Prison. The Soldiers having put her on Board, returned to the House (after
they had rifled her Pocket of four Shillings) where they found a Box of Clothes
and Linen, which they took, leaving the poor Woman not one Rag of Linen
or any Thing else but what she had on, saying, they had seized her Goods by

Shipt in an
open Vessel.

Landed in
Lancashire.

the *Bishop*'s Warrant. They were detained on Board in an open Boat, half-
deckt, and that so badly, that when it rained they could not sit dry. On the
6th of the Month called *July* they put to Sea, and next Day landed at *Peel* in
Lancashire: Upon Notice of their Landing, two Justices of the Peace made an
Order to send them back again in the following Form, *viz.*

" *Lancashire*

ISLE of
MAN.
1669.
*Order of two
Justices for
sending them
back again.*

" *Lancashire* ſs.

" WHEREAS Complaint is made to us whoſe Names are ſubſcribed,
" two of his Majeſty's Juſtices of the Peace for this County of *Lan-*
" *caſter*, that there hath lately been landed at *Peel* within the Pariſh of *Dalton*
" in this County, ſeveral Perſons late Inhabitants within the *Iſle* of *Man*, that
" is to ſay, *William Callow* and *Anne* his Wife, and *Jane Chriſten*, who have
" all Eſtates within the ſaid Iſland whereon to ſubſiſt, but have none elſewhere,
" and are likely to be burdenſome to his Majeſty's Subjects in theſe Parts, if
" they ſhall be permitted to ſettle, and have been baniſhed out of the ſaid
" Iſland, the Place of their Habitations, without any legal Proceedings, as is
" by them alledged, or doth any Way appear to us, and not ſent or con-
" fined to any certain Place of Baniſhment, by any legal Authority, but
" turned out as Vagabonds to the wide World, to the Scandal of the Laws
" and his Majeſty's Government. Theſe are therefore in his Majeſty's Name
" to require you and every of you, that you put them on board the Ship called
" the *Trinity* of *Ramſey*, which Veſſel brought them hither, and is now at *Peel*
" aforeſaid, the Maſter whereof is hereby required to receive them, and to
" convey them over to the ſaid Iſland, which if he refuſe to do, then you are
" to ſtay the Ship, and bring the ſaid Maſter before us forthwith to anſwer
" his Contempt, and farther to do and receive as to Juſtice appertaineth.
" Fail not hereof at your Peril. Given under our Hands and Seals the 10th
" Day of *July*, in the 21ſt Year of the Reign of our ſovereign Lord *Charles*
" *the Second* over *England*, &c. 1669.

*To the Conſtables within the
Hundred of* Lequeſdale, *and
eſpecially to the Conſtable of*
Dalton, *and to every of
them.*

" MATTH. RICHARDSON.

" WILLIAM KIRBY."

Purſuant to this Order, on the 6th of the Month called *Auguſt*, *William Cal-* *Returned to
the Iſland, but
not ſuffered to
land.*
low and *Jane Chriſten* were put on Board : (*Anne Callow*, then in Childbed,
being left behind) At the ſame Time *Evan Chriſten* and *Alice Coward* were
put into another Veſſel : And on the 8th they all arrived at *Ramſey* on the
Iſland, but were not ſuffered to land, but kept Priſoners on Shipboard under a
Guard of two Men, Day and Night till the 1ſt of *September*.

While they lay on Board they were informed that *George Pickering*, who had *Uſeful Obſervations.*
been active and forward in tranſporting ſome of them, had loſt his Lading and
Money, and had his Ship much damaged in *Ramſey* Haven ; and that *Richard
Bell* the Owner, who had joined with the Biſhop in tranſporting *Alice Coward*,
had been caſt away on the Coaſt of *Wales*, and that the Veſſel, Men, and
Lading, had been all loſt. Theſe Diſaſters adminiſtred Occaſion to the Sufferers, conſcious of their own *Innocence*, to make ſuch Obſervations reſpecting
the Divine Juſtice on Perſecutors and their Agents, as probably any other Perſons in their Circumſtances would have made.

On the 1ſt of *September* the Governour ſent a Letter to Captain *Aſcough*, to *Order to tranſport* W. Cal-
low *to* Vir-
ginia.
ſend *William Callow* to him by a Soldier. In their Paſſage thither they came
to *Ramiſh* Way, where *Nowel* the Deputy-Governour dwelt : There lay a
London Ship at Anchor, called the *Tangier-Merchant*, bound for *Virginia* ; of
which *Ralph Harwood* was Maſter. This *Harwood*, meeting *Callow*, told him,
that he had Orders to tranſport him to Virginia : *William* replied, *that it was
contrary to Law ſo to do* ; and adviſed him *to do as he would be done by*, aſking
him, *whether he would be willing to be taken from his Wife and Children, and
Eſtate, without Law, and baniſht to another Country.* The Captain replied, *that
he would not meddle with him till he had been before the Governour.* So he was
had to the Governour's Houſe, and being brought into his Parlour, the following Conference paſt between them, *viz.*

ISLE of
MAN.
1669.

*Conference
betwixt* W.
Callow *and
the Gover-
nour.*

Governour. *How doſt thou ?*

W. C. I am pretty well.

Gov. *Art thou willing to go to* Virginia *?*

W. C. I have no Buſineſs there.

Gov. *But we will ſend thee thither.*

W. C. That is a Queſtion.

Gov. *But we will ſend thee.*

W. C. I deſire to know by what Law.

Gov. *By my Lord's Order.*

W. C. I deſire to be tried according to the Laws of this Place.

Gov. *Thou haſt been tried.*

W. C. I deny it : I was not.

Gov. *Thou haſt been baniſht often, and ſtill comeſt to trouble us and others, and thou art too long unpuniſht, but we will ſend thee far enough now.*

W. C. Send me as far as thou canſt : Thou canſt not ſend me from my God.

Gov. *Upon my Credit thou ſhalt go to* Virginia *with Captain* Harwood.

W. C. He has nothing to do with me until I be legally convicted, and proceeded with according to Law.

Gov. *Thou haſt been tried according to Law, and thou wouldſt not conform.*

W. C. I deny it : I was never tried by Law, nor never came into any Court to be convicted by Law.

Gov. *What I do I will anſwer it, and I have written an Order for Captain* Harwood *to take thee away to* Virginia, *and thee ſhalt go, upon my Credit.*

W. C. I do appeal to the Law of this Place to be tried by.

Gov. *Thou ſhalt go, and thy Appeal I deny* ; and then read the Order he had written.

W. C. I deny it : Thou haſt no Power to do it.

Gov. *What I do, I will anſwer it, and I will warrant him.*

W. C. Thy Warrant will ſtand him in little Stead out of this Place.

Gov. *If thou wilt conform to the Law thou mayſt be cleared.*

W. C. The Benefit of the Law I deſire, and if not of the Laws of this Place, I deſire the Benefit of the Laws of *England.*

Gov. *Thou ſhalt not.*

W. C. I make my Appeal to the higheſt Court in *England,* to the King and his Council, and if there had been a Parliament now ſitting, I would have made it to them alſo.

Gov. *I deny thy Appeal.*

W. C. I do call theſe Men to witneſs, that I do make my Appeal to the King and his Council, and my Cauſe is already before them, and I wait for their Anſwer.

Gov. *I deny it : I will not accept of it.*

W. C. If thou wilt not accept of it, but deny the King's Law to me : The Captain is a Subject ; I think he will not deny it, and tranſport me out of my Country, and from my Wife and Children, without legal Proceedings againſt me.

Captain. *Friend, I would have you ſubmit to the Governour, for I have a long Voyage to go, no leſs than a Thouſand Leagues.*

W. C. Haſt thou but a Thouſand Leagues to go ? That's not ſo far as *David* experienced, who ſaid, *that if he ſhould take the Wings of the Morning, and fly to the uttermoſt Parts of the Earth, the Lord's Hand would find him out.* And doſt thou think that he will not overtake thee, and find thee out at the End of a Thouſand Leagues ; yea he will, and reward thee according to thy Works, and the Cry of my Wife and ſix ſmall Children will be heard.

Gov. *Thou threatneſt the Captain.*

W. C. I do not threaten him : There is one that will reward him according to his Works, as he has in his juſt Judgments done to others before him ; for, *Curſed is he that parts Man and Wife.*

Gov. *Take him away, Soldiers, and put him on Shipboard.*

Two Soldiers took either of them an Arm, and haled him to the Boat, and then lifted him up on Shipboard ; when on Board, the Mafter and feveral of the Sailors were very kind to him, the Sailors refufing to go the Voyage if they carried him, faying, *they never heard of a Ship that carried* Quakers *againft their Will, that ever profpered :* Upon which the Mafter promifed them, that he would carry him no farther than *Ireland* ; and accordingly on the 2d of *September* he fet him on Shore about forty Miles North of *Dublin. William* went directly to *Dublin*, took Shipping, and was landed next Day at *White-haven.* About the fame Time *Evan Chriften* with his aged Mother, and *Alice Coward* alfo, arrived in *England* from the Ifle of *Whitehorn* in *Scotland*, whither they had been carried in a Fifhing-Boat, after long Confinement on board the Veffel which brought them back out of *Lancafhire* to the Ifland, as is before mentioned, where they were not fuffered to land.

ISLE *of* MAN. 1669.

He is by Force put on Shipboard. Seamen refufe to go the Voyage, and put him on Shore in Ireland.

Thus have we traverfed an almoft unparallel'd Series of Perfecution, carried on many Years together, by the arbitrary Power of an inexorable Prelate, againft a Chriftian and harmlefs People, for no other Caufe than the Exercife of pure Religion, and keeping of a Confcience void of Offence both toward God and Man.

The next Account we find of Sufferings in this Ifland, bears Date ANNO 1682. In this Year *Eleanor Stockdale*, being concerned to ex-hort the Inhabitants of *Douglas* to repent of the Evil of their Ways, was put into the Stocks, and after many Abufes caft into a Dungeon, and kept Prifoner eight Days : At the End of which, by Order of *Thomas Robinfon* a Magiftrate, and Prieft of that Town, fhe, with *Jane Hall* her Companion, were carried by two Soldiers of the Garrifon to a Veffel then lying there, to be tranfported ; but the Mafter of the Veffel, a *Scotchman*, refufed to receive them. Whereupon the Soldiers arrefted the Ship, and the Mafter and Mariners left it : But the Soldiers after fome Time departing, the Seamen returned and fet Sail, leaving the Women on Shore. The Soldiers took away from the faid *Eleanor* an Apron worth 5 s. 6 d.

Sufferings of E. Stockdale, *and* J. Hall.

ANNO 1683. *Robert Callow*, and the faid *Eleanor*, then his Wife, were profecuted in the Bifhop's Court for being married without a Prieft, on the 17th of the Month called *July* the faid *Eleanor* was committed Prifoner to the Fort of *Douglas*, and on the 21ft of the fame, the faid *Robert* was fent to *Peel-Caftle*, where he remained eighteen Days in Time of Harveft, to his great Prejudice, his Corn and Hay being in Danger of fpoiling. His Wife *Eleanor* remained in the Fort five Weeks, and then by Order of Bifhop *Leake* was removed to *Peel-Caftle*, where fhe was kept Prifoner eleven Weeks, and on the 8th of *November*, by Order of *Robert Heywood* Governour of the Ifland, was fent to *Ramfey* to be banifhed. She was pulled by Force out of her Huf-band's Arms at the Market Crofs in *Ramfey*, and thence dragged with Violence to the Boat (the Spectators much commiferating her Cafe) in order to be put on board a *Scotch* Veffel then in the Harbour , but the Shipmen hoifted Sail and left her : So fhe was carried back to *Ramfey*, and kept Prifoner about fourteen Months longer. On the 3d of the Month called *March* following, in the Night, fhe was taken out of her Bed, and carried by *Edward Curfey* a Cap-tain, and fome of his Company, to the Ship of *Martin Coltrup* then at Anchor in the Bay, and bound for *Warkinton* in *England*, but the Owner of the Veffel refufed to take her in, fo that between the Captain's Men pufhing her into the Ship, and the Seamen thrufting her off, fhe was much hurt : However at length they left her on Board, and the Ship failed ; but a contrary Wind bringing the Ship back to *Ramfey*, fhe was again fet on Shore. Three Days after fhe was carried on Board by Night, but the Ship was again driven back to the Harbour : The next Day and Night fhe was kept on Board with a Guard, and the Day following brought again on Shore ; and at Midnight carried on Board again, but the Wind being contrary was again fet on Shore : On the 17th fhe was put on Board again, and carried to *England*. On her landing there, *Richard Lamplugh*, a Juftice of the Peace in *Cumberland*, taking Notice

More Suffer-ings of Robert Callow, *and* Eleanor *his Wife.*

A Series of cruel Ufage of an inno-cent Woman.

ISLE of
MAN.
1684.

Eleanor Callow, *great with Child, imprisoned by Procurement of three Priests. Priests more cruel than Soldiers. Their Cruelty over-ruled by the Governour. Sent again to Prison with her sick Child. The Governour's angry Answer to a Constable.*

Imprisonment and Distress for Tithes.

Imprisonments.

Notice of the Illegality of the Proceeding againſt her, obliged the ſaid *Coltrup*, at the next Return of his Veſſel, to carry her back to the Iſland, where ſhe continued at Home with her Huſband twelve Weeks: After which

ANNO 1684. By the Procurement of three Prieſts, who bore great Sway in the Iſland, ſhe was again committed to *Peel-Caſtle*, being then great with Child. She petitioned the Prieſts for Liberty to ſtay at Home while in that Condition, but was denied, and continued ſeveral Months in Priſon till the Time of her Delivery drew nigh, when the Prieſts were again ſollicited on her Behalf, but they rigidly anſwered, *that ſhe might take a Bed in the Town for one Night, and return next Day to the Caſtle.* But the Soldiers of the Caſtle, more merciful than the Prieſts, repreſenting to the Governour the Weakneſs of her Condition, and her Petition on that Occaſion, he interpoſed his Authority, over-ruled the Cruelty of thoſe rigorous Eccleſiaſticks, and ſent her Home to her Huſband.

About half a Year after this, the Governour ſent both for her and her Huſband, and committed her again to *Peel-Caſtle.* She had at that Time her Child, about ſix Months old, ſick of the *Small-Pox:* This was repreſented by the Conſtable to the Governour, but he anſwered, that *She and her Friends had procured her Return to the Iſland contrary to his Order, and therefore he would not ſpare her, but ſhe ſhould either leave the Iſle, or live and die in Priſon.* Accordingly ſhe was ſent ſixteen Miles to Priſon, and obliged to take her ſick Child with her.

About this Time alſo, *Anne Callow* was committed to Priſon at *Ramſey,* and continued there about ſix Weeks for Tithes, and had afterward a Cow taken from her by Diſtreſs worth 19 s. Likewiſe *Robert Callow* and his Mother, for 20 s. demanded for Tithes, had Wheat and Hay taken from them to the Value of 2 l. 0 s. 9 d.

ANNO 1685. *Robert Callow* and *John Callow* were impriſoned in *Peel-Caſtle* for Tithes, at the Suit of *John Allen* Prieſt.

Having gone through the Account of Sufferings in this Iſland, we return to *England,* and proceed to relate the Occurrences of like Sort in the County of *Kent.*

George Fox being stoned by James Lancaster's wife, 1652
Drawing by Robert Spence, courtesy of Friends House Library, London.

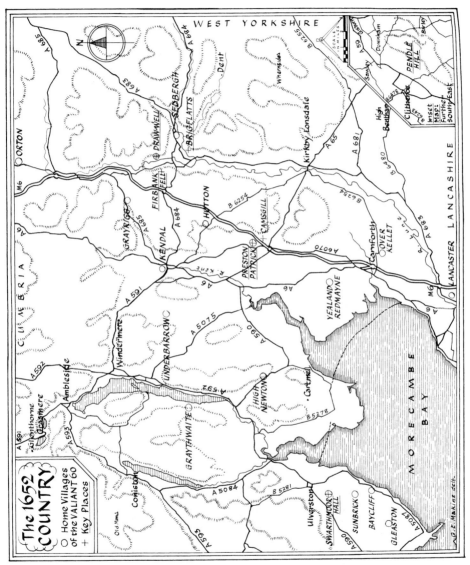

Courtesy of The Valiant Sixty by Ernest E. Taylor.

LANCASHIRE.

ANNO 1652.

*Many Abuses
of G. Fox.*

GEORGE FOX, preaching in this County, met with a Multitude of Abufes from the ignorant People, animated by defigning Priefts, whofe Intereft his Doctrine oppofed. He endured the Infults, Beatings, Stonings, Kickings, Railings, Revilings, and Contradictions of Sinners with Chriftian Patience and Magnanimity. The Tendency of his Preaching was to direct Men to the Guidance of the *Light* of *Chrift* in themfelves, the univerfal Teacher, which would prevent their being mifled by thofe who then affumed the Office of Minifters, and whom he boldly teftified againft as *Hirelings* and *Deceivers.* The Priefts, alarmed at fo daring an Attempt againft their Power and Profit, cried out with one Voice, like the *Jews* againft *Paul, Away with fuch a Fellow from the Earth, for it is not fit that he fhould live*; and, as if they had imitated the Perfecutors of the Protomartyr *Stephen,* when *they were not able to refift the Wifdom and the Spirit by which he fpake, then they fuborned Men which faid, We have heard him fpeak blafphemous Words.*

*His Trial at
Lancafter
Seffions.*

To anfwer this Charge, *George Fox* appeared at *Lancafter* Seffions, and forty Priefts all combined againft him. The Witneffes were a young Prieft, and two Priefts Sons ; thefe agreed in the general Accufation of *Blafphemy,* but in their Evidence of the fpecial Matter, and of the Words fpoken, they were confufed, and fo palpably contradicted by the Teftimony of many ferious and fubftantial Perfons who were prefent at the Meeting, where they pretended the Blafphemy was uttered, that his Oppofers were utterly foiled and went away afhamed :

*Many con-
vinced at his
Trial.*

While *George Fox,* having Liberty given him by the Juftices, declared the Teftimony of Truth with fuch Power and Efficacy, that many prefent were convinced, among whom were Juftice *Benfon* and the Mayor of *Lancafter* ; alfo *Thomas Briggs,* who became a faithful and zealous Minifter and Preacher of the Doctrine of Truth all his Life after.

The Priefts, thus difappointed, were very uneafy, and ufed their Endeavours to have perfuaded fome of the Juftices, and other Gentlemen of the County, to fign the following Petition, *viz.*

" To

*Quaker woman
on horseback.*

*Drawing by
Geoffrey Makins,
courtesy of* Margaret Fell:
Mother of Quakerism.

" *To the* Right *Honble the* Council *of* State.

" *The humble Petition of several* Gentlemen, Juſtices *of the Peace,*
" Miniſters *of the* Goſpel, *and* People, *within the County of* Lancaſter,
" *whoſe Names are ſubſcribed,*

" SHEWETH,

" THAT *George Fox* and *James Naylor* are Perſons diſaffected to Religion,
" and the wholſome Laws of this Nation, and that, ſince their coming
" into this Country, they have broached Opinions tending to the Deſtruction of
" the Relation of Subjects to their Magiſtrates, Wives to their Huſbands,
" Children to their Parents, Servants to their Maſters, Congregations to their
" Miniſters, and of a People to their God, and have drawn much People after
" them; many whereof (Men, Women, and little Children) at their Meetings
" are ſtrangely wrought upon in their Bodies, and brought to fall, foam at the
" Mouth, roar, and ſwell in their Bellies: And that ſome of them affirmed
" themſelves to be equal with God, contrary to the late Act, as hath been
" atteſted at a large Quarter Seſſions holden at *Lancaſter* in *October* laſt paſt,
" and ſince that Time acknowledged before many Witneſſes; beſides many
" other dangerous Opinions, and damnable Hereſies, as appears by a Schedule
" hereunto annexed, with the Names of the Witneſſes ſubſcribed.
" May it therefore pleaſe your Honours, upon the Conſideration of the
" Premiſſes, to provide, (as your Wiſdom ſhall think fit) that ſome ſpeedy
" Courſe may be taken for the ſpeedy ſuppreſſing of theſe Evils.

*A Petition
from the
Prieſts againſt
G. Fox and
J. Naylor.*

" *And your Petitioners ſhall ever pray, as in Duty bound.*"

To this Petition an Anſwer was written by *George Fox*, intituled, *Saul's*
Errand to *Damaſcus*, to which is a Preface, wherein the Caſe of this People at
that Time ſeems impartially related, *viz.*

*An Anſwer
thereto.*

" *To the* Chriſtian Reader.

" THESE are to let thee know, that the only wiſe God at this Time
" hath ſo by his Providence ordered it, in the North Parts of *Lanca-*
" *ſhire,* that many precious Chriſtians (and ſo for many Years accounted before
" the Nick-Name *Quaker* was heard of) have for ſome Time paſt forborn to
" concorporate in parochial Aſſemblies, wherein they profeſs themſelves to
" have gained little of the Knowledge of *Jeſus Chriſt*: And it is, and hath
" been upon their Hearts to meet often (and on the Lord's Day continually) at
" convenient Places, to ſeek the Lord their Redeemer, and to worſhip him in
" Spirit and in Truth, and to ſpeak of ſuch Things tending to mutual Edifi-
" cation, as the good Spirit of the Lord ſhall teach them, demeaning them-
" ſelves without any Offence given to any that truly fear the Lord.
" But true it is, that ſome Men, and Intereſts, of thoſe Parts, do take great
" Offence at them, and their Chriſtian peaceable Exerciſes; ſome, becauſe they
" have witneſſed againſt Pride and luxuriant Fulneſs, have therefore come
" armed with Swords and Piſtols (Men that never drew a Sword for the Intereſt
" of the Commonwealth of *England*, perhaps againſt it) into their Aſſemblies
" in Time of their Chriſtian Performances, and have taken him whom the
" Lord at that Inſtant had moved to ſpeak to the Reſt, and others of their
" Aſſembly, after they had haled and beaten them, and carried them bound
" Hand and Feet into the open Fields, in the Cold of the Night, and there
" left them to the Hazard of their Lives, had not the Lord of Life owned
" them, which he did in much Mercy. Others have had their Houſes broken
" in the Night, and entred by Men armed as aforeſaid, and diſguiſed, when

*The Preface to
that Anſwer.*

" they

LANCA-
SHIRE.
1652.

" they have been peaceably waiting upon God with their own and Neighbours
" Families ; and yet thefe humble perfecuted Chriftians would not (even in
" thefe Cafes of grofs and intolerable Affronts, acted equally againft the Peace of
" the Nation as againft them) complain, but expreffed how much, in Meafure,
" of their Mafter's Patience was given them, in breathing out their Mafter's
" gentle Words, *Father, forgive them, they know not what they do.* Who have
" at any Time born fuch an unheard of Perfecution with fo mild Spirits ?
" Only they in whom perfecuted Chrift dwells : Thefe poor Creatures know
" how their Mafter fared, and rejoice to fuffer with him, by whom alone they
" hope to be glorified, and are as well content to fuffer, as to reign with
" Chrift ; and yet a Neceffity lies upon us (if we will be the Lord's Difeiples)
" *to take up our Crofs daily, and follow him :* How is it then, that the Crown
" of Pride is fo long upon the Head of Perfecutors ? How is it that fuch Men
" fhould dare to divide the People of *England*, to trouble the *Council of State*,
" (in the Throng of Bufinefs concerning the Management and Improvement of
" the mighty Series of glorious Providence made out to this Infant Common-
" wealth) with fuch abominable Mifreprefentations of honeft, pious, peaceable
" Men, who defire nothing more than to glorify their God in their Genera-
" tion, and are and have been more faithful to the Intereft of God's People
" in the Nation, than any of the Contrivers of the Petition, as will eafily be
" made appear, if we may take for Evidence what they themfelves have often
" faid of the Parliament and Army, and their Friends and Servants, pub-
" lickly and privately ; and it is well known their Judgments are the fame,
" but that the Publication thereof will not fafely confift with the Enjoyment
" of their large Vicarages, Parfonages, and Augmentations, whereby they are
" lifted up above their Brethren, and exalt themfelves above all that are called
" God's People in thefe Parts.

" However, Reader, we need not fear, we hope the Lord will never fuffer
" that *Monfter* Perfecution again to enter within the Gates of *England*'s *White-*
" *hall.* They that fit in Council there know well enough, who it was that
" fo often affembled to confult how they might take *Jefus* by Subtilty and kill
" him. They were Men of no lower Condition than Chief Priefts, Scribes,
" and Elders of the People, and if ever thefe Petitioners fhould but appear
" before them to whom they have directed their Petition, my Heart deceives
" me if they be not accounted fuch.

" *Reader*, I would not *Preface* thee into a good Opinion of thefe fuffering
" Objects of fuch Men's Wrath ; but read their Paper here put into thy
" Hand, by them written upon the Occafion of this Petition, and feveral
" Snares and Temptations laid before them on purpofe to entrap them ;
" And if by them thou canft find Caufe to pity thefe oppreffed little Ones,
" have them in thy Remembrance when thou goeft to the Throne of Grace,
" where my Prayers fhall meet thine for them."

*The Fervour of
their Zeal.*

The fervent Zeal and earneft Concern many called *Quakers* in thofe Times
were under to declare the Truth they had received, conftrained them to feek
Opportunities for that Purpofe, either at the Clofe of the publick Worfhip,
before the People were difperfed, or at their coming out from thence : This
greatly offended the eftablifhed Teachers, who excited the worft of their
Hearers, on whom they have often the greateft Influence, to receive thofe
Meffengers with all Manner of defpiteful Ufage, as by the following Inftances
appears.

*Imprifonments
and grievous
Abufes of
many of this
People for
their publick
Teftimony.*

ANNIS 1654, 1655, 1656. *John Lawfon* of *Lancafter*, for preaching
to the People in the Steeple-houfe Yard at *Malpas* was let in the Stocks four
Hours, and afterward fent to the County Goal, where he was imprifoned
twenty three Weeks. At another Time for exhorting the People in the Steeple-
houfe at *Lancafter*, he was fent to Prifon till the Affizes, where he was fined 20 *l.*
and for Non-payment of that Fine was continued in Prifon above a Year after.

Edward

Edward Hulley, attempting to exhort the People affembled in the publick Worfhip-houfe at *Pately-Briggs*, was dragged out of the Place, and fo cruelly kickt on the Head and Belly, that it was thought they had killed him.

Henry Wood, for afking a Prieft, *Whether he did witnefs the Truth of what he taught?* was beaten backward. by the rude People, one of whom ftruck him fuch a Blow on the Face, that the Blood came out at his Eye : After which he was fent to Prifon and lay there thirteen Weeks.

Anne Kennebie, for fpeaking a few Words to the People in their publick Affembly at *Liverpool*, was fent to Prifon. The Prieft of that Place went to the Prifon to fee and deride her, while others with him beat and abufed her.

William Simfon and *Leonard Addifon*, fpeaking to the Prieft at *Blackburne* after Sermon, the People fell upon them, pluckt them by the Hair, and beat them cruelly.

For the like Caufes, *Jeremiah Tomlinfon, George Cowfon, John Moone, Edward Moone, Richard Cubbam, Thomas Hill, Benjamin Boult, Agnes Mackreath, Simon Whitehead, Peter Leatherhead, James Fletcher, William Gibfon, William Dewfberry, Thomas Hutton, Thomas Curwen, Walter Myers, Mary Clayton, Anne Clayton, Mary Howgill, Jane Afhburner, John Driver, James Simonfon, Thomas Rawlinfon, Richard Roper, Richard Waller, Thomas Salthoufe,* and *Leonard Fell*, were at feveral Times committed to Prifon in this County ; for as they efteemed it their. Chriftian Duty to exhort both Priefts and People to Repentance and Amendment of Life, they difcharged that Duty through many Afflictions, knowing that *as the Sufferings of Chrift abounded* in them, *fo their Confolation alfo abounded in him.* 2 Cor. i. 5.

The Superftition of thofe Times made it penal to travel but a few Miles on the Firft-day of the Week, though to a religous Meeting, for which Caufe *John Tompfon, William Tompfon, Eleanour Parkinfon, John Lawfon,* and *Thomas Bond,* had their Horfes feized and taken from them to the Value of 20*l.* Alfo *Peter Lawford,* for permitting a Meeting at his Houfe, was committed to Prifon. *Richard Weaver,* riding to a Meeting, had his Mare taken from him, and for complaining of the Injury done him to the Mayor of *Prefton,* was by him fent to Prifon.

Richard Hubberthorn and others were taken out of a Meeting, bound Hand and Foot, and fo carried and laid in the open Fields in a cold Winter Night, to the Hazard of their Lives. *Ralph Barnes* and *John Barnes* were taken from a Meeting at *Warrington* Heath, and committed to *Lancafter* Goal.

The diftinguifhing Plainnefs of this People in Habit and Deportment expofed them to many Abufes from the *Malice* of the *Priefts,* the *Ignorance* of the *People,* and the *Pride* of *fome in Authority,* of which the following Inftances are obfervable :

Many other Abufes thro' Malice and Ignorance.

James Smithfon, going to a Meeting, met his Landlord, formerly High-Sheriff, who, becaufe *James* did not pay him the ufual Homage of the Hat, rode furioufly to him, ftruck him till his Staff broke, and afterward beat him with his Hands. At another Time as they occafionally met, he afked *James, Whether no Honour was due to a Landlord?* He replied, *I do honour thee with my Rent when due.* Upon which he pluckt off his Hat, and ftruck him about the Head and Face till the Blood ran.

Edward Hulley, and others, paffing from a Meeting, the ufual Footway through the Grounds of *Henry Mugtroyde,* he ftopt them, and when they alledged, that *It was an Highway,* he anfwered, *'Tis fo to others, but fhall not be fo to you,* and forced them to go back. He alfo knockt down the faid *Edward,* and gave him many Blows over his Head and Face.

Anne Beck was ftruck to the Ground by the faid *Henry Mugtroyde* and his Son ; and at another Time, as fhe paffed the Streets exhorting the People, fhe was laid violent Hands on, put into the Stocks, fet in the Dirt, and there left.

As feveral of this People were returning from the interring of a Child of *John Sagar* of *Marfden,* they were affaulted and beaten with a Hedge-ftake by one *Edward Kipper,* who in his Fury threatned *to kill the firft of*

LANCA-
SHIRE.
1654,
1655, *and*
1656.

of them he met. In like Manner *John Liddell,* paffing on the Highway, was knockt down by a barbarous Ruffian who met him.   Alfo *Oliver Atherton* was ufed with like Barbarity as he was quietly travelling on the Road.

At a Meeting near *Zanchy,* where *Elizabeth Leavens* was preaching, a rude Company, headed by an Elder of their Church, pulled her down and abufed her much.   As fhe and others were going Home the People fell upon them, and grievoufly beat *William Birchall, James Challoner, Laurence Johnson,* and *James Laffal.*

Rife of thefe Abufes.

Thefe Injuries and Abufes were the Effect of a falfe and ignorant Zeal for *Religion,* which when it enters into Men of *ill Morals,* inftead of mending, makes them worfe, and increafes their Prejudice and Malice againft thofe who fincerely worfhip God in Spirit and in Truth.   Another Inftance of the lamentable Confequences of fuch a blind Zeal next follows, *viz.*

Murder of R. Barnes.

ANNO 1658. *Rebecca Barnes, Elizabeth Holme,* and others, coming from a Meeting near *Ormfkirk,* met with *David Ellifon* a Prieft, to whom *Rebecca* fpake fome difpleafing Words.   The Perfons, who accompanied the Prieft, fell to abufing her, while he animated them, crying out, *Down with her, down with her,* which his cruel Comrades effectually performed, for they beat, bruifed, and ftruck her on the Breaft fo cruelly, that within feven Days after fhe died. The Men and Women, who were in her Company, endeavouring what they could to keep the Blows off her, were forely bruifed with Hedgeftakes, and had much of their Blood fhed, they making no Refiftance, and one of them,

Bruifing of J. Barnes.

John Barnes, was forced to keep his Bed, through Weaknefs, fome Time after.

In the Month called *Auguft* this Year, *John Lawfon,* with about nineteen others, going to a Meeting, were apprehended by a Watch purpofely appointed by the Mayor of *Prefton,* and detained Prifoners twenty four Hours without any Caufe affigned.

ANNO 1659. In this and the preceding Years were taken by Diftrefs for Tithes,

Diftreffes for Tithes.

From	*l.*	*s.*	*d.*			*l.*	*s.*	*d.*
Richard Afhburner, for	2	3	4	demanded, Goods worth		6	17	0
Oliver Atherton	1	0	0			6	0	0
Samuel Barrow	0	2	3			0	10	0
Thomas Barrow	1	0	0			3	0	0
Richard Britton	1	10	0			4	11	8
James Chambers	1	7	0			4	0	0
Edmund Clayton	0	3	6			6	0	0
Thomas Curwen	0	12	0			2	10	0
Thomas Earle	0	1	2			0	5	0
Thomas Fell	1	4	0			4	0	0
William Greenbank	6	0	0			22	0	0
Richard Hargreaves	0	12	0			5	0	0
Edward Harrifon	2	13	0			10	17	0
Laurence Hay	0	1	6			0	3	6
Thomas Leaper	7	4	0			23	0	0
Roger Leatherbarrow	3	5	0			20	0	0
Richard Miers	3	0	0			15	0	0
John Minfhall	0	2	0			0	12	0
Edward Moon	0	0	10			1	3	4
Thomas Moon	0	0	10			3	9	0
George Pye	2	4	0			8	0	0
Thomas Pierfon	1	13	4			4	0	0
John Pierfon	0	2	0			0	9	0
William Simpfon	0	17	0			4	0	0
John Townfend	0	1	5			1	10	0
Robert Walker	3	17	4			10	18	4
Alice Woolhead	1	1	0			5	0	0

For 41 18 6 demanded,   Taken   172 15 10
                                                Several

Several of the Perfons laft named alfo fuffered Imprifonment for Tithes, namely, *Richard Afhburner, Richard Miers, Thomas Leaper, Oliver Atherton,* and *Thomas Curwen* ; befide whom, *Robert Stout* for the fame Caufe fuffered eighteen Months Confinement, *Thomas Atkinfon* five Months, and *Richard Cubham* a confiderable Time. *Robert Widders* was fued to an Outlawry for Tithes, and was imprifoned in *Lancafter* Caftle two Years and an Half. *Richard Apener*, for the fame Chriftian Teftimony againft the Payment of Tithes, alfo fuffered Imprifonment till Death.

LANCA-
SHIRE.
1659.

*Imprifonments
for Tithes.
R. Apener
died Prifoner.*

From *John Barrow, Thomas Atkinfon, James Taylor,* and *Richard Fell,* Goods were taken by Diftreffes for Tithes to the Value of 27 *l.* 13 *s.* 2 *d.* *Thomas Hill* alfo endured the fpoiling of his Goods for the fame Caufe.

For refufing to take an Oath on feveral Occafions, the following Perfons were fined and fuffered Diftrefs, *viz.*

	l.	*s.*	*d.*	
George Barrow, Thomas Cummin, John Hargreaves, Thomas Leaper, and *John Minfhall,* to the Value of	10	11	4	*Fines and Diftreffes.*
Thomas Green, Richard Hargreaves, John Sagar, Robert Walker, George Stythe, and *John Smith*	12	3	0	
William Seaman, John Smith, Richard Weaver, Peter Sharlton, and *John Townfon*	12	15	0	
	35	9	4	

Taken alfo from feveral Perfons for refufing Payments impofed for repairing the Steeple-houfes, Wages of the Parifh-Clerks, and the like Claims, for 1 *l.* 6 *s.*¹ demanded, Goods worth 4 *l.* 16 *s.*

ANNO 1660. In the Month called *June* this Year, four Conftables came with a Warrant to the Houfe of *Margaret Fell* at *Swarthmore*, where they apprehended *George Fox*, and carried him before *Henry Porter*, Mayor of *Lancafter*, who examined him as follows, *viz.*

Apprehenfion of G. Fox.

Mayor. *Why came you into the Country this troublefome Time ?*

His Examination.

G. *F.* To vifit my Brethren.

Mayor. *But you have great Meetings up and down.*

G. *F.* Though we have fo, our Meetings are known throughout the Nation to be peaceable, and we are a peaceable People.

Mayor. *You fee the Devil in People's Faces.*

G. *F.* If I fee a Drunkard, a Swearer, or a peevifh heady Man, I cannot fay, I fee the Spirit of God in him.

Mayor. *You cry againft our Minifters.*

G. *F.* Whilft we were as *Saul* fitting under the Priefts, and running up and down with their Packets of Letters, we were never called peftilent Fellows, nor Makers of Sects ; but when we came to exercife our Confciences towards God and Man, we were called *peftilent Fellows,* as *Paul* was.

Mayor. *You can exprefs your felves well enough : I won't difpute with you, but I will reftrain you.*

G. *F.* By whofe Order didft thou fend a Warrant for me ?

Mayor. *I have an Order, but will not reveal the King's Secrets : A Prifoner is not to fee for what he is committed.*

G. *F.* That is not Reafon ; how then fhall he make his Defence ? I ought to have a Copy of it.

Mayor. *There was a Judge that fined one for letting a Prifoner have a Copy of his* Mittimus. *I have an old Clerk, though I am a young Juftice.*

Then he called to the Clerk, *Is it not ready yet ?* meaning the *Mittimus.*

Mayor. *You are a Difturber of the Nation.*

G. *F.* I have been a Bleffing to the Nation in and through the Lord's Power and Truth, and the Spirit of God in all Confciences will anfwer it.

LANCA-
SHIRE.
1660.

G. Fox *sent*
to Prison.

Mayor. *You are an Enemy to the King* : *You endeavour to raise a new War,* and imbrue the Nation in Blood again.

G. F. I have never learned the Postures of War, but am clear and innocent as a Child concerning these Things, and therefore am bold.

Then the *Mittimus* was brought, the Goaler called, and commanded to put him into the Dark-house, and let none come at him.

Habeas Cor-
pus.

Bail was offered for his Appearance, but refused : After a considerable Time of close Confinement an *Habeas Corpus* was procured to remove him to *London*, and the Sheriff, well satisfied of his Innocence, permitted him to go up with some of his Friends, without any Guard, on his Promise to appear before the Judges at *Westminster*, on a certain Day, if the Lord permitted. He appeared accordingly, accompanied with *Robert Widders*, *Richard Hubberthorn*, and Esquire *Marsh* of the King's Bedchamber. The Charge against him was read in Court, but no Accuser appearing, Esquire *Marsh* signified to the Judges, that *it was the King's Pleasure* George Fox *should be set at Liberty*. Whereupon the Court ordered the *Sheriff's* Return of the *Habeas Corpus* to be laid before the King, being as follows, *viz.*

Return.

" **B**Y Virtue of his Majesty's Writ to me directed, and hereunto annexed,
" I certify, that before the Receipt of the said Writ, *George Fox*, in the
" said Writ mentioned, was committed to his Majesty's Goal at the Castle of
" *Lancaster*, in my Custody, by a Warrant from *Henry Porter* Esq; one of
" his Majesty's Justices of the Peace within the County Palatine aforesaid,
" bearing Date the 5th Day of *June* now last past, for that he the said *George*
" *Fox was generally suspected to be a common Disturber of the Peace of this*
" *Nation, an Enemy to our sovereign Lord the King, and a chief Upholder of*
" *the Quakers Sect, and that he, together with others of his fanatick Opinion,*
" *have of late endeavoured to make Insurrections in these Parts of the Country,*
" *and to embroil the whole Kingdom in Blood :* And this is the Cause of his
" Taking and Detaining. Nevertheless, the Body of the said *George Fox* I
" have ready before *Francis Mallet* Knight, one of his Majesty's Justices as-
" signed to hold Pleas before his said Majesty, at his Chamber in *Serjeant's*
" Inn in *Fleet-street*, to do and receive those Things which his Majesty's said
" Justice shall determine concerning him in this Behalf, as by the aforesaid
" Writ is required.

" GEORGE CHETHAM Esq; Sheriff."

Upon Consideration of the whole Matter and Circumstances, the King being satisfied of *George's* Innocence, gave Direction for his Release, which was done by the following Warrant from a Secretary of State, *viz.*

Warrant for
his Discharge.

" **I**T is his Majesty's Pleasure that you give Order for the releasing and
" setting at full Liberty the Person of *George Fox*, late a Prisoner in *Lan-*
" *caster* Goal, and commanded hither by *Habeas Corpus*. And this Signification
" of his Majesty's Pleasure shall be your sufficient Warrant. Dated at *White-*
" *hall* the 24th of *October* 1660.

" To Sir *Francis Mallet* Knight,   " EDWARD NICHOLAS."
" one of the Justices of the
" King's Bench.

Upon which Judge *Mallett* issued the following Order, *viz.*

The Judge's
Order.

" **B**Y Virtue of a Warrant which this Morning I have received from the
" Right Honourable Sir *Edward Nicholas* Knight, one of his Majesty's
" principal Secretaries, for the releasing and setting at Liberty *George Fox*, late
" a Prisoner in *Lancaster* Goal, and from thence brought hither by *Habeas*
" *Corpus*, and committed unto your Custody. I do hereby require you
" accordingly

" accordingly to releafe and fet the faid Prifoner *George Fox* at Liberty ; for L A N C A-
" which this fhall be your Warrant and Difcharge. Given under my Hand S H I R E.
" the 25th Day of *October*, in the Year of our Lord God 1660. 1660.

To Sir John Lenthall *Knt.*
  Marfhal of the King's Bench,   " FRANCIS MALLETT."
  or his Deputy.

Purfuant to this Order *George Fox* was fet at Liberty after twenty Weeks *His peaceful*
Imprifonment : Some of his Friends would have perfuaded *George* to have *Temper of*
taken the Advantage of the Law againft the Juftice and others who had pro- *Mind.*
ceeded fo illegally againft him, and been the Authors of his unjuft Confinement ; but he, like a meek and patient Chriftian replied, *I fhall leave them*
to the Lord : If the Lord forgive them, I fhall not trouble my felf about them.

About the Month called *January* this Year, a general Profecution of this *Many Impri-*
People, for refufing to take the Oath of Allegiance, was fet on foot : On the *fonments for*
9th of that Month, *Robert Alfton* and *Thomas Bond* were taken from their own *not Swearing.*
Houfes at *Chipping* by Soldiers, and without any Warrant or *Mittimus* carried
to Prifon at *Lancafter*. On the 13th a Conftable with armed Soldiers took
twenty fix Perfons from a Meeting at *Yelland*, kept them under a Guard. till
next Day, and then carried them unexamined to *Lancafter* Caftle. On the 20th
they took from the fame Place all that were met, and carried them to a neighbouring Juftice, who fent one Man, twelve Women, and a Boy to Prifon :
The Names of thofe who were apprehended at thefe two Meetings, with two
others, were as follows, viz. *John Backhoufe, Richard Barrow, Thomas Barrow,*
Chriftopher Bifbrown, Chriftopher Bifbrown jun. *John Bifbrown, John Bifbrown*
jun. *John Beakbean, Thomas Camm, Thomas Chorley, Edward Cumming, Thomas*
Dowethwell, Robert Hadwen, William Hugginfon, Robert Hubberfty, James Hut-
ton, William Johnfon, Thomas Leaper, Thomas Prefton, William Slith, William
Wefton, James Weathman, William Weathman, William Weathman jun. *Robert*
Widders, Thomas Widders, Alice Barrow, Anne Beakbean, Mary Athwenwheat,
Mary Bifbrown, Anne Cumming, Martha Croft, Elizabeth Fell, Frances Flem-
ming, Margaret Hadwin, Jane Hubberthorn, Margaret Lucas, Frances Prefton,
Anne Stout, Anne Weathman, and *Jane Widder.* To thefe add *Robert Drink-*
well, who was taken fhortly after by Soldiers ; alfo the following fixteen, taken
out of their own Houfes at *Wray* and Places adjacent, viz. *Robert Batefon, John*
Crofier, Richard Fletcher, Chriftopher Glover, Robert Glover, William Edmon-
fon, William Lamb, John Myers, Chriftopher Nelfon, John Prieftly, Chriftopher
Skirrah, Giles Skirrah, Thomas Skirrah, Thomas Skirrah jun. *Marmaduke Ta-*
tham, and *Thomas Wilfon.* Alfo on the 20th *Thomas Crofby, Jeremiah Lion,*
Ifaac Afhton, Henry Fofter, Henry Martland, John Bifpham, John Witherby, John
Afhton, Richard Johnfon, Godfrey Atherton, Peter Wefthead, George Pye, Peter
Leadbeater, Roger Leatherbarrow, John Underwood, and *John Smallfhaw,* were
forcibly taken out of a religious Meeting at *Biccurfeth* by Soldiers (who faid
they had Orders from the Earl of *Derby*) and fent to the Seffions at *Wigan,*
where the Juftices tendred them the Oath of Allegiance, and committed them
to *Lancafter* Goal for refufing it. On the fame Day, at *Knowlfey, Peter Laith-*
waite, Henry Hulgreave, William Bootle, Richard Beefly, Thomas Tarbock, Robert
Heyes, William Harrifon, and *Thomas Rofe,* being met together to worfhip
God, were apprehended by a Conftable, and by Warrant from a Juftice of the
Peace, before whom they had refufed to take the Oaths, were fent to the fame
Goal. Alfo on the fame Day, at *Lancafter,* a Party of Soldiers, fome with
Swords drawn and Piftols cockt, others with Mufkets and lighted Matches,
came to the Meeting and took away all the Men they found, and carried them
to the Caftle. On the 27th, the Meeting confifting of Women, only one Man,
they took them alfo, and fent them to the fame Prifon with fome others whom
they had taken from their own Houfes. The Names of the Men fo committed were, *John Lawfon, Peter Cathery, Thomas Hinde, Robert Mayor, Matthew*
Jepfon,

Jepfon, Matthew Baines, John Fowler, William Gunfon, John Jenkinfon, William Marfhall, John Walker, Robert Willfon, William Harrifon, Timothy Taylor, Robert Thornton, Francis Shirefon, Richard Hinde, George Cawfon, Henry Crofsfield, William Greenbank, Thomas Hodgfon, Robert Proctor, William Mafher, John Birlow, Chriftopher Barrow, Robert Taylor, Robert Bruce, William Baines, and *Thomas Green.*———And of the Women, *Mary Bruce, Dorothy Baines, Ellen Hodgkinfon, Anne Stubbs, Jennet Tenant,* and *Jane Dickenfon.*

On the fame Day *John Abraham, Ifaac Moffe, Abraham Garfide, Jonathan Bradfhaw, John Burgefs, Mary Ridgway, Mary Poole, Elizabeth Owen,* and *Elizabeth Fletcher,* were taken out of their Meeting at *Manchefter,* and by Order of one Juftice detained till the next Day, when, upon refufing to Swear, they were committed to Prifon.

On the 24th, at *Swarthmore,* forty three Perfons were taken, fome out of their Houfes, others from the Market, and fome from their Labour and Employments, by a Party of Horfemen, and without any Warrant, *Mittimus,* or Examination before a Magiftrate, committed to *Lancafter* Caftle, namely, *Thomas Hutton, Tobias Wilfon, John Chambers, Thomas Fell, Thomas Goad, Richard Fell, Richard Afhburner, Thomas Barwick, James Milner, Thomas Curwen, Richard Myers, Francis Pearfon, William Simpfon, Thomas Myers, Thomas Fell, Francis Pearfon* jun. *Thomas Haverigg, Paul Pennington, Edward Cowper, Leonard Afhburner, James Chambers, John Goade, William Hawthornthwaite, William Dodgfon, Thomas Wilfon, William Strickland, George Fell, Jafper Sharp, Robert Pennington, John Kirkby, Robert Salthoufe, William Salthoufe, James Parke, Thomas Rawlinfon, Daniel Thwaite, Nicholas Birkett, Thomas Benfon, John Holme, William Towers, William Atkinfon, Thomas Fifher, Edward Cowper,* and *Thomas Wilfon* jun.

On the 27th twenty Perfons, *viz.* four of them for refufing the Oaths, and the Reft for not giving Sureties for their good Behaviour, were committed to the fame Prifon, namely, *Ralph Barnes, Samuel Barnes, Thomas Barnes, John Barrow, Samuel Barrow, James Barton, Thomas Earle, Samuel Dunbabin, Richard Goofe, Gilbert Hoult, Richard Houlden, Henry Holbrook, John Minfhall, Samuel Minfhall, Savage Mafon, John Mercer, John Johnfon, John Seddon, Richard Tarbock,* and *Thomas Taylor.*

On the fame Day, at *Downham, James Whip, Thomas Tatham, Elizabeth Eafton, Mary Tatham, Elizabeth Lorrimer, Anne Driver,* and *Edward Hulley,* at whofe Houfe they were met, were apprehended by a Conftable, kept all Night, and next Day by a Juftice of Peace committed to Prifon for refufing the Oaths. The Conftable alfo took by Diftrefs from *Edward Hulley* an Heifer worth 2 *l.* 12 *s.* for pretended Charges of carrying them to Goal, he alfo extorted by Arrefts and other vexatious Methods from the faid *Edward's* Relations 3 *l.* 19 *s.* 6 *d.* on the fame Pretence, although all the Prifoners did bear their own Expences.

On the 10th of the Month called *February, Richard Madder, Edward Dawfon, Nehemiah Poole, Arthur Walker, Hannah Taylor, Mary Moffe,* and *Ellen Alred,* were taken out of a religious Meeting, and for refufing to Swear, committed to *Lancafter* Goal. And on the 17th of the fame Month, at *Haflenden, Abraham Hayworth, Henry Birtwifle, Richard Ratcliff, John Grime, Laurence Taylor, James Ratcliff, Henry Wood, John Cowper, Ifabel Wood, Mary Royfteron, Alice Royfteron, Agnes Robinfon, Katharine Doe, Ifabel Ratcliff, Elizabeth Birtwifle, Margaret Birtwifle, Mary Hayworth,* and *Elizabeth Hayworth,* being met together, were taken by a Conftable, and kept with a Guard all Night : Among them was the Wife of *Henry Wood,* who coming to fee her, was alfo detained, and committed to Prifon with the Reft for refufing the Oaths.

On the fame Day the following Perfons were taken out of the Houfe of *John Hartley* at *Trawden,* where they were affembled to worfhip God, by the High Conftable and Soldiers, and, for refufing to take the Oaths, committed to *Lancafter* Goal, where they lay above five Weeks, namely, *John Hartley, Peter Shackleton, James Smithfon, Robert Atkinfon, William Whaley, Nicholas Whitacre, John Smith, Samuel Driver, John Hargreaves, Jofeph Catherly,*
William

William Heape, John Sagar, Stephen Sagar, Eilen Pollard, Richard Mitchel, Richard Hargreaves, Elizabeth Hartley, Mary Wilkinson, Jennet Swaine, Jane Clayton, Anne Pollard, Jane Wregles, Mary Mitchel, Anne Parker, and *Alice Heape.*

On the 13th of the Month called *March, John West, Christopher West, William Hanson, Thomas Ackringly, Robert Ardington, Elizabeth Driver,* and *Anne Driver,* with *Thomas Patefield,* a poor labouring Man, at whose House they were met, were taken thence by Constables, and by two Justices, for refusing the Oaths, committed to *Lancaster* Castle. About this Time also, *Margaret Atkinson* was sent to Prison for reproving a Priest, *Alice Ambrose* and *Mary Tomkins* for declaring Truth in the Market-place, and *John Lawson* was committed, by an Order of Sessions, for refusing the Oath when tendred him in Court.

Beside the great Numbers already mentioned, we find that *John White* was taken from his own House, and sent to Prison, as were *William Tompson, John Tompson, John Moone, Henry Eccles,* and *Christopher Parkinson,* who had been taken at a Meeting, and *William Gibson,* who was committed for refusing the Oath of Allegiance. Also *James Smith* of *Poulton,* who after five Months Imprisonment, by means of an envious Priest, who had sworn the Peace against him, was brought to the Sessions, where the Priest, being called upon to shew the Cause of his pretended Fear, had nothing to say, but instead of assigning a Reason for what he had done, after some Pause moved the Court, that *James* might have the Oath of Allegiance tendred him, which the Justices complied with, and so instead of releasing the injured Man from his unjust Imprisonment, sent him back to Goal for refusing to Swear. About this Time also *William Brewer* and *John Thorne* were imprisoned, also *Henry Hales* of *Inskip,* and *Robert Biggs* of *Hollowmire.*

So that about the End of this Year, two Hundred and seventy Persons of this People were Prisoners together at *Lancaster,* mostly for refusing to take the Oaths, a Snare which few of them escaped, because by their constant and public lick Manner of assembling for Worship, they stood always exposed to the Malice of those who sought Occasion against them.

ANNO 1661. On the 16th of the Month called *June, Edward Lord, Ralph Ridgeway, Nehemiah Poole, Edward Dawson, Richard Madder, James Bold, John Alred, John Blinkhorne, Henry Wood, John Wood, John Abraham, Isaac Mosse,* and *Abraham Garside,* as they were coming out of a Meeting found the Passages beset with armed Men, who would not suffer them to depart till some Justices of the Peace came, who tendred them the Oath of Allegiance, saying, that *the Law had appointed that as a Means to discover* Papists, and upon their Refusal to take it sent them to *Lancaster* Goal.

*More Imprison-
ments for not
Swearing.*

At the Sessions and Assizes held this Summer, many of those who had been committed to Prison in the foregoing Year were set at Liberty, yet there remained about fifty Prisoners, which Number was soon after increased; for on the 1st of *September* a Warrant was issued from three of the Deputy-Lieutenants of the County and other Magistrates, directed to the Mayor of *Lancaster,* for apprehending all *Quakers* that should be found met together, by which Means the following Persons were sent to Prison, *viz. Thomas Cumming, Robert Wilson, Henry Crosfield, Thomas Harrison, William Mashter, Robert Taylor, George Escridge, Robert Walker, Thomas Hodgson, William Gunson, John Fowler, Timothy Taylor, Robert Bruce, William Taylor, Matthew Jepson, Robert Thornton, Bryan Hodgson, William Weaver, George Cawson, William Harrison, Robert Mayor, William Coward,* and *Richard Hinde.* Several others also, of those lately discharged, being taken again at a Meeting at *Cardmell,* were recommitted, and with them *William Pull, Philip Braithwaite,* and *Richard Simpson.*

At the Quarter Sessions held in the Month called *January* this Year, the following Remonstrance from the Prisoners in *Lancaster* Castle was presented, and read by the Clerk in open Court, *viz.*

" *To the Justices in the Commission for the Peace in this County,* and
" *now in the Town of* Lancaster, *or to any others whom this may*
" *concern, to read and consider in the Spirit of Meekness.*

" S H E W E T H,

*A Remon-
strance to the
Justices at
Quarter Ses-
sions.*

" THAT we the Subscribers, with others our fellow Prisoners, were by
" Order from some of you, or your fellow Justices of the Peace, ap-
" prehended and sent to Prison, where we have innocently and patiently suf-
" fered Bonds for the Space of fourteen Weeks (and some more) this Winter
" Season, although nothing can be justly laid to our Charge, as Matter
" of Fact, deserving such an Imprisonment, both to the Prejudice of our
" Health, the Ruin of our Estates, and the Expence of our Time, in our
" Separation from our Wives, Children, and Families, and from our La-
" bour in our lawful Callings in the Creation, whereby we might be in a
" Capacity to help others, and not to be burdensome to any, being, as you
" well know, Husbandmen and Tradesmen, upon whose Diligence and daily
" Labour, the Subsistence of our Families, as to the outward, consists, the
" Neglect whereof may in all likelihood impoverish them and us, and so
" bring an unnecessary Charge and Burden upon others, which if it should be
" incurred upon this Account, and by this Imprisonment, could not be laid
" to the Charge of the Oppressed, whose Suffering is but upon Suspicion, and
" not for any actual Transgression, but only for Conscience-sake, not for any
" Wrong, Injury, or Offence, either intended or acted against any Person or
" Power appointed of God for the punishing of evil Doers, and for the Praise
" of them that do well, for unto such our Souls are subject for Conscience-
" sake, and we desire nothing from you but that we may live quietly and
" peaceably in our own Houses, eat our own Bread, and follow our
" own Callings in the Fear of God, for the Good of all, and to meet to
" serve and worship our God, according as he requires of us : And if you
" will not grant these Things unto us, then shall we lie down in the Peace
" of our God, and patiently suffer under you, as we have done under those
" Powers whom the Lord God hath overturned by his Power ; and remember
" you are in his Hand, and if you trouble and afflict us for so doing, then
" will the Lord our God trouble and afflict you, (mind that) they are the
" Words of Truth to you. 2 *Thess.* i. 6, 7. Now you knowing that our
" Commitment was only upon Suspicion, and nothing can justly be laid to
" our Charge worthy of these our Bonds : We therefore put you in Mind
" hereby, to consider of our present Condition, and compare it with the
" Cause, and do unto us as you would be dealt with in Case of Conscience,
" and as you are Ministers of the Law, look into the *perfect Law of Liberty,*
" which saith, *Whatsoever ye would that Men should do unto you, do ye even
" so to them, undo the heavy Burdens, and let the Oppressed go free,* for the
" Lord requires it of you, *to do justly, and to love Mercy* ; and we do expect
" from you Justice and Equity, our Right and Privilege to labour in our
" Callings, that as becometh *Saints* we may serve our God, and as *Subjects* we
" may serve our King and Country in all just Requirings ; and this we leave
" to your Consideration, expecting to receive some Answer from you, tending
" to the Enlargement of us who are Prisoners.

    " Subscribed in the Behalf of our selves, and the rest of our fellow Pri-
     " soners, who are in Number about fifty, which suffer upon this Ac-
     " count."

Lancaster *Castle, the* 14*th of
the Eleventh Month* 1661.

            The

The Juſtices at that Seſſions took their Cauſe into Conſideration, and having their Minds diſpoſed to Compaſſion and Mercy, ordered all the Priſoners to be indicted, fined ſuch as were convicted in very ſmall Sums, and then cauſed them to be ſet at Liberty.

ANNO 1662. In this Year *Thomas Moon, William Brewer, John White, John Townſend,* and *John Moon,* for Demands of 2 *l.* 14 *s.* 5 *d.* for Tithes, had Cattle and Goods taken from them by Diſtreſs to the Value of 15 *l.* 19 *s.* Alſo *Gilbert Whiteſide* for a Claim of 1 *l.* 10 *s.* for Tithe, was committed to *Lancaſter* Caſtle, where he ſuffered twenty three Months Impriſonment. Taken alſo from *George Lydiatt, Roger Leatherbarrow,* and *Richard Johnſon,* for 19 *s.* 3 *d.* demanded for Steeple-houſe Rates, Goods to the Value of 3 *l.* 8 *s.* 2 *d.*

In this Year *George Braithwaite* and *George Holme* were impriſoned, and *John Sands* died a Priſoner for refuſing to Swear.

ANNO 1663. Taken from *Roger Hartley, Stephen Sagar, John Sagar,* and *Richard Hargreaves,* for Demands of 3 *l.* 5 *s.* for Tithes, Goods worth 11 *l.* 10 *s.* 6 *d.* There were alſo Priſoners this Year in *Lancaſter* Caſtle for Tithes, *Thomas Curwen, Richard Cubban, Iſaac Aſhton, Thomas Chaddock, Henry Woods, Richard Johnſon, John Smallſhaw,* and *Henry Hulgreave.*

In this Year *Oliver Atherton,* who had been in Priſon about two Years and an Half at the Suit of the Counteſs of *Derby* for Tithes, being a Man of a weakly Conſtitution, through long Impriſonment in a cold damp unwholſome Place, was brought ſo low and weak in Body, that there appeared no Hope of his Life, unleſs he might be removed from thence : His weak Condition was repreſented to the Counteſs in a Letter ſent her by his Son : The young Man returned to his Father on his dying Bed, and told him that the Counteſs denied him any Liberty, to which the dying Man faintly replied, *She hath been the Cauſe of ſhedding much Blood, but this will be the heavieſt Blood that ever ſhe ſpilt :* And ſoon after died. His Body was delivered to his Friends to be interred at *Ormſkirk,* where he had dwelt. In their Way thither they fixed on the publick Places at *Garſtang, Preſton,* and other Towns, a Paper with this Inſcription, " This is *Oliver* " *Atherton* of *Ormſkirk* Pariſh, perſecuted to Death by the Counteſs of *Derby* " for good Conſcience toward God and Chriſt, becauſe he could not give her " Tithes, &c." At the ſame Time three others of this People were confined in the ſame Priſon at the Suit of the ſaid Counteſs, one of whom writ a Letter on Behalf of himſelf and his fellow Priſoners, ſhewing *that it was not of Wil-fulneſs, Stubbornneſs, or Covetouſneſs, that they refuſed to pay her Tithes, but purely in good Conſcience toward God and Chriſt* ; and letting her know, *that if ſhe ſhould be ſuffered to keep them there alſo till Death, yet they could not yield to pay her :* And therefore deſired her *to conſider their Caſe in a Chriſtian Spirit, and not bring their Blood upon her alſo :* But ſhe continued inexorable toward them, who had already ſuffered thirty Months Impriſonment at her Suit : She alſo threatned to complain to the King and Council againſt the Town of *Garſtang,* for ſuffering the Paper concerning *Oliver Atherton's* Death to be put upon their Croſs. Her Anger on that Occaſion cauſed the People there to be more obſervant of what followed, and to make ſuch Reflections as to them occurred, when they took Notice that, *On that Day three Weeks when* Oliver Atherton's *Body was carried through* Ormſkirk *to be buried, the* Counteſs died, *and her dead Body was carried that Day ſeven Weeks through the ſame Town to her Burying-place.*

In the ſame Year alſo, *John Satterthwait* and *Samuel Sandys* died Priſoners for their Teſtimony againſt Tithes. And *Thomas Chorley, Thomas Waters, William Greave, John Stubbs, Thomas Davenport, James Brown, William Wilſon, Edward Satterthwaite,* and *George Holme,* were committed to Priſon for refuſing the Oath of Allegiance when tendred by the Magiſtrates.

In this Year *George Fox* was again impriſoned in *Lancaſter* Caſtle, and *Margaret Fell* ſoon after, of which take her own Account as publiſhed in the Collection of her Works, pag. 7, 8. *viz.* " *George Fox* went into *Weſtmorland* " and

LANCA-
SHIRE.
1663.

M. Fell's *Ac-
count of G.
Fox's and her
own Imprifon-
ment.*

" and *Cumberland,* and had fome Meetings among Friends, and came to
" *Swarthmore,* and they (the Juftices) fent out Warrants for him and took
" him, and fent him to *Lancafter* Caftle. About a Month after, the fame
" Juftices fent for me to *Ulverftone,* where they were fitting, and when I came
" there they afked me feveral Queftions, and feemed to be offended at me for
" keeping a Meeting at my Houfe, and faid, *They would tender me the Oath of*
" *Allegiance.* I anfwered, *They knew I could not Swear, and why fhould they*
" *fend for me from my own Houfe, when I was about my lawful Occafions, to*
" *enfnare me, what had I done ?* They faid, *If I would not keep Meetings at my*
" *Houfe, they would not tender me the Oath.* I told them, *I fhould not deny my*
" *Faith and Principles for any Thing they could do againft me, and while it*
" *pleafeth the Lord to let me have an Houfe, I would endeavour to worfhip him in*
" *it.* So they caufed the Oath to be read, and tendred it to me, and when I
" refufed it, telling them, *I could not Swear for Confcience-fake,* Chrift *Jefus*
" *having forbid it,* they made a *Mittimus,* and committed me Prifoner to *Lan-*
" *cafter* Caftle, and there *George Fox* and I remained Prifoners until next
" Affizes, and they indicted us upon the Statute for denying the Oath of
" Allegiance, for they tendred it to both of us again at the Affizes, and the
" Indictments were found againft us." But their Trial was put off till another
Affizes, and they continued Prifoners.

ANNO 1664. An *Abftract* of the Trial of *Margaret Fell* at the Affizes
holden at *Lancafter* the 29th Day of the Month called *Auguft* 1664.

Margaret Fell was brought to the Bar, and her Indictment read.

Judge. *Come, will you take the Oath ?*

M. F. There is a Claufe in the Indictment, that the Churchwardens informed of Something, which feemeth, that fhould be the Ground or Caufe of this
Indictment : I defire to know what that Information was, and what the Tranf-
greffion was, by which I came under the Law.

Judge. *Miftrefs, we are not to difpute that : You are here indicted, and you
are here to anfwer, and to plead to your Indictment.*

M. F. I am firft to feek the Ground and Caufe wherefore I am indicted,
for being that the Churchwardens did inform, my Queftion is, What Matter
of Fact they did inform of, for I was fent for from my own Houfe, from
amongft my Children and Family, when I was about my outward Occafions,
when I was in no Meeting, neither was it a Meeting-day ; therefore I defire
to know what this Foundation or Matter of Fact was, for there is no Law
againft the Innocent and Righteous, and if I be a Tranfgreffor, let me know
wherein.

Judge. *You fay well ; the Law is made for Tranfgreffors : But Miftrefs, do
you go to Church ?*

M. F. I do go to Church.

Judge. *What Church ?*

M. F. The Church of Chrift.

Judge. *But do you go to Church among other People ? You know what I
mean.*

M. F. What doft thou call a Church, the Houfe or the People ? The Houfe
you all know is Wood and Stone, but if thou calleft the People a Church, to that
I anfwer. As for the Church of *England* that now is, I was gathered unto the
Lord's Truth, unto which I now ftand a Witnefs, before this Church was a
Church. I was feparated from the general Worfhip of the Nation, when there was
another fet up than that which is now, and was perfecuted by that Power that
then was, and fuffered much Hardfhip ; and would you now have us deny our
Faith and our Principles, which we have fuffered for fo many Years, and turn
to your Church contrary to our Confcience.

Judge. *We fpend Time about thefe Things ; come to the Matter in Hand :
What fay you to the Oath, and to the Indictment ?*

M. F. I fay to the Oath, as I have faid in this Place before now : Chrift
Jefus hath commanded me *not to Swear at all,* and that is the only Caufe, and

no other, the righteous Judge of Heaven and Earth knoweth, before whofe Throne and Juftice we fhall all appear one Day, and his Eye fees and beholds us all at this Prefent, and he fees and hears all our Actions, for the Place of Judgment is weighty : And this I do teftify unto you here, where the Lord's Eye beholds us all, that for the Matter or Subftance of the Oath, and for the End for which it is intended, I do own one Part, and deny the other, that is to fay, I do own Truth, Faithfulnefs, and Obedience to the King, and all his juft and lawful Commands and Demands. And I alfo deny all Plottings, Contrivings againft the King, and all *Popifh* Supremacy and Confpiracy, and I can no more tranfgrefs againft King *Charles* in thefe Things, than I can dif-obey *Chrift Jefus's* Commands : And by the fame Power and Virtue of the fame Word which hath commanded me *Not to Swear at all,* the fame doth bind me in my Confcience, that I can neither plot nor contrive againft the King, nor do him nor any Man upon Earth any Wrong. And I do not deny this Oath, becaufe it is the Oath of Allegiance, but I deny it becaufe it is an Oath, becaufe Chrift Jefus hath faid I fhall *not Swear at all, neither by Heaven, nor by Earth, nor any other Oath.* If I might gain the whole World for fwearing an Oath, I could not, and whatever I have to lofe this Day for not fwearing of an Oath, I am willing to offer it up.

Judge, *What fay you to the Indictment ?*

M. F. What fhould I fay ? I am clear and innocent of wronging any Man upon the Earth, as my little Child that ftands by me ; and if any here have any Thing to lay to my Charge, let them come down and teftify it before you all, and if I be clear and innocent, you have no Law againft me.

Then Colonel *Kirby* and the Sheriff whifpered to the Judge, whereupon fhe thus fpake to the Colonel.

M. F. Let us have no Whifpering : If thou haft any Thing to lay to my Charge, or to fpeak againft me, come down here, and teftify againft me.

Judge. *Jury, take Notice fhe doth not take the Oath.*

M. F. This Matter is weighty to me, whatever it be to you, on many Accounts, and I would have the Jury take Notice of it, and to confider fe-rioufly what they are going to do : I ftand here before you upon Account of the Lofs of my Liberty and my Eftate : *Secondly,* I ftand here in obeying Chrift's Commands, and fo keeping my Confcience clear, which if I obey this Law, and King *Charles's* Commands, I defile my Confcience, and tranfgrefs againft *Jefus Chrift,* who is the King of my Confcience ; and the Caufe and Controverfy in this Matter, that. you are all here to judge of this Day is betwixt *Chrift Jefus* and King *Charles,* and I am his Servant and Witnefs this Day, and this is his Caufe, and whatfoever I fuffer it is for him, and fo let him plead my Caufe when he pleafeth.

Judge to the Jury. *Are you agreed? Have you found it ?*

Jury. For the King.

M. F. I have Council to plead to my Indictment.

The Court adjourned till after Dinner, when being met again, they proceeded.

M. F. I defire we may have Time till to Morrow Morning to bring in our Arreft of Judgment.

Judge. *You fhall.have it.*———*Mrs.* Fell, *you wrote to me concerning the Badnefs of your Prifons, that it rains in, and that they are not fit for People to lie in,*

M. F. The Sheriff knows, and has been told of it feveral Times, and now it is raining, if you will fend, you may fee whether they be fit for People to lie in or not.

Then Colonel Kirby *ftanding up to excufe the Sheriff, and to extenuate the Badnefs of the Place.*

M. F. faid, If you were to be in it your felves, you would think it hard, but your Mind is only in Cruelty to commit others, as *William Kirby* here has done, who hath committed ten of our Friends, and put them into a cold

LANCA-
SHIRE.
1664.

Room, where there was nothing but bare Boards to lie on, where they have lain several Nights, some of them above threescore Years of Age, and known to be honest Men in the Country where they live ; and when *William Kirby* was asked, *Why they might not have Liberty to shift for themselves for Beds ?* He answered, *They were to commit them to Prison, but not to provide Prisons for them.* And being asked, *Who should do it then ?* He answered, *The King.*

Judge.   *You should not do so : They ought to have Prisons fit for Men.*

Next Morning her Council pleaded in Arrest of Judgment, and found several Errors in the Indictment, which yet the Judge would not admit of ;

Sentence of Premunire passed upon her.

but passed Sentence of *Premunire* upon her.

M. F.   The Lord forgive thee for what thou hast done. This Law was made for *Popish* Recusants, but you pass Sentence but on few of them.

In her own Account of the Sentence passed upon her, which, she says, was, *That she should be out of the King's Protection, and forfeit all her Estate, real and personal, to the King, and suffer Imprisonment during Life.* She adds, " But the great God of Heaven and Earth supported my Spirit under this " severe Sentence, that I was not terrified, but gave this Answer to Judge " *Turner,* who gave the Sentence, *Although I am out of the King's Protection,* " *yet I am not out of the Protection of Almighty God.* So then I remained in " Prison twenty Months before I could get so much Favour of the Sheriff, as to " go to my own House, which then I had for a little Time, and returned to " Prison again." Where she continued about four Years, till released by an Order of the King and Council.

G. Fox's In-dictment quash'd.

At the same Assizes *George Fox* was also called, and his *Indictment* read, but he strenuously insisting upon many *material Errors* in the Indictment, and making the same plainly appear to the Judge and Court, they acknowledged the same to be sufficient to quash the Indictment, which accordingly was set aside : And he thereupon demanding his Liberty, and asking *Whether he was free from the Matter of that Indictment ?* The Judge answered *Yes :* But at the

The Oath again tendred him.

same Time tendred him the Oath again, and recommitted him to Prison till the next Assizes, which were held on the 16th of the Month called *March* 1664-5, when he was tried on another Indictment. An *Abstract* of his Trial was as follows,

The Indictment was read, and the Jury called over,

His Trial.

Clerk.   *Mr. Fox, Have you any Thing against any of the Jury.*

G. F.   I know none of them.

Then three Witnesses were sworn, who testified, that the Oath was tendred him last Assizes.

Judge.   *Come, come, this Thing was not done in a Corner, did you take the Oath the last Assizes ?*

G. F.   They gave me the Book to Swear on, and the Book saith, *Swear not at all :* But I told them, *If they could prove that after Christ Jesus and his Apostles had forbidden Men to Swear, they had allowed it, I would Swear :* Thus I said, and my Allegiance lies in Truth and Faithfulness, not in Swearing, and so should all your Allegiance lie, if you did well. I do not deny Swearing upon some Account, and own it upon others, but I deny it, because Christ and the Apostle have said, I should *not Swear at all.*

Judge.   *I shall not dispute with you, but in point of Law.*

G. F.   I have something to speak to the Jury concerning the Indictment. But the Judge would not admit it.

G. F.   Is the Oath only to be tendred to the King's Subjects ?

Judge.   *Yes.*

G. F.   Then look, and you will see the Word *Subject* is left out of the Indictment.

Judge.   *Take him away, take him away.*

Sentence of Premunire passed upon him in his Absence.

So the Goaler took him away, and when he was gone, the Jury brought in a Verdict for the King, and *George* was called no more, but Sentence of *Premunire* was passed upon him in his Absence.

Thus

Thus was he returned to his Place of clofe Confinement, where he had lain all the Winter before, *viz.* a fmoky Tower, fometimes fo thick with Smoke that he could fcarce fee the Candle, when burning, where he was at Times almoft fmothered : Befides, it rained in upon his Bed, and his Shirt was fometimes wet as Dung in attempting to ftop out the Rain. In fhort, he was fo ftarved with Cold and Wet, that his Body was much fwelled and benummed.

L A N C A-
S H I R E.
1664.

His hard and cruel Confinement.

In this Year *George Pye* of *Lydiatt*, for a Demand of 3 *l.* fuffered Diftrefs of fix Cows worth 20 *l.* Alfo *Robert Bruce* of *Hatluck*, for a Claim of 40 *s.* had his Goods taken away to the Value of 8 *l.* And *John Minfhall* of *Sankey*, for 30 *s.* claimed for Tithe, had a Steer, a Cow, and other Things taken from him worth 9 *l.* and for the fame Claim alfo fuffered eight Months Imprifonment.

Sufferings for Tithes.

Of thofe, who this Year had their Goods diftrained for Steeple-houfe Rates, were *William Wirefide*, *Mary Boult*, and *Gilbert Whitefide*.

In this Year alfo, or the next preceding, Goods were taken by Diftrefs for meeting together to worfhip God,

		l.	*s.*	*d.*	
From	*Robert Wales, Robert Briggs, T. Crofsfield, James Lancafter, Richard Cleaton,* and *Richard Fell,* to the Value of	21	14	0	*Diftreffes for Meetings.*
	Richard Walker, Giles Walker, Thomas Chorlay, Robert Widders, and *Thomas Leaper,* to the Value of	21	10	0	
		43	4	0	

Alexander Rigby had taken from him two Horfes worth 5 *l.* and *James Gregory* a Cow worth 3 *l.* Thefe two laft named, as alfo *Jonathan Rigby, George Bradfhaw, Ralph Wood, Alice Pemberton,* and *Margaret Bradley*, were committed to the Houfe of Correction for three Months. There were alfo imprifoned for their religious Meetings, *Thomas Warriner, James Hadwen, Robert Clark, Richard Borough,* and *William Jackfon.*

ANNO 1665. Taken by Diftrefs for Tithes,

		l.	*s.*	*d.*		*l.*	*s.*	*d.*	
From	*Thomas Moone,* for	1	6	0	demanded, Goods worth	14	0	0	*Diftreffes.*
	John Minfhall,	0	14	0		3	13	4	
	For Demands of	2	0	0	Taken	17	13	4	

* On the 20th Day of the fixth Month 1665, there having been a Meeting at the Houfe of *Thomas Sale* near *Bury*, which Meeting being ended, and fome Friends walking not far from the Houfe, there came two Conftables of *Bury*, and two Churchwardens, fo called, of the fame, with a Company of Men with them, who without any Warrant, violently took feven of us to *Bury*, before one called a Juftice, who demanded on what Account we were at *Thomas Sale's.* We faid, *In the Fear of God, to worfhip him in Spirit and in Truth :* And the next Day two Juftices, fo called, examined us apart, labouring to enfnare us, yet neverthelefs, being guided by one Spirit, we anfwered one and the fame Thing in Effect ; and although they could prove nothing againft us, but only being met together in the Name and Fear of God, they fent feven of us to *Lancafter* Goal, *viz.* Thomas Sale, James Sikes, John Afhton, Arthur Walker, Thomas Yates, Richard Mather, and John Wood, who left behind them thirty five Children, befides our Wives and the reft of our Families, all which we have given up into the Hands of God, having Hope in him, who in his tender Love and fatherly Pity hath called us, and made known unto us the Riches of his Goodnefs

Proceedings at a Meeting in T. Sale's Houfe.

* This Article is inferted in the very Words of one of the Sufferers,

Goodnefs through Jefus Chrift our Lord and Saviour, for whofe Sake we are freely given up to bear our Teftimony amongft this ungodlike Generation, rejoicing greatly that we are thought worthy to fuffer for his Name's Sake, whofe Name we blefs, and to whom be fung Praifes, over the Heads of our Perfecutors, for ever and ever.

Diftrefs for for refufing to Swear.

John Berley of *Lancafter* for 11 s. and 8 d. Fine, for refufing to Swear when fummoned on a Jury, had fifteen Sheep taken away which coft him 3 l. 5s. 4 d. *John Townfon,* chofen Conftable, and refufing to take the ufual Oath for that Office, had a Cow taken from him worth 4 l.

William Satterthwaite, Robert Pennington, Thomas Pennington, George Benfon, Thomas Docwra, and *Michael Wilfon,* were taken from a Meeting at *Hawk-fhead,* and by the Juftices fent to Prifon for refufing the Oaths. And for the fame Caufe *James Hartley* and *John Brewer* alfo fuffered Imprifonment ; and *William Hutton* and *John Greenwood* had their Goods taken by Diftrefs.

Francis Benfon, for being at a Meeting, had his Coat and Hat taken from him, and his Daughter her Petticoat. There were alfo imprifoned this Year for Meetings, *James Fell, Leonard Fell, Chriftopher Milner, William Holme, Bernard Benfon, William Rigg, Thomas Sale, James Sikes,* and *Thomas Yates.*

Reginald Walker, Elizabeth Wilfon, and *Michael Wilfon,* for Demands of 2 d. each for *Eafter-Offerings,* fuffered Diftrefs of their Clothes and other Things to more than twenty Times that Value.

As *William Clayton* was preaching in a Meeting at *Padifham,* the Prieft of that Parifh, attended by a Conftable with a Warrant, came into the Meeting, pulled *William* out into the Street, and tore his Coat. The Conftable then carried him before the Juftices, who tendred him the Oath of Allegiance, and upon his Refufal to take it, committed him to Prifon till the next Seffions, when the Juftices fined him 5 l. for being at an unlawful Affembly, and committed him to the Houfe of Correction for three Months. The Officers, for pretended Fees and Charges of carrying him thither, took his Coat off his Back. The Keeper put him into the Dungeon five Days and Nights, till fome moderate People of the Town procured him the common Liberty of the Houfe for the reft of the Time.

James Sikes, of *Heyfide,* for abfenting himfelf from the National Worfhip, had a Cow and a Calf taken from him worth 4 l.

We return to *George Fox,* whom we left laft Year under Sentence of *Premunire* in *Lancafter* Caftle. About the Month called *May* this Year, he was removed to *Scarborough* Caftle, and there confined in a Room next the Sea-fide, fo open that the Wind and Rain came in, without Chimney or Fire-place, fo that his Clothes were wet, and his Fingers fwelled as big again as ufual, nor could he, though he was at fome Expence about it, keep out the Weather : They fuffered few or no Friends to come at him, fo that he was, as to them, like a Man buried alive. The Deputy-Governour told him, *that the King, knowing he had a great Intereft in the People, had fent him thither, that if there fhould be any Stirring in the Nation, they fhould hang him over the Wall, to keep the People down.* To which he anfwered, *If that be defired and permitted you, I am ready, for I never feared Death nor Sufferings, but am known to be an innocent, peaceable Man, free from all Stirrings and Plottings, and am one that feeks the Good of all Men.* At length, his Patience having furmounted their Cruelty, and his Innocence pleading for him, the Keepers became more favourable and refpectful to him, fo that he wanted not the common Accommodations of a Prifoner, and when the Officers and Soldiers had Occafion to fpeak of him, they would fay, *He was as ftiff as a Tree, and as pure as a Bell, for we could never bow him.* He remained a Prifoner feventeen Months.

ANNO 1666. In this Year *George Fox* was releafed from his Imprifonment by Order of the King and Council. And the Governour of the Caftle gave him the following Paffport,

LANCA-
SHIRE.
1666.

G. Fox's *Paſſ-
port.*

" PERMIT the Bearer hereof, *George Fox*, late a Priſoner here, and
" now diſcharged by his Majeſty's Order, quietly to paſs about his law-
" ful Occaſions without any Moleſtation. Given under my Hand at *Scar-*
" *borough* Caſtle the 1ſt Day of *September* 1666.

" JORDAN CROSSLANDS,

" *Governour of* Scarborough *Caſtle.*"

Sufferings for Tithes,

In this Year *George Benſon, Richard Walker*, and *William Satterthwaite,*
were committed to Priſon for refuſing to pay Tithes ; as were *Richard Johnſon*
and *John Smallſhaw*, the Former for 2 s. and the Other for 1 l. 10 s. demanded
by *Edward Morton* Prieſt, at whoſe Suit they remained Priſoners near two
Years. Six others for Demands of 4 l. 16 s. 4 d. for Tithes, ſuffered Diſtreſs of
Cattle and other Goods to the Value of 15 l. 12 s. 8 d.

*and for Meet-
ing*

James Fell, Chriſtopher Milner, William Holme, William Salthouſe, and *Thomas
Fiſher*, were taken from a Meeting at *Swarthmore*, and ſent to Priſon ; as were
George Benſon, Reginald Holme, John Dixon, Michael Wilſon, Edward Hird, and
Reginald Walker, who had been taken at a Meeting in the Houſe of *Giles
Walker* of *Walker-Ground.*

ANNO 1667. *Thomas Keckwick*, of *Bold*, was ſued to an Outlawry at
the Suit of *Orlando Bridgman* Impropriator, for Tithes, and after eleven Weeks
Impriſonment had four Horſes and Cows taken from him to the Value of
26 l. 8 s. 8 d. And at another Time for a Demand of 8 s. ſuffered Diſtreſs of
Goods worth 1 l. 6 s. Taken alſo from ſeveral others for 1 l. 8 s. 6 d. demanded,
Goods to the Value of 4 l. 19 s. 4 d.

On the 6th of *October* this Year, *Leonard Fell* was caſt into Priſon for
Tithes, at the Suit of the Prieſt of *Aldingham*, but was diſcharged about a
Fortnight after by the Death of his Proſecutor.

John Townſon and *John White* were impriſoned in *Lancaſter* Caſtle on Writs
de Excommunicato capiendo for a Demand of 6 d. from the Former, and 8 d. from
the Latter, toward the Repairs of the Steeple-houſe.

*Cruel Impri-
ſonment of
J. Sagar.
Perſecution*

ANNO 1668. *John Sagar*, proſecuted in the Eccleſiaſtical Court for
Tithes, was *excommunicated* for not appearing there at a Time when he was
cloſe ſhut up in Goal, and in Conſequence of that *Excommunication* was detained
in Priſon four Years and an Half. His Wife, afflicted at the Loſs of her
Huſband, and the Difficulty of ſupporting four Children in his Abſence, became
diſtracted : The Proſecutor would not permit him the Liberty of ſo much as
once viſiting his Wife in that doleful Condition. *James Whip*, of *Twiſden*, was
alſo excommunicated and ſent to Goal.

*Diſtreſs for
Tithes.*

In this Year *James Taylor, Thomas Barrow, Thomas Atkinſon*, and *Laurence
Newton*, had Cattle and Sheep taken from them by Diſtreſs for Tithes, to the
Value of 28 l. 5 s. Several others alſo for Demands of 4 l. 14 s. 2 d. for Tithes,
ſuffered Diſtreſs of Goods to the Amount of 17 l. 16 s. 10 d.

On the 5th of the Month called *April* 1668, *John Aſhton, John Haydock,
Thomas Lorimer, Hugh Taylor, Henry Wood*, and *Thomas Sale*, were committed
to *Lancaſter* Goal from a Meeting at the ſaid *John Aſhton*'s Houſe. One of
them, *Hugh Taylor*, died in Priſon, and the Reſt continued there fifteen Weeks.
On the 3d of the next Month, thoſe who would have met again at the ſame
Place were kept out by Force, and when met in the Street, were beaten,
dragged away on the Ground, puſhed into the Mire and Hedges, and uſed
inhumanly. On the 18th of *September*, a *Lieutenant* with Soldiers and others
came to a Meeting at *Henry Robinſon*'s Houſe in *Padiſham*, and furiouſly
dragged away *William Clayton* then preaching ; whom, with the ſaid *Henry
Robinſon, Francis Dunn*, and *James Whipp*, they carried before a Juſtice of the
Peace, who ſent them to Priſon till next Seſſions, where *Dunn* and *Clayton*
were fined 5 l. each, and the other two 3 l. 6 s. 8 d. each, and for Non-payment
were committed to the Houſe of Correction, where they lay ten Weeks. On

*Death of
H. Taylor.*

LANCA-
SHIRE.
1668.

the 22d of *November* twenty two Persons, taken at a Meeting in the same Place, were sent to the House of Correction, and detained there seven Weeks. *Leonard Fell* and *Thomas Briggs*, after a Meeting at *Swarthmore*, were taken, by an Officer with Soldiers, from their own Dwellings, and sent to Prison. At the next Sessions they were fined and recommitted.

ANNO 1669.   Taken by Distress for Tithes,

Distresses for Tithes.

		l.	*s.*	*d.*
From *Abraham Hayworth* for 10 s. demanded, Goods worth	}	2	10	0
Henry Birtwisle, for the like Demand, an Heifer worth	}	1	13	4
Abraham Hayworth, for 15 s. demanded, a Cow worth	}	2	10	0
Thomas and *Alice Beakbain*, for 3 l. 14 s. 5 d. demanded, a Cow and Horse worth	}	5	15	0
		12	8	4

Imprisonments and Distresses.

In this Year *Reginald Walker*, for 16 s. demanded for Tithe of Wool, was imprisoned in *Dalton* Castle eighteen Weeks.

Roger Langworth, Anthony Shaw, Alexander Hatton, and *Heskin Fell,* were sent to Prison for meeting together to worship God, and *Heskin Fell,* while in Prison, was fined 20 l. for suffering a Meeting at his House. Others also suffered by Distress for Meetings to the Value of 45 l. 9 s. 6 d.

Sufferings for Tithes.

ANNO 1670.   Taken by Distress for Tithes from several Persons, for 2 l. 5 s. 8 d. demanded, Goods worth 13 l. 9 s. 4 d.

In this Year *Reginald Walker* was again imprisoned seven Weeks at *Kendal,* at the Suit of *John Ambrose,* Priest of *Grassmore.*

On the 31st of the Month called *July* this Year, the Friends assembled at *John Ashton's* House were taken without Warrant, and put into a Court-house all Night, and next Day carried before *Laurence Rawthorn* of *Newhall,* a Justice of the Peace, who sent *Thomas Lorimer, Roger Longworth, James Tomson, Heskin Fell, James Radcliff, Abraham Crossly, Anthony Shaw, Charles Dawson,* and *Alexander Hatton,* to the House of Correction in *Manchester.* About the same Time certain Informers meeting some Friends going homeward from *Rosendale,* took their Names, and gave Information upon Oath that those Persons were met at a Meeting at *Henry Birtwisle's* House, of which the Informers, who had not been there, could not be legal Evidences. Nevertheless, upon that Information their Goods to the Value of above 35 l. were taken away. They appealed to the Quarter Sessions, but were for some Time denied a Copy of the Information, so that two Sessions past before they could obtain an Hearing: At the third Sessions, though it was fully proved that the Witnesses had sworn against three Persons, as being at the Meeting, when they had only seen them, one at two Miles, another at Half a Mile, and the third at a Quarter of a Mile, Distance from thence, yet they found no Redress, one of the Justices declaring, that seeing the *Quakers* had Meetings at certain Houses, if Witnesses saw them coming from any of those Houses it should be sufficient to convict them.   This Instance may serve to shew the Prejudice and Partiality of some Magistrates, and what slight Presumptions would pass for Proofs with those whose Minds were inclinable to Severity and Rigour against the Prosecuted on these Occasions.

Prejudice of Magistrates.

Distress for Marriage.

Thomas Beakbean, for a pretended Marriage Fee, had Goods taken from him worth 7 s. though the Priest who claimed it had no Concern in marrying him: But he and his Wife took each other in Marriage before Witnesses in a publick Assembly of the *Quakers.*

Distresses.

ANNO 1671.   Taken from *Mary Hargreaves* and *John Hardiman,* for Demands of 1 l. 17 s. for Tithes, Goods worth 5 l. 7 s.   And from *Edward Dawson,* to the Value of 45 s.

Many

LANCA-
SHIRE.
1671.

Many Diftreffes were made for Meetings in this and the next preceding Year, by which Goods and Chattels were taken away to the Amount of 274 *l.* 1 *s.* 3 *d.* ¼ *d.* Befide which, when one of the Informers made Complaint to the Qurrter Seffions of 3 *l.* Charges he had been put to, they granted him a Warrant by which they took from feveral Perfons Goods worth 16 *l.* 8 *s.* 8 *d.*

John Minſhall, Samuel Barrow, George Birch, Thomas Barnes, Thomas Taylor, and *Robert Barton,* were committed to Prifon for refufing to pay toward the Repairing of *Farnworth* Chapel. Three of them lay in Prifon above eighteen Months, though the Demand on fome of them was but 3 *d.* and on none of them above 18 *d.*

Imprifonment and Diftrefs for Tithes.

ANNO 1672. *John Smallſhaw,* for fmall Tithes of but 6 *s.* Value, was fent to Prifon, where he lay near two Years, and for the fame Tithe had a Mare taken from him worth 40 *s.*

Robert Atkinfon, Elizabeth Barrow, Richard Brittain, Laurence Newton, and *Thomas Atkinfon,* fuffered by Diftrefs of Cattle and Goods to the Value of 11 *l.* 13 *s.* 6 *d.* And from feveral others for Claims of 16 *l.* 13 *s.* 4 *d.* for Tithes, Goods were taken away to the Value of 49 *l.* 10 *s.* 6 *d.*

John Curwen, imprifoned on a *Significavit,* at the Suit of *Theophilus Aimes* Prieft of *Beacliff,* was detained feven Weeks, and had his Cattle and Goods taken away to the Value of 30 *l.* *Leonard Fell* was alfo imprifoned at the Suit of the fame Prieft for a frivolous Demand of Tithe-hay ; but 'twas obferved that within about three Weeks after his Commitment his Profecutor died.

Marriage-Fees.

In this Year *Suſanna Roſe,* Widow, was profecuted by *Thomas Marfden,* Vicar of *Walton,* for a Demand of 1 *s.* 4 *d.* for a Marriage-Fee, fhe having been married after the *Quakers* Method, to her deceafed Hufband. For refufing to comply with this unrighteous Demand fhe fuffered feventeen Weeks Imprifonment in *Lancafter* Caftle.

Falfe Accufation againft a married Woman.

Elizabeth Hirt, of *Weft-Houghton,* was committed to the Houfe of Correction at *Manchefter* by the Procurement of *John Anger* a Prieft, who dwelt at *Deane* near *Boulton,* upon a Charge of having two Children unlawfully begotten. She was detained there about ten Weeks, till the Quarter Seffions, and then re-leafed upon producing a Certificate figned by feveral Witneffes prefent at her Marriage.

Releafe of Prifoners.

In this Year *Richard Clayton* and *Francis Dunn* were difcharged out of Prifon by the King's Letters Patent.

ANNO 1674. *Roger Haydock* was profecuted in the Ecclefiaftical Court at *Chefter* for Tithes of about 30 *s.* Value, and was committed to *Lancafter* Goal on the 3d of the Month called *May* this Year, where he continued Prifoner about eight Months. But on an Appeal, appearing to have been only a Servant to his Brother, he was difcharged at that Time: But was foon after, together with *Hefkin Fell,* recommitted by two Juftices : The Form of their *Mittimus* was as follows,

Mittimus of R. Haydock and others.

" *Lancafter* ſs.

" FORASMUCH as *Roger Haydock, Hefkin Fell* of *Coppull,* and
" * *Thomas Cotterill* of *Sherington* Gent. within the Parifh of *Standiſh*
" within the County aforefaid and Diocefe of *Chefter,* have difobeyed and con-
" temned the Procefs of the Ecclefiaftical Court, for not appearing at Days
" and Times appointed, to anfwer in a Caufe depending in the faid Court.
" Thefe are therefore in his Majefty's Name ftrictly to charge and command
" you forthwith upon Receipt hereof to apprehend the Bodies of them the faid
" *Roger Haydock, Hefkin Fell,* and *Thomas Cotterill,* and bring them forthwith
" before us or one of us, or any other of his Majefty's Juftices of the Peace
" within this County, to find fufficient Sureties for their and every of their due
" Obedience to the Procefs, Proceedings, Decrees or Sentences of the Eccle-
" fiaftical

---

* *Thomas Cotterill* was not a *Quaker,* and was not fent to Prifon ; 'Tis probable he com-plied with the Profecutor.

" fiaftical Court : And if any of them fhall refufe fo to do, that then you
" fhall forthwith convey him or them fo refufing to the common Goal, there
" to remain until he or they fhall willingly do the fame. See you fail not
" herein at your Peril. Given under our Hands and Seals at *Eccleſton* the 21ſt
" Day of *March* 1674.

" CHRISTOPHER BANNISTER.
" HENRY HOUGHTON."

The Caufe for which *Heſkin Fell* was profecuted, was a Claim of 1 *s.* 8 *d.* for
Tithe of Hens, Hay, *&c.* for three Years.

*Proſecution
for Tithes.*

Richard Cubham, Edward Lion, and *George Shaw,* all of *Bickerſtath,* were
profecuted in the *Exchequer* for Tithes, at the Suit of the Lady *Katharine Pye,*
and were committed to Prifon at *Lancaſter* in the Month called *March* 1674.
During their Imprifonment the Profecutor's Agents broke their Gates and
Hedges, entred their Lands, and carried away their Corn at Pleafure. In this
Year alfo *Roger Harſnep, George Pye,* and *Roger Leatherbarrow,* were profecuted for Tithes, the Firſt at the Suit of *Alexander Baggerly,* Prieſt of *Aughton,*
and the two laſt at the Suit of Dr. *Smallwood.*

*Excommuni-
cations for
Steeple-houſe
Repairs.*

Iſaac Aſhton and *Hannah Kennedy,* for refufing to pay 5 *s.* 5 *d.* each, and *Anne
Atherton,* for refufing to pay 6 *s.* 8 *d.* toward the Repairing the Steeple-houfe
at *Ormſkirk,* were profecuted in the Ecclefiaftical Court and excommunicated.
Richard Johnſon was alfo profecuted in that Court, excommunicated, and imprifoned, for not paying 12 *s.* 6 *d.* toward the Repairs of the Steeple-houfe at
Sephton. But after a few Weeks was releafed by the Judge of Aſſize. Some Time
before this, *John Fowler* and *George Cawſon* had fuffered four Months Imprifonment at *Lancaſter* for a fmall Demand for Steeple-houfe Repairs.

*Diſtreſſes for
Meetings.*

Robert Salthouſe and *James Harriſon* fuffered Diftrefs of Goods for Meetings
held at their Houfes, the Former to the Value of 6 *l.* and the Latter of 11 *l.* 6 *s.*
For a Meeting at *James Smithſon's* in *Marſden,* on the 30th of the Month
called *Auguſt* 1674, Goods were taken from feveral Perfons by Diftrefs to the
Amount of 45 *l.* 18 *s.* Alfo *Richard Colburne* of *Clitheroe,* for being at a religious Meeting, fuffered Diftrefs of a Cow worth 4 *l.* 5 *s.*

*Sufferings for
Tithes.*

ANNO 1675. *Thomas Bond, John Walker,* and *William Baines,* were Prifoners for Tithes in *Lancaſter* Caftle in the Month called *March,* and continued
there about nine Weeks, one of them for a Demand of 3 *s.* and another but
of 9 *d.*

In *September, Roger Harſnep,* after a Profecution in the Bifhop's Court for
Tithes, at the Suit of *Alexander Baggarly,* Prieſt of *Aughton,* was committed
to *Lancaſter* Goal, where he lay about fixteen Months. In the fame Month
Roger Haydock was committed to the fame Prifon, at the Suit of *Ralph Briddock,* Bifhop of *Cheſter,* by Warrant from two Juftices grounded on a *Signifi-*

*The Biſhop's
Severity.*

cavit out of the Ecclefiaftical Court. The Bifhop writ a Letter to the Goaler,
charging him not to let the faid *Roger* have any Liberty : The Judge of Aſſize
alfo, at the Bifhop's Importunity, gave the Goaler the like Charge concerning him.

*Impriſonment
for Tithes, and
Diſtreſſes for
Meetings.*

In the Month called *January, Robert Hubberſty, Francis Flemming, William
Waithman,* and *James Waithman,* were committed to *Lancaſter* Goal on an *Exchequer* Profecution, at the Suit of *Hugh Phillips,* Tithe-farmer under the Dean
of *Worceſter.* In this Year alfo, *John Grime* had an Horfe-load of Meal worth
about 20 *s.* taken from him without any Warrant or legal Proceeding, by *Laurence Ormond* Tithe-farmer. And in the fame Year, the Diftreffes made for
Fines upon the Act againſt Conventicles amounted to 34 *l.* 1 *s.* 1 *d.*

*Impriſonment
for not Swear-
ing.*

Heſkin Fell, for refufing to take an Oath in the Bifhop's Court at *Cheſter,*
when cited thither for *Eaſter-Offerings,* was pronounced Contumacious, and by
Warrant from two Juftices committed to the Common Goal at *Lancaſter.*

ANNO

---

* She was the Widow of *Oliver Atherton,* whofe Death and Burial is before related,
pag. 311.

ANNO 1676. *Alice Haydock*, Widow, was profecuted for Tithes by *Ralph*   L A N C A-
Briddock, Bifhop of *Chefter*, and was imprifoned at *Lancafter* in the Month   S H I R E.
called *July.*   1676.

On the 3d of the Month called *April*, *Elizabeth Wildman* of *Tatham*, Widow,   *Profecutions*
about fixty Years of Age, was committed to *Lancafter* Goal by a Writ *de*   *for Tithes.*
excommunicato capiendo, at the Suit of *Thomas Sharp*, Prieft of *Tatham*. After
about nine Months Confinement fhe died there on the 3d of the Month called
January following.

Robert Walker, after three Years and an Half Imprifonment for Tithes, be-   *Death of*
ing kept very clofe by his Profecutor's Order, in the Winter Seafon, contracted   R. *Walker.*
much Cold, and being of a tender Body, fell fick and died. He was imprifoned on a *Significavit* from the Ecclefiaftical Court, at the Suit of *Edward*
Garthford, Prieft of *Lancafter*, for a Demand of 10 s. for fmall Tithes.

Henry Birtwiftle, for a Claim of 10 s. for Tithes, had an Heifer taken from   *Diftrefs.*
him worth 3 *l.* 6 *s.* 8 *d.*

John Moone, of the Parifh of *Garftang*, was imprifoned in *Lancafter* Goal   *Imprifonment*
an whole Winter, at the Suit of *Thomas Butler*, for a Demand of 6 *l.* 0 *s.* 4 *d.*   *and Diftrefs.*
for Tithes, for which he had alfo his Goods taken from him to the Value
of 20 *l.* and upwards. The faid *John Moone*, in his own Account of his Imprifonment, expreffes himfelf thus, " *The Lord was with me in the Prifon, and*
" *made me more to rejoice than thofe that have Abundance of Riches, of Corn,*
" *of Wine, and Oil.*"

In this Year, for Claims of 9 *l.* 11 *s.* 3 *d.* ½ *d.* for Tithes, were Cattle,   *Diftreffes.*
Sheep, and other Things taken by Diftrefs to the Value of 30 *l.* 19 *s.* 8 *d.* From
John Vipon was taken a Piece of *Kerfey* worth 1 *l.* 10 *s.* And from feveral
others Corn out of the Field worth 5 *l.* 6 *s.* 10 *d.*

Mary Walker, for a Meeting at her Houfe, was fined 20 *l.* and *William Wilfon*   *Fine for*
was fined the like Sum for preaching there, alfo feveral others prefent had their   *Meeting.*
Goods taken away to the Value of 3 *l.*

On the 13th of *December*, *James Dilworth* of *Thornly*, for a Meeting at his
Houfe, had two Oxen taken from him worth 9 *l.* *Leonard Fell*, for preaching
in a Meeting at *Windermere*, fuffered Diftrefs of Malt to the Value of 20 *l.*
And *William Rigg*, *John Bownas*, and *Thomas Pennington*, for being there, had
Goods taken from them worth 1 *l.* 10 *s.* 8 *d.*

William Heape, for a Meeting held at his Houfe in *Marfden*, had five Beafts
taken from him worth 14 *l.* And feveral others, for being at the fame Meeting,
Goods to the Value of 2 *l.* 0 *s.* 6 *d.*

For a Meeting at *Freckleton*, *Thomas Tomlinfon*, *Henry Tomlinfon*, and *John*
Townfon, fuffered Diftrefs of Cattle and Goods to the Value of 22 *l.* 10 *s.* Thefe
Diftreffes were taken by Warrant granted by *Edward Rigby* of *Prefton*, a per-
fecuting Juftice, who in the Excefs of a mifguided Zeal, threatned, *that he*
would root the Quakers *out of the Hundred where he dwelt*: And farther faid,
that *all the Laws yet made againft the* Quakers *were too fhort*, and that *he*
would be of the firft that fhould move for a Law to have them tied to, and drag-
ged at either an Horfe's or Cart's Tail. Such a virulent Temper, added to the
Rigour of the Laws, made the Sufferers Cafe fometimes very grievous.

In *October* this Year, *Charles Lee* of *Clitheroe*, a labouring Man, for
a Meeting at his Houfe, had taken from him four Horfes with their Ac-
coutrements, one Heifer, a Cow, and four Calves, worth 26 *l.* 11 *s.* 8 *d.* And
in the next Month *Alexander Salfbury*, for preaching at a Meeting in the Houfe
of *Thomas Garner*, was fined 20 *l.* and had his Cattle taken away at feveral
Times to the Value of 60 *l.*

ANNO 1677. For a Meeting at *Franley* on the 24th of the Month   *Profecutions*
called *June*, were taken from *Thomas Crofby*, *Jofeph Coppuck*, and *John John-*   *of feveral*
fon, Goods worth 8 *l.* 5 *s.*   *Kinds.*

John Veepan, *William Whaley*, *Richard Hargreaves*, *John Bordman*, and *John*
Grime, after a Profecution in the *Wapentake* Court for 3 *s.* 6 *d.* demanded for

LANCA-
SHIRE.
1677.

*Grievous Suf-
ferings.*

*Falfhood of
Informers.*

Exchequer.

R. Long-
worth's *Mit-
timus.*

Tithes, had taken from them Cattle, and other Goods, to the Value of 15 *l.* 7 *s.* 4 *d.*

George Pye, for 5 *l.* 13 *s.* 4 *d.* demanded for Tithes, had Judgment given againſt him on the Statute for treble Damages, upon which he had taken from him four Cows and other Goods worth 21 *l.*

Robert Withers, of *Overkellet,* was ſued by *James Greenwood* Tithe-farmer, for five Years Tithe of Hay, for which he obtained a Judgment for treble Damages 6 *l.* 15 *s.* and for five Years Tithe of Corn, for which Judgment was given for 65 *l.* 15 *s.* being treble the Demand and Coſts : For all which Diſtreſs was made, and his Cattle, Sheep, and Corn taken away to the Value of 98 *l.* 2 *s.* 10 *d.*

In *October, George Rigg* and *Edward Stones,* Informers, gave Intelligence of a Meeting at *Height* to *Miles Dolding* Juſtice, who upon their Oaths convicted thirty five Perſons, and granted his Warrant for Diſtreſs, by which Goods were taken from ten of them to the Value of 35 *l.* 17 *s.* 10 *d.* Of the Perſons at that Time convicted, *two* were at a great Diſtance in another County, a *third* was two Miles from the Place, and a *fourth* was at Home with her Child, having lately lain in : But it was common with the Informers to Swear at all Adventures, againſt thoſe who uſually were at the Meetings, whether preſent at that Time or not. And ſuch Miſtakes as theſe were eaſily overlookt by the Juſtices, who ſcreened the Offenders under the plauſible Character of *uſeful Men,* and the *King's Witneſſes.* In this Year alſo ſeveral were proſecuted in the *Exchequer* on old Statutes made againſt *Popiſh* Recuſants, to the Forfeiture of two Thirds of their real Eſtates, the Rent of which was ſeized by the Sheriff for the King's Uſe. The Sums ſo taken amounted to 60 *l.* 4 *s.* 3 *d.*

ANNO 1678. *Roger Longworth,* of *Bolton,* occaſionally travelling into *Cheſhire,* was by two officious Juſtices ſent to Priſon. A Copy of his *Mittimus* follows, *viz.*

" *Com.* Cheſter ſs.

" **F** O R A S M U C H as by Reaſon of ſeveral Expreſſions which we have
" this Day, at *Holme* in the County of *Cheſter,* heard from a ſtrange Per-
" ſon, who calls himſelf *Roger Longworth,* of *Bolton* in the County of *Lancaſter,*
" we do ſuſpect that the ſaid *Roger Longworth* is a *Papiſt,* and thereupon ac-
" cording to his Majeſty's Commiſſion, under the great Seal of *England,* to us
" and others directed, we have this Day tendred unto him the ſaid *Roger Long-*
" *worth* the Oath of Obedience, and the Oath of Supremacy, both which
" Oaths the ſaid *Roger Longworth,* being above the Age of eighteen Years,
" hath this Day refuſed to take. Theſe are therefore in his Majeſty's Name to
" require and command you forthwith upon Sight hereof to receive into your
" Cuſtody the Perſon of the ſaid *Roger Longworth,* whom we have herewith
" ſent you, and him there ſafely keep until the next general Quarter Seſſions
" of the Peace, to be held in and for this County of *Cheſter,* without Bail or
" Mainprize. For ſo doing this ſhall be your Warrant. Given under our
" Hands and Seals at *Holme* this 28th Day of *February, Anno rni Caroli ſecundi*
" *Dei Gra. Angliæ, &c. Triceſimo, Annoq; Dom.* 1678-9.

To the Keeper of   " THO. MANWARING *Bart.*
Cheſter *Caſtle.*   " JEFFERY SHACKERLY *Knt.*"

*Sufferings for
Tithes.*

After he had been detained in Priſon above two Months, he was ſet at Liberty by a private Order from the ſaid Juſtice *Manwaring.*

In this Year *Andrew Lund, Henry Townſon,* and *John Townſon,* for trivial Demands of Tithes, were impriſoned in the *Fleet* at *London,* where they had been above two Years, and continued about two Years after, till the Death of their Proſecutor,

Thomas

Thomas Skerray, of *Wrea*, Hufbandman, and *Agnes Skerray* of the fame, Widow, were imprifoned on Writs *de Excommunicato capiendo* at the Suit of Lord *Morley*, of *Hornby*, for Tithes. Alfo *Charles Lee*, of *Clitheroe*, Hufband-man, for 3 *s.* 4 *d.* Tithe, at the Suit of Sir *Ralph Afhton*, of *Whaley.* They both remained Prifoners about two Years.

In or about this Year alfo, Seizures were made on *Exchequer* Procefs for two Thirds of the real Eftates of many Perfons in this County, to the Amount of 74 *l.* 17 *s.* 4 *d.* Some of thofe Seizures were very exorbitant, amounting to five or fix Times the Sums demanded.

At a *Wapentake* Court, held for the Hundred of *Lonfdale*, feveral Judgments were obtained, and Diftreffes thereupon made next Day, by which were taken

	l.	*s.*	*d.*	
From *Thomas Atkinfon*, for 1 *l.* 13 *s.* 4 *d.* Cattle and other Goods worth	4	0	0	*Diftreffes for Tithes.*
Richard Britton, for 1 *l.* 9 *s.* 3 *d.* a Gelding worth	3	6	8	
John Barrow, for 5 *s.* 1 *d.* an Heifer worth	1	10	0	
Thomas Barrow, for 1 *l.* 18 *s.* 6 *d.* two Cows worth	5	10	0	
Ellen Braithwaite, for 6 *s.* 7 *d.* a Cow and Calf worth	1	15	0	
Elizabeth Barrow, Widow, for 18 *s.* a Cow worth	3	10	0	
For Demands of 6 *l.* 10 *s.* 9 *d.*　　Taken	19	11	8	

All thefe Goods and Cattle were taken and fold by the Bayliffs, without producing any Warrant or Writ authorizing them either to levy or fell the fame.
ANNO 1679. Taken by Diftrefs for Tithes,

	l.	*s.*	*d.*
From *William Whaley*, for 2 *l.* 2 *s.* a Cow worth	4	0	0
Stephen Sagar, for 10 *s.* Flannel worth	0	18	6
Peter Shackleton, for 1 *l.* 1 *s.* a Cow worth	5	0	0
William Hatton, for 1. 0 *s.* 8 *d.* a Stack of Hay worth	1	10	0
James Fletcher, for 6 *s.* 3 *d.* Goods worth	1	5	0
For Demands of 4 *l.* 19 *s.* 11 *d.*　　Taken	12	13	6

Thomas Leaper, of *Copenwray*, was profecuted by *James Greenwood* Tithe-farmer, for eight Years Tithe, on the Statute for Treble Damages, and had Cattle and Corn taken from him to the Value of 41 *l.* 16 *s.* 4 *d.*

James Smith, of *Coulton*, was committed to *Lancafter* Caftle by a Writ *de Excommunicato capiendo*, for a Demand of 1 *l.* 10 *s.* for Tithe, at the Suit of *Henry Rowe*, of *Wigan*, Tithe-farmer.

Richard Yearwood, *Gilbert Holt*, and *Thomas Barnfall*, were committed to *Lancafter* Caftle by Writs *de Excommunicato capiendo*, at the Suit of *Edward Goodall*, Vicar of *Prefcott*, whofe Demand upon all the three did not amount to 20 *s.* After their Commitment the Prieft feveral Times directed the Goaler, both by Word of Mouth and Writing, to keep them under a clofe Confine-ment. The faid *Gilbert Holt* died a Prifoner there about four Years after.

On the 31ft of the Month called *March* this Year was a Meeting at *Macclesfield* in *Chefhire*, to which the Mayor and two other Juftices came, and took what Names they pleafed. After a fhort Time, the Meeting ftill con-tinuing, they came again. At their firft Coming they found *James Harrifon*, of *Bolton* in *Lancafhire*, preaching, for which they fined him 20 *l.* and at their coming again, he ftill preaching, they called that a fecond Offence, and fined him 40 *l.* which Convictions and Fines they certified to *John Hartley*, a Juftice near *Manchefter* in *Lancafhire*, who iffued his Warrant to the Conftables of *Bolton* to levy the Fines. They made Diftrefs of the faid *Harrifon*'s Houfhold Goods of about 40 *l.* Value, taking all they could find, not leaving fo much as a Skillet to boil the Children's Milk in : But before they proceeded to any farther Seizure, an Appeal was entred on his Behalf to the Quarter Seffions,
where

Fines for Meetings.

where the Conviction was adjudged illegal, for that they had made two Offences of once Preaching. But though the Conviction was set aside, yet he could not obtain the Restitution of his Goods.

In the Month called *May*, *Richard Cubban*, for a Meeting at his House in *Bickerstaff*, was fined 20*l*. and *John Bispham* was also fined 20*l*. for preaching there. *Roger Harsnep* and *Richard Beesly*, for being at the same Meeting, were fined 8*s*. each. On the 9th of *November*, as *James Harrison* was preaching at a Meeting in his own House, the Constables came and pluckt him away. They caused him to be fined, and by a Warrant from *Thomas Laver* and *John Kenyon* Justices, made a Seizure of Leather and other Goods to the Value of 10*l*. 19*s*. *Phineas Pemberton*, for himself and Wife being at the said Meeting, had Goods taken from him to the Value of 4*l*. 15*s*. 4*d*. In order to

Feasting of Justices and others.

A Bayliff's sudden Death.

Distresses.

convict the Persons met at *Bolton*, the Justices, Informers, and Witnesses, with the Attendants, ate and drank in one Afternoon as much as cost 50*s*. which the Constable engaged to pay for. *Thomas Russel*, an Under-Bayliff, was so drunk, that he was found in the Street wallowing in his Vomit about three in the Morning, and some Time after died suddenly.

Many Persons in this County were fined this Year for Absence from the National Worship, and had their Goods taken by Distress to the Value of 9*l*. 12*s*. 1*d*.

ANNO 1680. Taken this Year for Tithes from several Persons, Corn and other Things to the Value of 15*l*. 16*s*. 2*d*.

Imprisonments on Writs de Excom. Cap.

Distresses.

Thomas Crosbie and *Joshua Crosbie* were taken by an Apparitor and a Bayliff, and committed to *Lancaster* Prison on a Writ *de Excommunicato capiendo*.

Matthew Read, of *Heighton*, for a Meeting at his House, had taken from him two Oxen, an Heifer, and fifteen Loads of Corn, worth 20*l*. 10*s*. And *William Whaley*, of *Marsden*, for Preaching, suffered Distress of his Cattle to the Value of 49*l*. 1*s*.

Imprisonments for Tithes.

ANNO 1681. *Henry Birtwistle* and *George Hayworth*, were imprisoned by a Writ *de Excommunicato capiendo*, at the Suit of *John Duckworth*, Priest of *Haslington*, for small Tithes.

Also *Henry Wood* was sent to Prison, and detained about two Years, at the Suit of the Priest of *Bramble*, for a pretended Claim of ten Years Tithe, seven of which the Priest's Servants had long before taken for his Use.

We shall next insert the Copies of two Warrants, by the Former of which Goods were taken to the Value of 15*l*. 11*s*. 7*d*. and by the Latter to the Amount of 25*l*. 13*s*. 6*d*.

1. A Copy of the *Warrant* for distraining the Goods of *George Hargreaves*.

" *Com.* Lancaster.

Warrant for distraining the Goods of G. Hargreaves.

" WHEREAS it appeareth unto us, as well by Witnesses upon
" Oath, as by notorious Evidence and Circumstance of the Fact,
" that upon the 16th Day of *October* last past, being *Sunday*, there was a
" numerous Meeting or Conventicle, under Colour or Pretence of religious
" Worship, in other Manner than according to the *Liturgy* or Practice of the
" Church of *England*, at the House of *George Hargreaves*, in *Pendle* within
" this County, Clothier, and by and with his Consent, at which said Meeting
" or Conventicle were many more than five Persons above the Age of sixteen
" Years, Subjects of this Realm, besides those of the Family, when and where
" *George Hargreaves* aforesaid did wittingly and wilfully suffer *Isaac Ashton*, of
" *Clitheroe*, to pray, preach or teach within his House, but did not read the
" Book of Common-prayer, contrary to a late Act of Parliament intituled,
" *An Act for preventing and suppressing seditious Meetings and Conventicles*, for
" which Offence *George Hargreaves* aforesaid hath forfeited the Sum of 20*l*.
" according to the Act aforesaid. These are therefore, in the Name of our
" Sovereign Lord the King, strictly to charge and command you forthwith after
" your

" your Receipt hereof to demand of the faid *George Hargreaves* the Sum of
" 20 *l.* forfeited by him as aforefaid, and if he fhall refufe to pay the fame,
" you are forthwith to levy it upon his Goods and Chattels by Diftrefs and
" Sale thereof, rendring to him the Overplus, if any be ; and the Money
" fo levied you are to pay unto us, or one of us, as the Act aforefaid doth
" direct : And you are not to fail of the Execution and Return hereof within
" ten Days, as you will anfwer the Contrary at your Perils. Dated the 15th
" Day of *November, Anno Dom.* 1681.

To the Conftables, &c.

" NICHO. TOWNLY.
" THO. BRADDYLE."

2. A Copy of a *Warrant* for Diftrefs on *Ifaac Afhton* and others.

" *Burg. de* Clitheroe *in Com.* Lancafter.

" FORASMUCH as we have this Day received a Certificate under
" the Hands and Seals of *Nicholas Townly* and *Thomas Braddyle* Efquires,
" two of his Majefty's Juftices of the Peace for the County Palatine of *Lan-*
" *cafter,* That whereas *Ifaac Afhton,* of *Clitheroe* aforefaid, Diftiller of Strong-
" Waters, ftands convicted before them the faid Juftices, for that he, upon
" *Sunday* the 16th Day of *October* now laft paft, did take upon him to teach
" and preach in a Conventicle holden at the Houfe of *George Hargreaves,* in
" the Foreft or Chafe of *Pendle* and County aforefaid, Clothier, contrary to
" the late Act of Parliament intituled, *An Act to prevent feditious Conventicles,*
" for which he hath forfeited the Sum of 20 *l.* it being the firft Offence of
" this Nature by him committed, for what appears before the faid Juftices.
" And whereas *John Fifh,* of the fame Town and County, Glazier, ftands
" convicted before the faid Juftices for being prefent at the faid Conventicle,
" whereby he hath forfeited the Sum of 10 *s.* it being the fecond Time of his
" Conviction for an Offence of this Nature. And whereas alfo *John Spencer*
" of the fame Town and County, Labourer, ftands convicted before the faid
" Juftices only 5 *s.* it being the firft Offence of that Nature that hath appeared
" before the faid Juftices. And therefore they do impofe the feveral Fines
" abovementioned, viz. upon *Ifaac Afhton* 20 *l.* upon *John Fifh* 10 *s.* and upon
" *John Spencer* 5 *s.* according to the faid Act of Parliament. Thefe are there-
" fore in his Majefty's Name to will and require you, and every of you,
" immediately upon Receipt hereof to demand of them the faid *Ifaac Afhton,*
" *John Fifh,* and *John Spencer,* thefe feveral Sums impofed upon them : And
" if they or any of them fhall refufe to pay the fame, that then you levy the
" faid feveral Sums by Diftrefs and Sale of the Goods of him or them fo re-
" fufing, returning the Overplus if any fhall remain, and you are to give an
" Account of your Proceedings herein to us, whereof fail not at your Peril.
" Given under our Hands and Seal of the Borough this 21ft Day of *November,*
" *Anno Dom.* 1681.

To the Conftables of
Clitheroe, *&c.*

" WILLIAM APPLETON,
" EDWARD ROBINSON,
" *Bayliffs of the faid Borough.*"

ANNO 1682. *John Afpinal,* of *Caffel,* was committed to *Lancafter* Caftle
on the 5th of the Month called *April,* by Juftices Warrant, grounded on a
Significavit out of the Ecclefiaftical Court, at the Suit of the aforefaid *John
Duckworth,* Prieft of *Haflington,* for Tithes.

*John Fell, John Curwen, John Cowel, William Salthoufe, James Geldert,
Thomas Fifher, and William Towers,* after a Profecution in the *Exchequer* for
Tithes, at the Suit of *Mary Woodburn* Tithe-farmer, had Corn, Cattle, and
other Goods taken from them by Sequeftration, to the Value of 64 *l.* 16 *s.* 3 *d.*

Alfo

LANCA-
SHIRE.
1682.

Diftrefs for Meetings.

Alfo *John Walker*, *Alice Bakebean*, *Chriftopher Widdow*, and *John Lees*, for Demands of 10 *l.* 17 *s.* 6 *d.* for Tithes, fuffered by Diftrefs to the Amount of 27 *l.* 7 *s.*

Thomas Turbuck, of *Sutton*, for being at a religious Meeting, had his Bedding taken away to the Value of 1 *l.* 13 *s.* 4 *d.* Alfo *William Holgate*, for a Meeting at his Houfe, fuffered the Lofs of his Houfhold Goods worth 9 *l.* 8 *s.* 6 *d.* And for a Meeting held in *November* this Year, at the Houfe of *James Strettell* in *Manchefter*, Goods were taken from feveral Perfons to the Amount of 29 *l.* 18 *s.*

Imprifonment of R. Bar-
row.

ANNO 1683. On the 12th of the Month called *January*, *Robert Barrow* was taken preaching in a Meeting at *Lancafter*, and by the Mayor committed to Prifon.

Diftrefs on M. Fox.

Margaret Fox, for fuffering Meetings at her Houfe in *Swarthmore*, was fined by the Name of *Margaret Fell*, Widow, and had taken from her, at one Time, Cattle worth

	l.	*s.*	*d.*
	30	0	0
And at another Time, to the Value of	40	0	0
	70	0	0

Fines for Meetings.
An hard Hearted Profe-cutor.

When *Thomas Lower*, on her Behalf, demanded a Copy of the Warrant in order to an Appeal, the Officers faid, *They durft not give it, the Juftices having charged them to the contrary.* So they fold her Cattle, and rendred no Account thereof. Taken alfo this Year from *Robert Salthoufe* and others, for Fines for Meeting, Goods worth 7 *l.* 9 *s.* 6 *d.*

John Leigh and *William Wilde* were profecuted at the Suit of *William Richard-fon* Tithe-farmer, and committed to Prifon by Juftices Warrant, grounded on a *Significavit* from the Ecclefiaftical Court. The Profecutor was fo rigid, that he got the Goaler bound in 40 *l.* Penalty not to fuffer them to come down to the Gate of the Caftle. He alfo got a Warrant and took Goods worth 22 *s.* for his Charges of carrying them to Prifon.

More Profecu-tions for Tithes.

John Moon, of *Carhoufe* near *Garftang*, Hufbandman, was profecuted at the Suit of *Thomas Butler* of *Kirklands*, for Tithes, and on the 21ft of the Month called *Auguft*, at *Lancafter* Affizes had a Verdict given againft him for 4 *l.* 7 *s.* on the Statute for treble Damages amounting to 13 *l.* 1 *s.* for which the Bay-liff took, by an Execution, his Corn in the Barn and on his Ground, with all his Houfhold Goods, not leaving him a Bed to lie on, the Whole amounting to 35 *l.*

In *November*, *Alice Bakebean* was profecuted in *Hornby* Court, at the Suit of *Anthony Proctor*, Prieft of *Arch-holm*, and, for 25 *s.* demanded for Tithes, had her Goods diftrained to the Value of 5 *l.*

For Clerk's Wages.

ANNO 1684. *Alice Bakebean* was profecuted by *John Colts* Parifh-Clerk, for 4 *d. per Annum*, for his Wages for five Years, and had her Goods taken away to the Value of 10 *s.*

For Tithes.

Robert Withers was profecuted on the Statute of treble Damages for Tithes, at the Suit of *James Greenwood*, of *Bolton*, Tithe-farmer ; the Tithe proved was 7 *l.* 11 *s.* 6 *d.* for the treble of which, being 22 *l.* 14 *s.* 6 *d.* he had taken from him five Beafts worth 27 *l.* 15 *s.* He had alfo taken from him on ano-ther Profecution for 4 *l.* 18 *s.* Tithe, Goods worth 20 *l.* Alfo *Chriftopher Duck-worth*, for Tithe of 4 *l.* Value, had his Goods taken away to the Value of 18 *l.* 3 *s.* 4 *d.* And *Michael Crabtree* and *William Crabtree*, for a Demand of 1 *s.* 3 *d.* for Tithe, had Pewter and wearing Apparel taken away to the Value of 2 *l.* 2 *s.* 6 *d.*

For refufing to Swear.

John Vipon, *John Ecroyd*, *Roger Hartly*, *John Hardman*, *Stephen Sagar*, *Wil-liam Kippax*, *Edmund Pilling*, *Peter Shackleton*, *Anne Whaley*, *James Rufton*, *John Hargreaves*, and *James Whitaker*, were committed to Prifon on Writs *de Excommunicato capiendo* for refufing to anfwer upon Oath, when profecuted in the Ecclefiaftical Court for Tithes, at the Suit of *Edmund Afhton*, of *Whaley*, Impropriator.

In this Year Corn was taken out of the Field for Tithes from feveral Per-fons, to the Amount of 22 *l.* 17 *s.* 5 *d.*

In

In this and the preceding Year, the Diftreffes made on the Conventicle Act, and otherwife, for religious Meetings, amounted to 304*l.* 7*s.* 10*d.* befide the feveral particular Cafes herein after mentioned, *viz.* On the 5th of *October*, at the Interment of the Wife of *Henry Tomlinfon*, *John Hayton* fpake a few Words by Way of Exhortation to the People; certain Informers, appointed by Juftice *Langworth* to be there, brought him to the Juftice, who fent him to the Houfe of Correction, and alfo fined him 20*l.* for Preacing, and the Owners of the Burying-ground 20*l.* for the Place; for which, and other Fines impofed for being at the faid Burial, Goods were taken by Diftrefs to the Amount of 60*l.* 7*s.* 1*d.* One of the Perfons diftrained on at that Time was *Henry Tomlinfon*, who, when his Cattle were expofed to Sale in the Market, publickly acknowledged them to be his, and was thought thereby to hinder their Sale. For this the aforefaid Juftice committed the faid *Henry* to Prifon. On the 9th of the fame Month *John Townfon*, for a Meeting at his Houfe, fuffered Diftrefs of his Cattle to the Value of 36*l.* 10*s.* And *Henry Houlden*, *Thomas Tomlinfon*, and *Henry Tomlinfon*, had their Goods taken away, for being at that Meeting, to the Amount of 5*l.* 16*s.* 8*d.* About the fame Time the faid *Thomas Tomlinfon*, for a Meeting at his Houfe, fuffered Diftrefs of Goods to the Value of 9*l.* 12*s.*

At the Summer Affizes this Year, *Richard Cubban, Godfrey Atherton, John Minfhall, William Crowdfon, John Bifpham, Daniel Bifpham, Richard Bufby, Alexander Roylance, James Frodfham, Thomas Hiccock, William Griffith, Gilbert Potter, Eleanor Billings, Henry Fofter, Jofeph Coppuck, Jofhua Crofbie*, and *Henry Walton*, then Prifoners for being at a Meeting, having been indicted at the Quarter Seffions for a Riot, were brought to Trial before Judge *Jefferies*, who fined them 20*l.* a piece: They were recommitted to Prifon, where the faid *Henry Fofter* ended his Days on the 18th of *November.*

In *September*, *Daniel Abraham, James Goddard*, and *Leonard Fell*, were fent to Goal for Abfence from the National Worfhip. The two Former continued there about a Month, and the Other longer. In the fame Month *William Rawlinfon, Abraham Rawlinfon, Elizabeth Saunders, Mary Benfon, Henry Stones*, and *Edward Robinfon*, were committed to Prifon, and in the next Month *Barbara Satterthwait*, and *Ifabel Foreft*. In this Year alfo, *Nathanael Difborow, John Barnes, Gilbert Potter, Matthias Fofter, John Dunbabin, John Gibfon, John Chorley, Samuel Dunbabin, Sufan Wright, Mary Cocker, Mary Southworth, Patience Sixfmith, Hugh Crofby, Richard Holcroft, Efther Holcroft, Elizabeth Gibfon, Elizabeth Barnes, Martha Coombs, Robert Burton, Thomas Keckwick, Daniel Keckwick, Gerge Birch, John Barrow, Savage Mafon*, and *Matthew Mafon*, having been taken in religious Meetings at the Houfe of *James Wright* in *Warrington*, were committed to Prifon; where fome of them were detained ten Months.

The pious Difpofition, and fweet Frame of Mind wherein thefe Chriftian Sufferers endured their Confinement, is excellently expreffed by one of them, *viz. Mary Southworth*, a religious Maiden, afterward married to *Henry Mollineux*, in the following Poem, which we recommend to our Readers Perufal, *viz.*

MEDITATIONS concerning our Imprifonment, only for Confciencefake, 1684, in *Lancafter* Caftle.

THO' the Eternal Wifdom, *Sion*'s King,
    Be pleas'd to try his Babes by Suffering;
Tho' fome departing from the Sinners Way,
And walking *Sion*-ward become a Prey;
Yea, though through Tribulation *Ifrael* muft
Enter the promis'd Land, yet Heaven is juft,
And tenderly fupports his patient Ones,
Altho' he chaftens his beloved Sons:

And tho' in Prifons outwardly they be
Confin'd, the Son of Love doth fet them free,
And leads in verdant Plains of Liberty ;
The frefh fat Valleys where fweet *Shiloh* flows,
Upon whofe fertile Banks the Lilly grows ;
Where though he by fome Exercifes prove,
He folaceth with Flagons of his Love.
Then why fhould any murmur ? *Jefus* thus
Extended fignal Favours unto us.
Here are we with the hidden Manna fed,
Tho' with Tranfgreffors we be numbred :
Here can we Profpects from our Tow'r furvey
With much more innocent Delight than they
That range at large ; yea here we may defcry
The pleafant Path, hid from the Vult'rous Eye.
Wherein the Righteous follow Chrift their King
And tender Shepherd, to the living Spring
Of Joy, and to his Name high Praifes fing.
Nor can the proudeft Walls (tho' ne'er fo high
The Monuments of grave Antiquity)
Be terrible to fpotlefs Innocence,
That knows the Rock of Ages a Defence.
Tho' fome be from their Families remov'd,
Here *Mary*'s Choice may better be improv'd.
And Chrift takes Care of his, altho' they fit
As unconcern'd, weeping at *Jefus* Feet.
He'll be a Father to the Family
Of fuch as for his Name in Prifon lie,
And fill their Hearts with everlafting Joy.
Thefe rugged Walls lefs grievous are to me,
Than thofe bedeckt with curious Arras be ;
T' a guilty Confcience, to a wounded Heart,
A Palace cannot palliate that Smart :
Tho' drunk with Pleafure, dull with Opiates,
Some feem as fenfelefs of their fad Eftates,
Till on their dying Beds Confcience awakes.
But tho' the Righteous be in Bonds confin'd,
They inwardly fweet Satisfaction find,
Neither can ftately Roofs, Gates, Bars, nor all
The Art of Man fupprefs the Cries and Call,
Or Supplication, or the pooreft Sigh,
Of *Ifrael*'s Seed, for his Redeemer's nigh,
Who will regard the Cries, and hear the Groans
Of his afflicted tribulated Ones ;
And will in his appointed Time arife
Utterly to confound his Enemies :
Altho' by them he for a Seafon prove
His Children dear, he'll yet in Time remove
The Scourge, and caft the chaftning Rod afide,
When *Ifr'el*'s Faith and Patience he hath try'd.

Now, though fome rage becaufe we cannot bow
Unto their vain Traditions, fince we know
The bleffed Truth, which hath engag'd to give,
Our Hearts to him, in whom alone we live.
Yea, tho' for this fome fret, and ftorm and rage,
And ftudy to afflict God's Heritage :
Their Wrath's reftrain'd by one, that if he pleafe
Can curb the furious, rolling, raging Seas,

As in a Moment, and upon the Wave
Teach his to walk, and by his Prefence fave
From finking, as of old, his Arm's the fame,
Eternal Praifes to his holy Name.
He is our Shield, our Sun that penetrates.
Our clofeft Rooms, and fweetly confolates
Our waiting Souls, and with his quickning Ray
Changes black Nights of Sorrow into joyful Day.
So that 'tis not the Terrors of the Night,
Nor Darts that fly by Day, that can affright
The righteous Souls, who walk in holy Fear ;
They know their Captain of Salvation's near,
The bleffed Prince of Peace, their Joy, their King,
The only Fountain whence true faving Comforts fpring.

Sixth Month 1684.

Such pious Meditations as thefe indicated a Freedom of Spirit, not to be reftrained by outward Bondage, and Bodily Confinement.

On the 19th of the Month called *January*, *James Ratcliff*, *Nicholas Raw-* *Imprifonments* *thorne*, *John Rawthorne*, *John Hargreaves*, *Alice Hargreaves*, *Abraham Hay-* *for Meeting.* *worth*, *Richard Mather*, *William Jackfon*, *Henry Crook*, and *Henry Hargreaves*, were in Prifon for meeting together. A few Days after, they were indicted *Indictment at* at *Manchefter* Seffions, and recommitted to Prifon. About the fame Time *Seffions.* *Francis Flemming* was fent to Prifon for Abfence from his Parifh Church, fo called. In this Year alfo *William Satterthwait* and *Edward Satterthwaite* were fent to Prifon by a Commiffion of Rebellion, for refufing to anfwer upon Oath in the Trial of a Title to an Eftate. And *Thomas Skirrow* was imprifoned for refufing to anfwer upon Oath in the Court of *Exchequer*. Some Time before this, two bold Informers came to the Houfe of *Abraham Hayworth* of *Rofindale*, *Falfe Informa-* when the Meeting there was breaking up : They went and made Informa- *tions.* tion that *James Ratcliff* preached there, who was not at that Meeting ; how-ever the Juftices upon this Evidence fined him 20*l.* for which the Officers broke open five Doors, and took away twelve Kine and an Horfe worth 39*l.* *Jonathan Rigby*, of *Blackrod*, for a Fine of 20*l.* had taken from him four Cows, an Horfe, Hay, and Houfhold Goods, worth 27*l.* *John Rofthwait* a Cow worth 2*l.* 15*s.* and *Alice Ratcliff*, her Bedding, Pewter, &c. worth 15*s.* Great Numbers were fined for abfenting themfelves from the National Worfhip, fo that the Sums taken by Diftrefs for that Caufe amounted to 118*l.* 5*s.* 11*d.* And for the fame Caufe *Daniel Abraham* and his Wife, and *Margaret Fox*, were Prifoners at *Lancafter* about fixteen Days, and *Leonard Fell* about two Months.

ANNO 1685. *Richard Britton*, *George Barrow*, *John Gurnall*, *Miles Bir-* Exchequer *kett*, and *Jennet Dixon*, were profecuted in the *Exchequer* for Tithes, at the Suit *Profecutions.* of *Thomas Prefton*, of *Holcar*, Efq; and by a falfe Return of *Non eft Inventus* (though they were fo far from abfconding, that they offered themfelves to the Baylifs) a Sequeftration was obtained againft them, by which their Cattle and Goods were carried away to the Value of 82*l.* 1*s.* 8*d.*

Henry Mitchel was fent to Prifon by Juftice's Warrant, on a *Significavit* from *Ecclefiaftical* the Ecclefiaftical Court ; and *George Hayworth* and *Henry Birtwifle* were com- *Procefs.* mitted by Writs *de Excommunicato capiendo*, at the Suit of Sir *Edmund Afhton* Impropriator. *John Backhoufe* was profecuted on the Statute for treble Damages, and for 5*l.* 7*s.* 4*d.* Tithe, had Cattle taken from him worth 21*l.* And *Richard Lancafter*, for 6*l.* 2*s.* 2*d.* demanded, fuffered by Diftrefs the Lofs of Cattle to the Value of 26*l.* Several others had Corn and Cattle taken away, for Tithes, to the Amount of 9*l.* 3*s.* 10*d.*

William Atkinfon and *Nathan Kenerdy*, for nine Weeks Abfence from the National Worfhip, had Goods taken away from them to the Value of 3*l.* 5*s.* 6*d.* And *Richard Johnfon*, *Richard Prophet*, and *John Fletcher*, were

LANCA-
SHIRE.
1685.

*Treble
Damages.*

*Imprisonments
on Writs* de
Excom. Cap.

Tithes.

fent to Prifon from a Meeting at *Hartfhaw*, but after three Months Confinement were releafed at the Summer Affizes this Year, when moft of the other Prifoners in this County were alfo difcharged by Virtue of King *James*'s Proclamation for a general Pardon.

ANNO 1686. Taken from *Mary Simpfon*, of *Cartmell*, by a Profecution for treble Damages for Tithe, Goods worth 11 *l.* Taken alfo this Year, for Tithe of Corn in kind, to the Value of 44 *l.* 18 *s.* 9 *d.*

ANNO 1687. In the Month called *October, Richard Hargreaves, John Sagar, John Hudfon, Roger Hartley, Nicholas Holgate, Jeffery Shackerly, John Horabin, Robert Atkinfon, George Birch*, and *Peter Barnes*, were committed to Prifon on Writs *de Excommunicato capiendo*, at the Suit of Sir *Edmund Afhton* Impropriator, for Tithes.

ANNO 1689. Taken from fundry Perfons this Year, out of the Fields for Tithes, Corn, &c. to the Amount of 79 *l.* 14 *s.* 10 *d.*

ANNO 1690. The Tithe of Corn taken in kind this Year from the People called *Quakers* in this County, amounted to 134 *l.* 14 *s.* 5 *d.*

Quaker women in prison.
Drawing by Geoffrey Makins, courtesy of Margaret Fell: Mother of Quakerism.

Index of People

(Page references as in Besse*)*

Index of Places